Graphics

Leland Wilkinson

MaryAnn Hill
Erin Vang

Graphics

References

SAS is a trademark of SAS Institute, Inc.
MS-DOS is a trademark of the Microsoft Corporation.
Lotus 1-2-3 is a trademark of Lotus Development Corporation
dBase is a trademark of Ashton-Tate, Inc.
McDonald's is a trademark of McDonald's, Inc.
SYSTAT and SYGRAPH are registered trademarks of SYSTAT, Inc.

Citation

The correct bibliographic citation for this manual is as follows:

SYSTAT: Graphics, Version 5.2 Edition. Evanston, IL: SYSTAT, Inc., 1992. 600 pp.

SYSTAT, Inc.
1800 Sherman Avenue
Evanston, IL 60201-3793
Tel. 708.864.5670
FAX 708.492.3567

Contents

Tutorial 1

Cognitive science and graphic design   2

Overview 3

Common options   **4**

Bar

5

Category

6

Pie 7

Box 8

Density 9

Stem 10

Plot

11

3-D data plots

12

SPLOM

13

Function

14

Probability 15

Quantile

16

Icon

17

Map 18

Using SYGRAPH commands 19

1 Tutorial

Tutorial 1

This chapter is the first thing you should read when you are ready to start using SYGRAPH. Please set this manual down next to your computer and try things in the tutorial. If you really hate tutorials, at least skim this chapter.

Is SYGRAPH for you?

This is a very unusual graphics package. As you can see by browsing through the menus, SYGRAPH can draw more different kinds of business and scientific graphs than any other computer graphics package. If all you want in a graphics package is to produce simple bar and pie charts for meetings or newsletters, then this package is a lot more than you need. Of course, SYGRAPH can produce bar and pie charts, but you can get other programs to do them in less time and for less money.

You may notice that, although it contains more different types of graphs than any other computer graphics package, SYGRAPH nevertheless lacks some "glitzy" features like pseudo 3-D highlighting and exaggerated perspective effects. This is because SYGRAPH was designed by an expert in graphics perception. Features that have been shown in published research to interfere with accurate perception of graphical material have been omitted from this package even though some who do not know this research may find them attractive.

Finally, SYGRAPH is unusual in another way. SYGRAPH includes intelligent scaling, positioning, and plotting routines. Variable labels, for example, will not collide or overlap with each other when large numbers of categories are plotted. Plotting scales and cutpoints need not be selected from menus. They are chosen automatically via sophisticated statistical analyses of the data being plotted. Thus, many plots that would require numerous menu selections in other graphics packages can be accomplished with a single choice. The options in SYGRAPH were designed so that you should rarely have to "touch up" a graph.

Starting up

Let's make some graphs right away. We'll start with a bar graph because it is typical of many of the types of graphs you can do with SYGRAPH. We assume that you have installed the program. If you have not, turn to the *Getting Started* volume. Otherwise, start up the program:

● Double-click the SYGRAPH or SYSTAT application icon

If you have purchased SYSTAT and SYGRAPH both, you'll double-click SYSTAT, because SYSTAT contains SYGRAPH. If you just bought SYGRAPH, double-click SYGRAPH.

**1.1
Opening a data
file**

We have prepared a file called US that contains data about the 48 continental United States in 1970. We are not discriminating against Alaska and Hawaii. For several reasons, our tutorial will be simpler by leaving them out at this time. We have chosen 1970 instead of a more recent census because of some interesting features in these data.

The statistics in this file are from various sources documenting state statistics for the year ending in 1970 (*U.S. Statistical Abstract*, 1970; *The World Almanac*, 1971). POPDEN is people per square mile. PERSON is the number of F.B.I. reported incidences, per 100,000 people, of personal crimes (murder, rape, robbery, assault). PROPERTY is incidences, per 100,000 people, of property crimes (burglary, larceny, auto theft). INCOME is per-capita income. SUMMER is average summer temperature and WINTER is average winter temperature. RAIN is average inches of rainfall per year. Two additional variables used in some of the analyses are not listed. They are LABLAT (latitude in degrees of the center of each state) and LABLON (longitude of the center).

STATE$	REGION$	POPDEN	PERSON	PROPERTY	INCOME	SUMMER	WINTER	RAIN
ME	NewEngland	32	21	588	3054	69	22	43
NH	NewEngland	80	14	556	3471	70	22	39
VT	NewEngland	47	19	608	3247	69	16	33
MA	NewEngland	719	51	1181	4156	74	30	43
RI	NewEngland	879	51	1355	3858	70	32	40
CT	NewEngland	613	43	1106	4595	72	30	46
NY	MidAtlantic	376	169	1374	4442	74	28	35
NJ	MidAtlantic	941	70	1096	4241	75	35	42
PA	MidAtlantic	259	53	645	3659	76	32	41
OH	GreatLakes	257	71	1097	3738	74	31	37
IN	GreatLakes	142	56	1027	3687	75	29	39
IL	GreatLakes	196	117	1104	4285	76	26	33
MI	GreatLakes	154	144	1644	3994	75	27	31
WI	GreatLakes	80	21	872	3632	69	19	30
MN	Plains	48	38	1017	3635	73	12	25
IA	Plains	50	21	808	3549	74	20	33
MO	Plains	67	101	1266	3458	78	32	35
ND	Plains	9	9	557	3012	72	10	15
SD	Plains	9	23	654	3027	75	17	15
NE	Plains	19	46	790	3609	79	23	28
KS	Plains	27	51	1147	3488	81	32	28
DE	Southeast	273	82	1312	4107	76	34	45
MD	Southeast	392	156	1339	4073	77	35	43
VA	Southeast	114	65	1028	3307	79	41	45
WV	Southeast	71	31	418	2603	76	35	39
NC	Southeast	101	93	758	2888	79	42	43
SC	Southeast	83	71	930	2607	81	50	49
GA	Southeast	77	75	1026	3071	79	45	47
FL	Southeast	123	125	1607	3525	82	66	49
KY	South	79	55	754	2847	78	36	41
TN	South	93	69	707	2808	81	40	45
AL	South	66	74	704	2582	82	51	59
MS	South	46	45	374	2218	82	49	50
AR	South	36	56	735	2488	82	41	49
LA	South	79	103	968	2781	82	55	60
OK	South	36	51	927	3047	83	37	31
TX	South	42	90	1243	3259	83	53	35
MT	Mountain	5	28	924	3130	68	19	11
ID	Mountain	8	31	1011	2953	75	29	11
WY	Mountain	3	28	953	3353	70	26	15
CO	Mountain	21	89	1654	3604	73	29	15
NM	Mountain	8	73	1314	2897	79	36	10
AZ	Mountain	15	93	1848	3372	90	50	7
UT	Mountain	13	34	1355	2997	77	28	14
NV	Mountain	4	100	1789	4458	71	28	8
WA	Pacific	50	55	1552	3848	68	29	33
OR	Pacific	21	64	1477	3573	68	39	40
CA	Pacific	126	119	1955	4290	68	52	16

Open the file:

- Select **Open...** from the **File** menu
- Highlight the Data Files folder and click Open
- Highlight the US data file and click Edit

You should see the Data Editor with the above data. The file also has some additional variables that we will use later.

Bar charts
1.2
Drawing a bar graph

Now, let's draw a bar graph. You should already be familiar with SYGRAPH's menus and dialog boxes from the *Getting Started* volume.

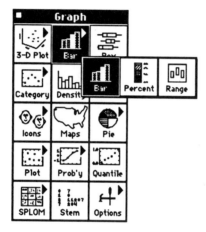

First, press and hold the mouse button on **Bar**. A submenu pops up offering **Bar, Range,** or **Percent**. Slide the pointer over to the item you want and release the mouse button. All three items present the same dialog box and work the same.

- Select **Bar/Bar** from the **Graph** menu
- Select the Y variable from the left selection list: INCOME
- Select the X variable from the right list: REGION$
- Click OK

You should see on your screen the graph below.

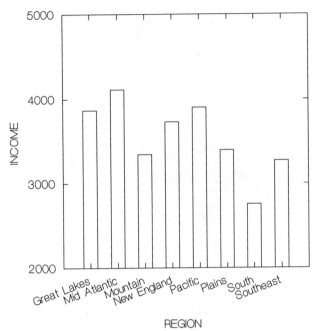

Notice that SYGRAPH automatically chooses scale values and angles the value labels to fit on the lower scale. The axes are labeled with the variables you chose (INCOME and REGION); notice that SYGRAPH even took the dollar sign off REGION$. We will see later how to change all these details to suit your preferences.

Every aspect of this graph can be modified. The important thing to notice is that when you don't want to bother with details everything is done automatically.

Notice that in our data there are several states in each REGION and only one bar on the graph. SYGRAPH computes the mean (average) of INCOME in each REGION to plot a bar. If there is only one value in the dataset corresponding to each bar, then you will see that as the height of the bar.

**1.3
Printing your
graph**

Let's make a hard copy of the graph. There are several ways to do this, as you learn in *Getting Started*. The most obvious now, since we already have a graph sitting in the View window, is **Print graph**.

- Select **Print graph** from the **File** menu
- Click **Print**

We assume that you have a printing device hooked up to your machine and that you have chosen it, if necessary, from **Chooser** in the Apple menu.

Hmm... Not pleased with the result? If you have a high-resolution device such as a LaserWriter, you can print graphs at whatever resolution your device (and screen) can handle. High-resolution graphics are slower, so you may want to stick with low-resolution for now. Generally, you will want to do fast, low-resolution graphics when you are just exploring your data and high-resolution only when you are ready to print up final copies of your results.

In the following examples, we'll try graphs just on the screen. You probably don't want to bother with [High-resolution]. If you do want to bother, just do the following. If you get impatient later, just come back to these instructions and turn [High-resolution] off.

- Select **Options/Global settings...** from the **File** menu
- Click [High-resolution]
- Click OK

If you want a high-resolution copy of your graph, you'll need to produce the graph again and then use **Print graph.**

1.4
Changing the axes

You may not want four axes, like a box, around your bar graph. You can change this easily. Suppose you only want the X axis.

- Select **Bar/Bar** from the **Graph** menu
- Click [Axes]
  - Choose the icon with the X axis
  - Click OK
- Click OK

Notice that the **Bar** dialog box remembered what you drew last. Therefore, we don't need to select variables all over again. We need only add the [Axes] option and click OK.

(*All* the dialog boxes "remember" the last graph that was drawn with them: the variables you selected *and* any options you may have chosen. If you want to select new variables, just click [Clear] to start anew.)

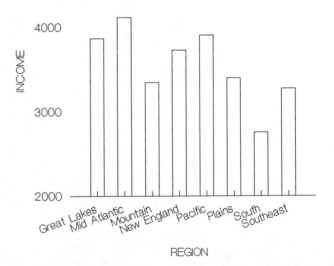

Notice that only the bottom axis is drawn. [Axes] uses all four axes by default: before you clicked a different icon, the box-shaped icon was blackened in the dialog box.

1.5
Changing scales

You may have noticed that the scale values for INCOME were printed even though we chose one axis. You can manipulate the scale values separately with [Scale] in the [Axes] dialog box. It works exactly like the [Axes] option except that only the scale values or labels are affected. Keep in mind that the two options work independently.

So, select **Bar/Bar** again. Notice that the [Axes] dialog box has a little black box in its upper right corner reminding you that SYSTAT has remembered your choice. You can click the black box off to restore the default, you can click the [Axes] button to go through its dialog box and make new choices, or you can do nothing and continue to have bar graphs with only the X axis.

Defaults   *Your choices*

We want to keep the one axis configuration, and we want to change to one scale, also. We'll get a bar chart that shows the general INCOME comparisons but no details.

- Select **Bar/Bar** from the **Graph** menu
- Click [Axes]; choose the single-scale icon under the still-chosen axis icon
- Click OK

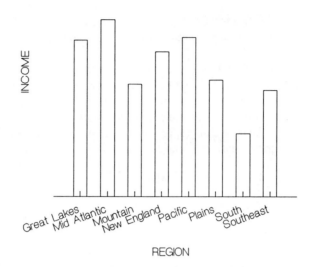

Try your own combinations of axes and scales.

1.6
Labeling axes

You may not want to use the names of the variables to label the axes. Sometimes longer labels are more clear. The [X label] and [Y label] options in the [Axes] dialog box let you do this.

If you need to place single or double quotation marks (" or ') in your text, then you should surround the whole thing with the opposite marks.

```
"Carol's Total Sales"
```

Let's label the axes and also switch to no axes and two scales.

- Select **Bar/Bar** from the **Graph** menu
- Click [Axes]
  - Click off the selected [Axes] choice
  - Choose the L-shaped [Scales] icon
  - Specify the [X label]: Census Region
  - Specify the [Y label]: Per Capita Income
- Click OK

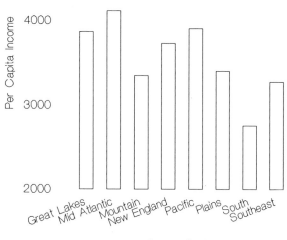

1.7
Scale limits

Notice that our bar graph has a minimum income of $2000 and a maximum of $5000. SYGRAPH chooses this range based on the data. It searches for round numbers below and above the minimum and maximum values in the data, respectively. You may want to modify these values to standardize your graph on a different scale.

Each type of graph in SYGRAPH has [Min] and [Max] options to govern these values. When there is only one scale possible in a graph, the [Axes] dialog box has only [Min] and [Max]. For graphs with more than one scale, you must specify the scale separately for each axis with the options [X min], [X max], [Y min], [Y max], and sometimes [Z min] and [Z max]. (For two-dimensional graphs, the horizontal axis is called X and the vertical axis is called Y.)

Here is an example for our bar graph. We set [Y min] to 0. Since we do not specify [Y max], the maximum value for the scale will be chosen from the data. Meanwhile, let's go back to the original axis and scale settings.

- Select **Bar/Bar** from the **Graph** menu
- Click [Axes]
  - Set [Y min] to 0
  - Choose the box-shaped [Axes] icon and the L-shaped [Scale] icon
  - Delete the [X label] and [Y label]
- Click OK

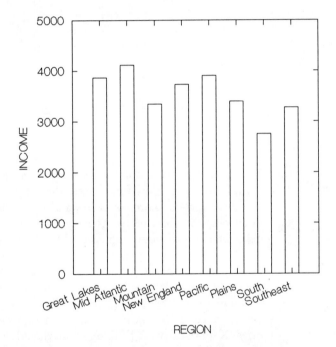

1.8
Tick marks

SYGRAPH chooses a number of tick marks that will produce round numbers and a pleasing display that fills the frame. Sometimes you might want fewer or more tick marks. To do this, use the [Tick] options in the [Axes] dialog boxes.

Here is our bar chart with 8 tick marks on the vertical (Y) axis instead of the 4 chosen by SYGRAPH. Usually, you will have difficulty choosing a number of tick marks that produces a better display than that chosen by SYGRAPH, but having this option can help when the data are unusual. There is no limit on the number of ticks, but if you choose too many, the scale values will overlap.

- Select **Bar/Bar** from the **Graph** menu
- Click [Axes]
  - Set [Ticks] to 8
- Click OK

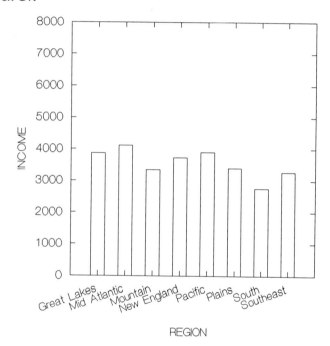

1.9
Pip marks

You can also make finer tick marks between those with scale values. These are called pip marks in SYGRAPH. For example, if you want to put 4 pip marks between each tick on our bar chart, set [Pips] to 4 in the [Axes] dialog box. This makes a break at each $500 interval on the graph. You can choose any number of pip marks for any axis.

- Select **Bar/Bar** from the **Graph** menu
- Click [Axes]
  - Delete the [Ticks] setting
  - Set [Pips] to 4
- Click OK

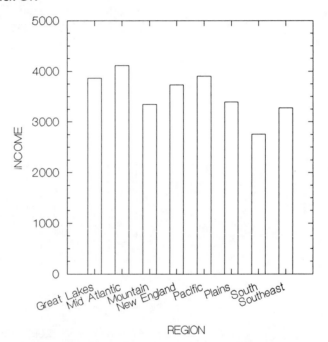

1.10
Ticks inside or outside

You can place tick and pip marks inside or outside the frame of a graph. Normally, SYGRAPH places tick marks inside the frame. If you click [Ticks out], they will be placed sticking out. Figure 10 shows our bar graph with the ticks and pips placed out.

- Select **Bar/Bar** from the **Graph** menu
- Click [Axes]
  - Click [Ticks out]
- Click OK

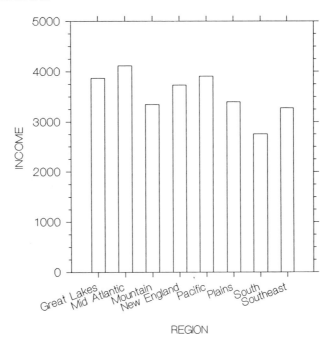

1.11
Reversing a scale

Now we're going to do something goofy. We're going to reverse the scale on the vertical (Y) axis to make an upside down bar graph. To reverse a scale, simply click [X reverse] or [Y reverse].

Why would you want to do this? Maybe you like upside down graphs. Some of us are glass-half-full/empty, yin/yang head/toe kind of people. Others like to do special graphs that require reversing scales. Age-sex pyramid graphs and back-to-back histograms are two examples that require reversed scales for half the graph. You can take a look at some of these graphs in the more advanced examples later. Just remember, any graph with one or more scales that make sense reversed can be reversed in SYGRAPH.

- Select **Bar/Bar** from the **Graph** menu
- Click [Axes]
  - Click off [Ticks out]
  - Delete the [Pips] setting
  - Click [Y reverse]
- Click OK

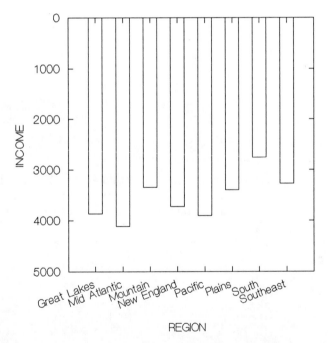

1.12 Transposing a graph

Bar graphs are normally vertical. Why not make them horizontal? Most graphs provide a [T'pose] option to flip them sideways.

Here is an example of this. In many ways, it is more pleasing than the previous graphs because it has a simple numerical scale at the bottom, clear labeling of the bars on the side, and otherwise clean features.

You must remember this: [T'pose] affects *everything* in a graph. [X label] becomes [Y label] and so on. In other words, specify a graph as you would ordinarily and then add the [T'pose] option to rotate the whole thing. Everything will be transposed appropriately, including the labels and scales.

- Select **Bar/Bar** from the **Graph** menu
- Click [Axes]
  - Choose the second [Axes] icon (Y axis only)
  - Click off [Y reverse]
- Click [T'pose]
- Click OK

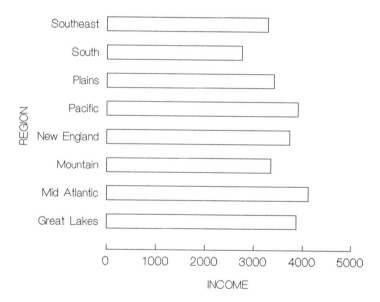

1.13
Filling a graph

You can fill bars, symbols, or other fillable features in a graph with the [Fill] option.

The [Fill] dialog box gives you white, black, and 6 different fill patterns. Either choose one of the samples or else specify one by number: 0 for white, 1 for black, 2–7 for the patterns, and a decimal number between 0 and 1 for a percentage "screen" of black.

Here is our bar graph filled with the shaded pattern to accentuate the bars.

- Select **Bar/Bar** from the **Graph** menu
- Click the little black box in the [Axes] button to return to defaults
- Click [Fill] and choose the last pattern (or type a 7 in the box)
- Click OK

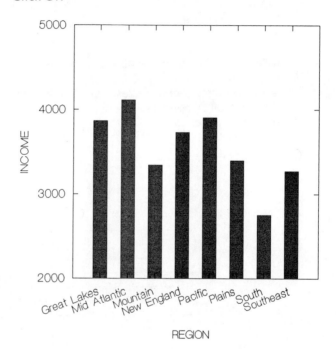

1.14
Coloring a graph

You can choose different colors for a graph with [Color] the same way you specified fill patterns. Either choose a color by name or by specifying a wavelength in nanometers. Nanometers! Why use a number for a color? Usually you don't want to, but there are times when you will want to control color (hue) by a numeric variable in your file. Wavelength is the most appropriate scale to use in these instances because it allows you to calibrate colors with published charts.

Some approximate nanometer wavelengths are:

Red   615
Orange   590
Yellow   575
Green   505
Blue   480
Violet   450

Your graphics device (screen or printer) must support color for this to work, of course. If your graphics device supports color mixing (e.g. a CRT or color camera), then you can specify color more continuously in nanometers wavelength, e.g. 543. SYGRAPH will hold brightness and saturation constant. If you do not know anything about color perception and the use of colors in graphs, you should read further about color in the next chapter.

Here is our bar graph in green. Since we choose solid "black" fill, the inside of the bars are green. We will see later how to modify the color of other parts of the figure.

- Select **Bar/Bar** from the **Graph** menu
- Click [Fill] and choose the solid pattern
- Click [Color] and choose [Green]
- Click OK

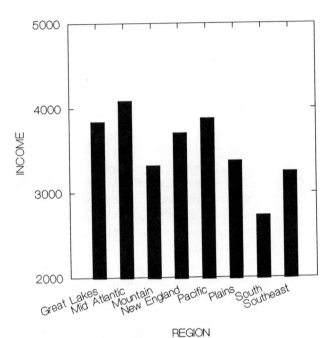

Pie charts

1.15
Making a pie chart

We've used the bar chart to illustrate many of the standard options to SYGRAPH commands. Now let's try another command to make a different graph. The pie chart is one of the most common methods for displaying portions of a whole. To display relative proportions of total per-capita income, we can use **Pie** the same way we used **Bar**.

Many of the options we have tried with bar graphs work also with pie charts. We will not try them here, however. You can try a few. Obviously, options like [T'pose] and the [Axes] options are meaningless. Others can have curious results.

- Select **Pie/Pie** from the **Graph** menu
- Choose the Y variable: INCOME
- Choose the X variable: REGION$
- Click OK

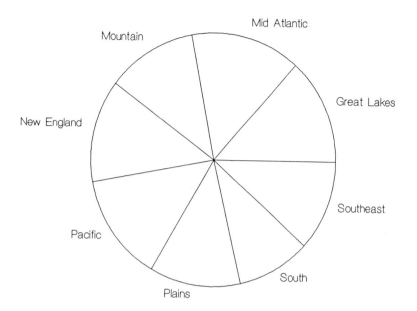

Scatterplots

One of the most common statistical displays is the two-way data plot called a scatterplot. These are easy to do in SYGRAPH with **Plot**.

1.16
Making a
scatterplot

Let's consider another variable in addition to income and region of the country. Population density might be related to income because of differences between urban and rural economies.

- Select **Plot/Plot** from the **Graph** menu
- Choose the Y variable: INCOME
- Choose the X variable: POPDEN
- Click OK

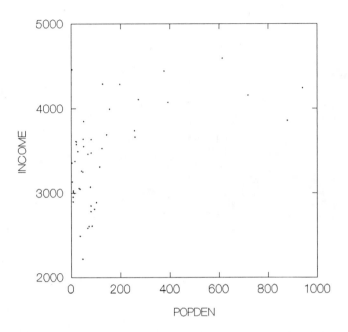

As you can see, **Plot** has most of the options we reviewed with **Bar**. For example, all the axis and scale options apply to **Plot** in the same way they do to **Bar**.

1.17
Smoothing a
scatterplot

The points appear to follow a curve rather than a straight line relating INCOME to POPDEN. Let's allow SYGRAPH to fit a curve through the data without our making any presuppositions about its form. To do this, use **Plot** again with [Locally weighted] smoothing. This option implements LOWESS, a robust smoothing algorithm developed by Bill Cleveland at Bell Telephone Laboratories.

- Select **Plot/Plot** from the **Graph** menu
- Click [Smooth] and choose [LOWESS]
- Click OK

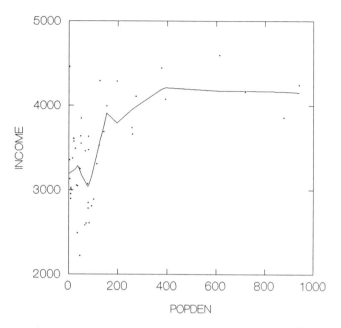

Notice that despite local jagged features, the line is curved. The exact form of a plausible function relating INCOME to POPDEN is not unambiguous, but we might say a log or square root function is plausible. Both of these functions are steeper for smaller values of POPDEN than for larger.

**1.18
Transforming a
plot scale**

Let's try a logarithmic function. SYGRAPH allows you to log the vertical or horizontal scale on any base logarithm (e.g. 2 or 3 or 10). The base of the log won't affect the appearance of the plot, but for most data, base 10 is easiest to understand. We're going to log the X axis (POPDEN), which will squeeze together large values of population density more than small. This should straighten our line.

Instead of smoothing by LOWESS this time, let's fit a regression line by using [Linear] choice for [Smooth]. This smoothing method fits a line through the points such that the sum of the squared vertical deviations of each point from the line is as small as possible.

In addition, we will request [Confidence bands] on the fitted line. By specifying a value of .95, we get an interval such that 95 out of 100 intervals computed this way on new samples would be expected to cover the "true" regression line relating INCOME to POPDEN. Statisticians might object to the use of a confidence interval here, because new samples are difficult to define precisely for these data and because the values are "spatially autocorrelated." That is, data for contiguous states are related, so that geography affects the relationship we are analyzing.

Nevertheless, we will forge ahead with imperfect data and examine our plot, keeping in mind that the confidence interval is only approximate.

- Select **Plot/Plot** from the **Graph** menu
- Click [Smooth] and choose [Linear]; specify .95 for [Confidence bands]
- Click [Log] and specify base 10 for [X log]
- Click OK

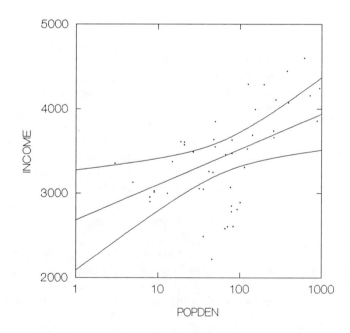

1.19
Labeling points

Some of the points in the plot are far from the fitted line. In fact, another condition for the confidence interval to be valid is that the points cluster in an even band along the line. Clearly, it would be valuable to identify the points that fit poorly. This is easy to do with the [Label symbols with variable name] option in the [Symb'l] dialog box.

Let's use the two letter post-office abbreviation of the state names to label the points. These are stored in the character variable STATE$. This time, we will leave out the confidence interval and just plot the line.

- Select **Plot/Plot** from the **Graph** menu
- Click [Smooth] and delete the [Confidence bands] value
- Click [Symbol] and specify STATE$ for the [Label symbols...] option
- Click OK

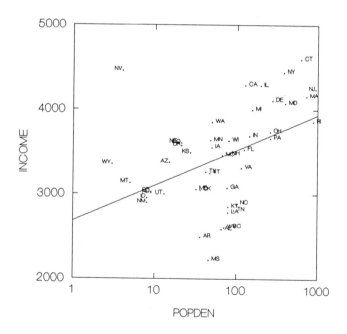

Notice in the figure that Nevada has an extremely low population density and extremely high per-capita income. We need not go into the explanation for this except, perhaps, for those not familiar with U.S. social customs. It is also an interesting reminder of the pitfalls of statistical summaries that this level of income is not shared by all or even half the people in the state. Notice, also, that a number of southern states with moderate populations lag below the expected per-capita income levels. When you become more familiar with SYGRAPH, you might want to enter the data for 1980 or 1990 to see if conditions have improved.

You may also have noticed a defect in SYGRAPH. Some of the labels overlap. SYGRAPH does its best to avoid this by reducing the size of the type and printing to the left or right of the plotting symbols. When labels collide, you may have to replace some of them with missing values (blanks) in the data or move the points slightly.

**1.20
Influence plots**

Let's try an exotic plot at this point. You may not understand everything about it, but it gives you a chance to see how statisticians diagnose problems with a graphical summary. As we mentioned earlier, the confidence interval we computed is somewhat questionable with these data, partly because Nevada and the southern states fall outside an even band we might expect. The following graph displays the influence of each point on a certain aspect of the fitted line, namely its slope.

If we standardize INCOME and the log of POPDEN such that their standard deviations (spread) are the same, then the slope of best fitting lines relating the two variables would vary between −1 and +1. The influence of a point measures how much the slope would vary if the point were eliminated from the calculations of the slope. A large influence value (say, .4 or −.3) would mean that eliminating that point would substantially affect the computed slope (by as much as .4 or −.3). We might, for example, expect that Nevada would have a negative influence on the regression line because leaving it out would allow the line to tilt more steeply (more positive slope) when we didn't have to include the square of the deviation of Nevada from the line in our calculations.

- Select **Plot/Influence** from the **Graph** menu
- Select the Y variable: INCOME
- Select the X variable: POPDEN
- Click OK

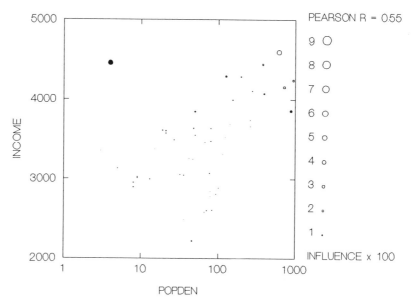

We see that, indeed, Nevada has a negative influence on the *slope* of the line. The legend to the right of the plot shows influence values. The one comparable to the size of the symbol for Nevada is approximately .05, indicating that the correlation (slope of the line when both standard deviations are equal) would increase by .05 if Nevada were eliminated from the data. Empty circles correspond to positive influences and filled ones to negative. The empty circle at the top right indicates, for example, that Connecticut has a positive influence comparable to Nevada's negative.

Incidentally, you can label the symbols on this influence plot, but it would be somewhat cluttered. As you can see from the palette of options in each dialog box, you can combine a huge number of options on any graph, and if you put your mind to it, you can construct the most confusing graph imaginable.

One warning about influence plots. The size of the symbols reflects influence on the correlation coefficient but not on the intercept of the regression line. Notice in this example that the southern states appear to be pulling the whole line lower than it should be. Since we are assessing influence on the slope of the line only, this other type of influence is not reflected in the plot.

1.21
Plotting symbols

So far, we have been using the default plotting symbol. You may have noticed that a different symbol, a circle, was used in the influence plot. You probably noticed back in example 1.19 that the [Symbol] dialog box offers numerous choices.

Let's use a new symbol in our scatterplot. A filled circle would be much more visible than the standard point. We produce it by choosing the circle and clicking the solid [Fill] pattern. You can use any other symbol on your keyboard by typing it in the box, enclosing it in quotation marks (e.g., '@').

- Select **Plot/Plot** from the **Graph** menu
- Click off [Smooth]
- Click [Symbol]
  - Delete the [Label symbols…] specification from before
  - Choose the circle plotting symbol from the LaserWriter choices
  - Choose the solid [Fill]
- Click OK

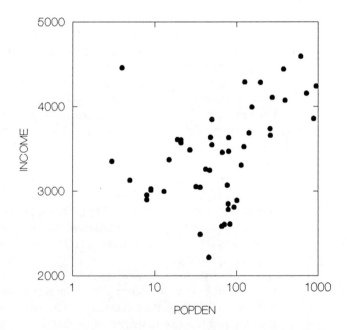

1.22
Symbols from data values

You can also choose your symbols from a data file. This way, you can use a different plotting symbol for each case or group of cases.

Here is a scatterplot with the first letter of each state at the latitude (LABLAT) and longitude (LABLON) of each state. To make the plot correspond roughly to a Mercator map projection, you should first trace a rectangular plotting frame—say, 3 inches high by 4 inches wide—with the ruler option (discussed in *Getting Started.*)

- Select **Plot/Plot** from the **Graph** menu
- Click [Label]
  - Specify STATE$
- Click OK

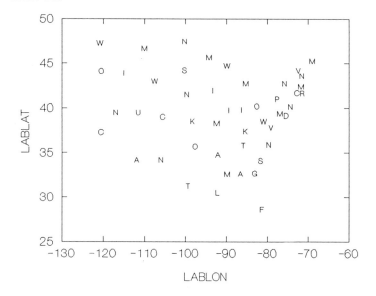

This plotting symbol option is handy for denoting subgroups. For example, you could have a character variable in your file with one symbol for males and another for females. This way, the plot symbols would reveal the distribution of gender across the plotting space.

**1.23
Varying symbol
sizes**

You can make your plotting symbols smaller or larger by using the [Size] option in the [Symbol] dialog box. You can choose from those shown or specify a number. If you specify a number, then you get a symbol that many times the size of the standard symbol. Typing .5 in the box, for example, produces symbols half the size of the standard one. If a symbol has a size less than .001, it is not plotted at all. This is handy for plotting axes in special positions or drawing lines without symbols. We'll take advantage of this feature later.

If you changed the plotting frame for the plot in 1.22, you might want to go back to square graphs now.

Here is a scatterplot with symbols half again as large as usual.

- Select **Plot/Plot** from the **Graph** menu
- Click [Clear] so we can pick new variables
- Select a Y variable: PERSON
- Select the X variable: PROPERTY
- Click [Symbol]
  - Choose the pentagonal plotting symbol
  - Choose the white [Fill]
  - Specify 1.5 for [Size]
- Click OK

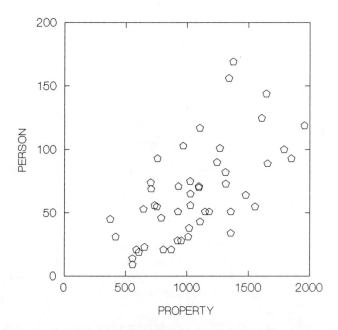

**1.24
Varying symbol
sizes with a
variable**

You can use a variable to control the size of plotting symbols. This way, you can use one scatterplot to represent three variables. SYGRAPH uses the value of the variable you specify to determine the diameter of the plotting symbol. Keep in mind, however, that viewers are more likely to notice area rather than diameter when judging the size of many symbols. For this reason, you should usually use the square root of your controlling variable to determine the size of plotting symbols with area, such as circles and squares.

Here is an example. First, let's use **Math...** to set a new variable RAI to the square root of RAIN (average annual rainfall). If the Editor window is not open, first reopen the US data file (with **Open...** from the **Files** menu), making sure the [Edit] box is checked.

- Select **Math...** from the **Data** menu
- Fill in the statement: Let RAI = SQR(RAIN/30)
- Click OK

We divide by 30 before rooting to keep the areas of the plotting symbols within a reasonable range on the plot, thus preventing overlaps.

Since this plot will look like a map, you might want to go back to a rectangular plotting frame, like in Example 1.22.

- Select **Plot/Plot** from the **Graph** menu
- Click [Clear] so we can pick new variables
- Select a Y variable: LABLAT
- Select the X variable: LABLON
- Click [Symb'l]
    - Choose the circle plotting symbol
    - Choose the white [Fill]
    - Specify RAI for [Size]
- Click OK

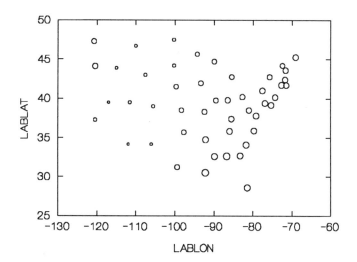

1.25
Grid marks

Sometimes you may want a grid on your graph to allow closer visual inspection. This is easy to do with the [Grid] option in the [Axes] dialog box, which works much like the [Axes] and [Scales] options.

Here we use the per-capita income data. We've added a lot of options to make a more attractive graph and to review how options can be combined. We've put pip marks in for the logarithms to show the relative scaling. Do you see why we set [X pips] to 9 instead of 10? If not, just count along the scale. The bold numbers correspond to the tick marks and the light ones to the pips.

1, 2, 3, 4, 5, 6, 7, 8, 9, **10**, 20, 30, 40, 50, 60, 70, 80, 90, **100**, 200, 300...

In case you didn't know it already, this plot is called a semilog plot because one scale is logged.

Again, you might want to switch back to a square plot.

- Select **Plot/Plot** from the **Graph** menu
- Click [Clear] so we can pick new variables
- Select a Y variable: INCOME
- Select the X variable: POPDEN
- Click [Symbol]
  - Delete RAI from the [Size] box
- Click [Axes]
  - Specify 9 for [X pips] and 10 for [Y pips]
  - Choose the third [Grid] option
  - Specify [X label]: Log of Population Per Square Mile
  - Specify [Y label]: Per Capita Income
- Click [Log] and specify base 10 for [X log]
- Click OK

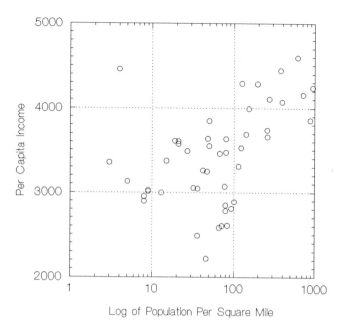

Function plots
1.26
Plotting a curve

SYGRAPH plots functions without any data. **Function** is handy for students of algebra, calculus, and analysis. Scientists will also find it useful for superimposing theoretical functions on their data plots. Just type the function you want plotted, e.g.

```
Y = X*X*X
Y = X^3
```

These two expressions are equivalent. Both are written in a language called BASIC. If you know BASIC, then any standard numerical BASIC function can be plotted. If you don't know BASIC, you can examine the additional examples in this manual or any introduction to BASIC. You can use any variable names you wish. For example,

CUBE = LINE^3
SOUP = BOUILLON^3

will result in the same plot as above. SYGRAPH simply examines the expression you type for any names that are not part of BASIC and then uses them for the range and domain. The graph is labeled with the names you use in the equation.

Notice that SYGRAPH picks the range and domain over which to display the plot. You can use the [Min] and [Max] options in [Axes] to change these values, but the ones SYGRAPH picks should be suitable for many functions. It does the picking by computing trial values and examining their behavior (first and second numerical derivatives, etc.) at various points.

- Select **Function** from the **Graph** menu
- Specify an equation: Y = X^3
- Click OK

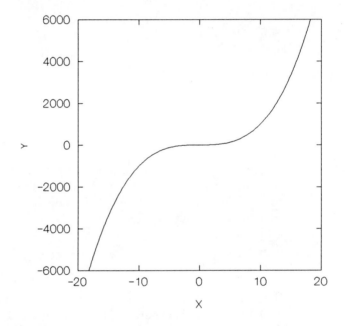

1.27
3-D function plot

Here's a simple three dimensional function plot. All we do is add another variable to our equation. This is a saddle function. We add one option, [Hide], which you usually want. It slows things down a bit, but it causes portions of the surface in the background to be hidden behind portions in the foreground.

- Select **Function** from the **Graph** menu
- Click [Clear] to specify a new equation: Z = X^2 – Y^2
- Click [Hide]
- Click OK

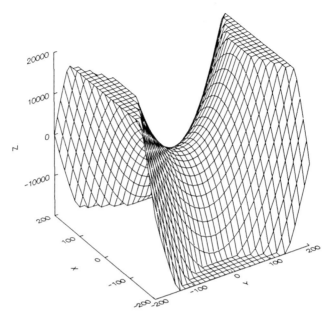

3-D data plots

You can do 3-D plots with **3-D Plot**.

1.28
3-D spike plot

Here is an example for our income data. We're plotting INCOME against LABLAT and LABLON, so that the XY plane is like a map of the U.S. and the vertical (Z) axis is income. We've added one other feature to the plot so that you can see it better: [Spike], which drops a line to the XY plane from each point.

You should be able to see the southern states in the foreground with lower per-capita income and the northwest and northeast with higher. (Again, you might want a rectangular plotting frame.)

- Select **3-D Plot/3-D Plot** from the **Graph** menu
- Select the variables: INCOME * LABLAT * LABLON
- Click [Spike] and click OK to accept the default
- Click OK

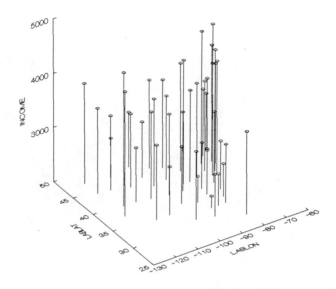

We could go on but we think you're getting the idea...

There is no way we can try every feature of SYGRAPH in a tutorial. The important thing is to get a feel for how the program is organized. At this point, you should turn off your machine and go to bed. Tomorrow, you should begin with the next chapter. If you're really impatient, you can skip the next chapter and go directly to the reference section. If you do, you will miss all the pearls of wisdom you'll need to make well designed graphs. You'll use SYGRAPH to make a bunch of chart-junk and sully our reputation. Were there world enough and time...

2   Cognitive science and graphic design

Cognitive science and graphic design   2

Overview

This chapter has nothing to do with SYGRAPH. It has everything to do with graphics. If you are anxious to start using SYGRAPH, skip this chapter and go directly to the reference section. If you do skip, we hope you will return to read this chapter sometime, because it is about designing good graphs.

The function of quantitative graphics

Graphics can have many functions. They can entertain. They can persuade. The function of *quantitative* graphics, however, is to inform. By presenting graphics to others, we are attempting to communicate information through a wide and complex channel: the human visual system. In communicating this information, we may entertain or persuade or do other things, but if we distort the information underlying our graphics, we have failed.

Many designers of quantitative graphics confuse these functions or subordinate the goal of informing to other goals. Sometimes this is intentional, as in graphic propaganda, but often it is inadvertent, as in popular newspaper graphs that distort their message with bright colors and "perspective" views.

If we think of quantitative graphics as a mode of information processing, then we can use the tools of cognitive psychology to evaluate displays. In this chapter, we will cover the basics of visual information processing, principals of graphic design, and then conclude with examples of good and bad graphs. If you want to read more in this area, you should look at Frisby (1980); Haber and Hershenson (1980); Levine and Shefner (1981); Spoehr and Lehmkuhle (1982); Tufte (1983); Chambers, Cleveland, Kleiner & Tukey (1983); and Cleveland (1985).

Visual information processing

The visual system can be represented by several abstract components. Figure 2.1 shows these components schematically. The *graphic image* is a composite of physical aspects that contain the information we are communicating. The image may originate on paper, on a computer screen, or in another medium. For our purposes, the image is the set of critical features that stimulate the retina to fire its neurons such that the remainder of the visual system in the brain can process the information.

Iconic memory is the first component of memorization. Cells in the retina fire neural impulses when they absorb a quantity of photons from a light stimulus. They continue to fire for a short time after the stimulation ceases and thus serve as a brief store for the image itself.

Short-term memory holds essential features of the stimulus so that it can be integrated into the framework of long-term memory. A famous study by George Miller (1956) and others since have indicated that short-term memory can hold at least four and perhaps as many as seven or eight "chunks" of information. These "chunks" can be made up of other chunks from long-term memory, so that short-term memory can be used to build up arbitrarily complex constructs. This is why we have used two arrows between short and long-term memory to indicate feedback. Some psychologists working in verbal learning claim that short-term memory is acoustical, meaning that information is rehearsed subvocally until it can be integrated into long-term memory. Others, such as Shepard (1978) and Kosslyn (1980), have shown that visual perceptual units can be stored in short-term memory as well. In either case, perceptual chunking in short-term memory allows time for long-term memory encoding to occur. This process takes about 20 seconds or so for each chunk of information.

Long-term memory contains the permanently remembered information from the perceived graph. We use "permanently" advisedly, since there is no compelling evidence to show that we ever forget anything once it is encoded into long-term memory (assuming no physiological damage from toxins like alcohol or physical deterioration associated with aging). Forgetting is more likely a failure to draw connections between associated information stored in memory. "Forgotten" information can often be recovered by a careful reconstruction of associated information, experiences, and sensations.

2.1 Abstract representation of the visual system

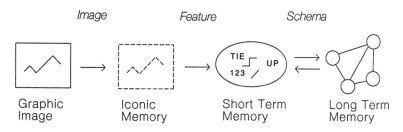

© 1989, SYSTAT, Inc.

Above the diagram, we have indicated components of the information that are processed at each stage. Information passed from the graphic image to iconic memory depends on the optical quality of the image. If a graph has poor contrast and fuzzy lines, for example, critical aspects will not register in the iconic store. Knowing this, we should attempt to keep graphic images clean, with high contrast and crisp delineation. If we use colors, we should avoid faint pastels, muddy tones, and other low intensity shades.

Features of an image are transmitted from the iconic store to short-term memory. If a graph is cluttered by many features (e.g. 15 curves), we know that this information cannot be held in short-term memory after a few seconds of looking at the graph. Knowing this, we should limit the essential features in one graph to a manageable number, unless we expect our viewers to spend considerable time processing the information.

Finally, information in short-term memory is integrated into long-term memory via schemas. We have used a "network" symbol to represent long-term memory because current theories frequently use this descriptive structure. Schemas are networks of associations that integrate information. If we abstract a graph of sales over years, for example, we might recall that sales increased in a straight line over the years involved. We might remember this straight line by associating it with a verbal description of the formula describing sales from years (some mathematicians and actuaries might remember a graph this way). We might instead keep a visual image of the slope of the line relative to the frame around the graph and associate this image with remembered values of the axes (e.g. "millions of sales in the 1960s").

Psychologists disagree on exactly how information is stored in long-term memory. There is evidence that information can be stored as a set of linked propositions and other evidence that it can be stored as linked icons, or visual mental representations. It may be stored both ways. We need not resolve this controversy to decide how to use graphic designs, however. In either case, we should realize that the information in a graph will be stored most effectively if it can be associated with other information. Unusual scales, break points in graphs, or puzzling anchor points for data values may all interfere with the process of storing the fundamental information in a graph—e.g. the change in one variable relative to another.

The psychophysics of perception

We have seen a representation of the path from graphic image to long-term memory. While this structure has implications for the design of good graphs, we still need to understand how images are perceived. The visual system, like our other sensory systems, encodes information in various forms. Perhaps because quantitative graphs are relatively recent visual icons in human history, we process them with the same tools we use to perceive three-dimensional scenes and two-dimensional pictures. Sometimes these tools cause us to distort the very information we are attempting to perceive accurately.

The power law

Early in the nineteenth century, Weber noticed that the increment in stimulation required to produce a just noticeable difference between two stimuli was proportional to the size of the stimuli: the bigger (more intense) the stimuli, the bigger the difference needed to notice a difference between the two. For example, we can easily see two objects separated on our desk. We have more trouble discriminating between two objects a quarter mile from our desk if they are separated by the same distance.

Not long after Weber's discovery, Fechner derived a scale for sensation. Assuming that Weber's just noticeable differences in sensation were equivalent at all levels of stimulation, Fechner computed a logarithmic function relating the magnitude of sensation (S) to the intensity of stimulation (I). In Fechner's function, sensation increases logarithmically with stimulation, so that differences in sensation are produced by the same ratios of stimulation:

$$S = k \log(I)$$

In the 1950s, Stevens (following the work of Plateau in the 1800s) proposed a power function for sensation instead of Fechner's logarithmic curve. Using a wide variety of stimuli, Stevens fit his data with a power function:

$$S = kI^{p}$$

There is still some controversy over whether Stevens' and Fechner's curves describe perceptual data and even the possibility that both are correct under different experimental conditions. Figure 2.2 shows both curves for a typical application. The important thing to notice is the downward curvature of both. In practical terms, increasing the size of symbols on a graph will not increase the *perceived* size in the same increments. Increasing the darkness of a filled area will not increase the perceived darkness in the same increments. This downward bias should make us wary of using area, darkness, and volume in graphs when we have other methods for representing quantitative variation that are less susceptible to these distortions.

Stevens and his associates measured a wide variety of auditory, visual, and tactile stimuli. For our purposes, it is most useful to note that the value of the exponent in the power function varies across types of graphical stimuli. For length judgments, it can range from .9 to 1.1; for area, from .6 to .9; and for volume, from .5 to .8 (Baird, 1970; Cleveland, 1985).

2.2 Power and log curves relating stimulus intensity and magnitude of sensation

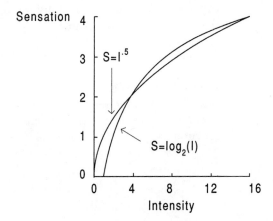

2.3 Circle areas and densities follow power law

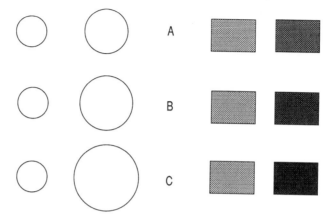

Figure 2.3 illustrates the perceptual bias. In which pair of circles (A, B, or C) is the right circle twice the area of the left? What about the densities on the right: which is twice as dark as its partner?

We drew each pair using a different exponent in the Stevens power function to modify what would otherwise be twice the area of the circle on the left or twice the density of the rectangle on the left. Pair A has an exponent of 1.0, pair B has .95 and pair C has .90. The answer, then, is that the right circle in pair A is twice the area of the circle on the left, and the right rectangle in pair A is twice as dark as the one on the left.

These examples should alert you to the dangers of using area and shading to represent numerical quantities. One solution might be to adjust areas, shadings, and other features in a graph to fit the psychometric functions derived from perceptual experiments. This is easy to do in a computerized graphing package. We shall see, however, that there are usually alternative ways to represent quantitative variation without resorting to shading, area, or other features governed by exceptionally flat psychometric functions.

Visual illusions

PICTURE: a representation in two dimensions of something wearisome in three.

—Ambrose Bierce, *The Devil's Dictionary*

Pictures have a dual reality (Haber & Hershenson, 1980). We live in a three-dimensional world in which pictures are two-dimensional, yet pictures can represent three-dimensional objects. Consequently, our perception of graphs (pictures) is influenced by the tools we have for perceiving three-dimensional space. Sometimes, these tools interfere with accurate perception of a graph.

Figure 2.4 shows some well known two-dimensional illusions. The first (A) is horizontal-vertical illusion in which two equal line segments are distorted by relative orientation. The second, (B), is the Muller-Lyer illusion, in which equal line segments are distorted by intersecting angles. C is the Poggendorf illusion, in which the diagonal segments lie on a common line but are displaced by the verticals. D is a Delboeuf figure, in which the sizes of the center circles are equal but distorted by their surrounds. Finally, E is a Ponzo illusion, in which the perceived sizes of two equal circles are distorted by the surrounding perspective angle. Coren and Girgus (1978) document many other illusions.

2.4 Visual Illusions

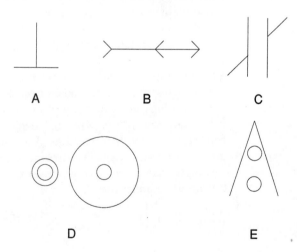

A   B   C

D   E

Gregory (1969) and others believe that many of these illusions evoke three-dimensional depth cues that are inappropriately applied in two-dimensional contexts. The Muller-Lyer and Ponzo illusions, for example, distort size judgments by surrounding stimuli with angular pseudo-depth cues. The Delboeuf figure may involve "tunnel" cues often used in three dimensional processing. These features make it difficult to judge absolute size in two dimensions, because we are accustomed to using depth cues for three-dimensional size judgments.

Whatever the explanation for these illusions, keep in mind that judgments involving angles and figure-ground relations (such as in illusion D) in graphs often are biased. If we can find alternatives to angle representations, such as parallel straight line segments, we will often be more successful in communicating information accurately.

Gestalt psychology and figure-ground separation

Early in this century, Gestalt psychologists proposed that "the whole is more than the sum of its parts." In graphical terms, this means that elements in a graph look different when viewed alone from when viewed in the context of the entire graph. The Gestalt psychologists showed, for example, that when objects are placed near each other, they are perceived as part of an integral pattern. Furthermore, similar objects in an overall display tend to be perceived as part of a unified pattern. Other features of objects, such as symmetry and continuity, affect how we perceive them when embedded in more general patterns. This perceptual organization is not always inherent to the retinal image—we impose organization on the image in order to process it.

Figure-ground effect is a closely related phenomenon. Objects can be framed or placed against a background in ways that change their appearance. An object that contrasts with its background, for example, tends to look more integrated than one that does not. Cleveland, Diaconis, and McGill (1982) proposed an interesting example of this effect. They showed that when point clouds of scatterplots are surrounded by larger or smaller frames, people's perceptions of the correlation between the represented variables changed.

Figure 2.5 shows an illustration of this effect using data generated by SYSTAT and plotted in SYGRAPH. The data are identical in both plots. The lesson is clear. If you want to get tenure or win the Nobel Prize, make your axes too big for the data.

2.5 The top scatterplot looks more correlated

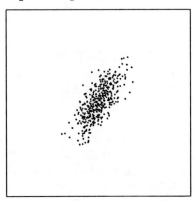

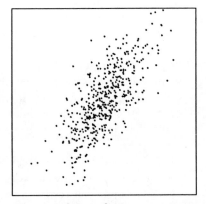

The perception of color

Color is one of the most popular media in computer graphics. Unfortunately, it is also one of the most difficult to use effectively. We want graphs to look pretty, and so we choose color to represent scales or categories. In doing so, we often overlook the complexities involved in perceiving color.

Color is not a physical characteristic of objects or light. It is a purely psychological phenomenon, a "fabrication of the visual system" (Levine & Shefner, 1981). The colors we see are the summation of stimulation by light photons of three different pigments in our retina. The firings of neurons associated with these different pigments are integrated in the visual system to construct every color we see. Because perceived color is a summation of stimulation, the same perceived color can be produced by an infinite number of different physical characteristics in an object and/or light source.

Any three different wavelengths of light can be added (or subtracted) in different quantities to produce the entire visible spectrum, but wavelengths corresponding roughly to RED, GREEN, and BLUE are used in our visual system. For similar operating reasons, color computer terminals and televisions mix the same basic colors.

Most of us were introduced to color theory via Newton's spectrum, which appears to be a linear ordering from short (deep violet) to long (deep red) wavelengths. Some computer displays use this spectrum to represent dimensions (e.g. COOL-WARM temperature, or LOW-HIGH altitude). Because of the way our visual system sums wavelengths, however, we do not perceive the spectrum linearly. We perceive it as an open circle or horseshoe, with deep red and deep violet at each end of the opening and green at the opposite closed portion. Deep red appears closer to deep violet than to green, for example. You can see a scaling of this circle in the MDS chapter of the Statistics manual. Thus, if we want to use color to represent a linear ordering, we should probably choose a segment of the spectrum, say, from green to red.

Another complication affects our use of color in graphics. A spectral color of a given *hue* can be mixed with white light to make it appear pale. Mixture affects not only the *saturation* of a color, but its energy or *brightness* as well. Pure spectral colors do not appear equally vivid or bright. SYGRAPH controls approximately the brightness and saturation of colors on most graphics devices when you choose to manipulate hue.

Colors are best used to represent categories instead of scales. We might use red symbols for an experimental group and green for a control group, for example. Perception of color categories is innate, cross-cultural and not dependent on language. Infants, for example, show clear boundaries between colors (Bornstein, Kessen, & Weiskopf, 1976). When using colors for category definition in a graph, it is a good idea to choose contrasting colors (e.g. RED-GREEN, or RED-YELLOW-GREEN-BLUE) to enhance these boundary discriminations.

Colors can create visual illusions. A gray patch against a green background will appear reddish, for example. You may have noticed a similar contrast effect after working at a green computer screen. The world looks pink when you look away from the screen. Colors also affect area judgments. In three dimensions, a blue disk appears to be farther away than a red disk of the same size, controlling for saturation and brightness. In two dimensions, a red area will look larger than a blue area, probably because of a three-dimensional illusion. Cleveland and McGill (1983), for example, found that people judged red areas on maps to be larger than blue. Durrett (1987) contains several informative papers on the use of color for computer graphics.

Graphic design

We can apply psychological principles to the design of graphs and we can supplement them with aesthetic principles. Cleveland (1985) integrated both areas in a landmark book. After a survey of statistical and psychological research, including some of his own, Cleveland derived an approximate ordering of graphical features from most to least accurate in representing quantitative variation. Figure 2.6 presents this hierarchy.

The criterion for constructing this hierarchy is the linear agreement between quantitative information presented graphically to subjects and the actual values underlying the graphical representation. In a variety of experiments, tasks involving modes higher up in the hierarchy were performed more accurately than tasks lower in the hierarchy. Thus, all other things being equal, we should prefer a bar chart to a pie chart for presenting comparative information, since a bar chart provides a common scale, and a pie chart involves angle judgments. Simkin and Hastie (1987) have found exceptions to this rule when proportional judgments are involved, but Cleveland's basic hierarchy has proved useful in practice.

Sometimes we have no choice. Time series plots, scatterplots, and mathematical functions often require angle judgments because slope is intrinsically angular relative to a horizontal or vertical orientation. In these cases, experimental evidence indicates it is important to choose scales that make the physical slope of the graphed function as close to 45 degrees as possible (Cleveland & McGill, 1988).

Bertin (1983) and Tufte (1983) have written about graphics more from a design point of view. Both stress economy and simple graphic icons. Although both speak of maximizing the information in a graph, we should qualify this rule with what we know about the visual system. In graphs intended for a glance, such as in slide presentations, Mies Van der Rohe's dictum "Less is More" is a better rule. If a graph contains too many visual modes, its information is unlikely to make its way into long-term memory. On the other hand, if we are presenting graphs in a publication, we can tolerate a high degree of complexity—provided components of the graph can be processed in "chunks" to make their way from short-term to long-term memory. By now, you should know there is no simple rule to discriminate good and bad graphics. The appropriateness of a graph depends on the conditions in which it is presented and the information to be communicated.

2.6 Cleveland graphic elements hierarchy

BETTER

1. Position along a common scale

2. Position along identical, nonaligned scales

3. Length

4. Angle - Slope

5. Area

6. Volume

7. Color hue - Color saturation - Density

WORSE

Some examples

A few examples should illustrate the psychological and design principles we have seen. In the following figures, we have contrasted two alternative graphs of the same information. The upper graph is less effective in communicating the information than the lower.

Perspective
mania

Figure 2.7 illustrates a three-dimensional bar graph. These perspective bar charts are popular in business programs. We cannot think of a single instance in which a perspective bar graph should be used for any application. Like all perspective plots, the depth information is confusing and gives rise to several visual illusions. The actual height of the bars is difficult to establish. Some users ruin the plot further by adding color coding to the bars which enhances the pseudo perspective illusions.

The lower graphs in the figure are less glamorous but more effective. If you wish to compare trends between the two grouping variables, the line graph in the middle of the figure is particularly useful. It is easy to see where the profiles are parallel, and their heights and values are easily identified on the common scale. If you are more interested in highlighting differences at each comparison point, the multi-value bar chart at the bottom of the figure is more suitable. Here, the graphic focus is on each pair of bars, facilitating individual comparisons. Finally, you should consider a dot plot (Cleveland,1985), which can be done with **Category** in SYGRAPH. Dot plots are similar to bar graphs but they do not connect the data points to a base the way bars do.

You may have noticed that SYGRAPH has a full assortment of 3-D graphs. We had to make *some* concession to the marketplace. Nevertheless, before you use them, please consider 2-D alternatives.

2.7 Three-dimensional bars versus lines

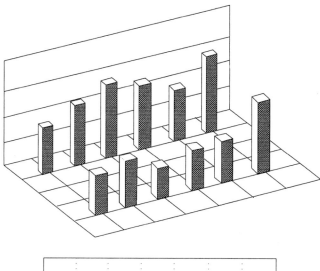

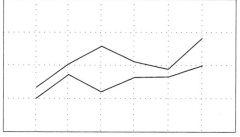

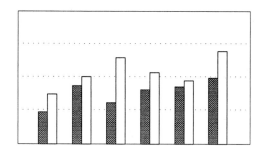

Pseudo
perspective bar
charts

A nasty relative of the perspective bar chart is the pseudo perspective bar chart. Illustrators frequently feel the need to make two dimensional bars look like blocks or skyscrapers. Doing so makes it difficult to reference the top of the bar against a scale. It is never clear whether the "front" or "back" of the bar is intended to be the height indicator. Figure 2.8 shows an example of this type of graph. The upper figure is a double bar graph with pseudo perspective to enhance the display. The same information is contained in the lower graph: less glitzy, but more informative and aesthetically more pleasing. As with Figure 2.7, this information could be represented with a simple line graph, especially if parallelism of the profiles were of primary interest.

2.8 Pseudo perspective bars versus two dimensional bars

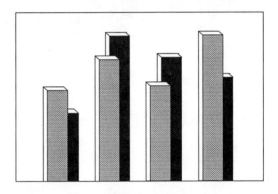

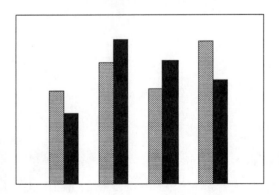

Pseudo perspective line graphs

The graph in the next figure was adapted from a chart of grain production in China and the Soviet Union featured in a leading national newspaper. The point of the article was to highlight the widening gap between Soviet and Chinese grain production. Although the graph shows production on the vertical axis against years on the horizontal, it does little to make the point. First, the pseudo three-dimensional perspective makes it difficult for us to line up the two trends. Shifting the upper trend to the left to simulate perspective ruins the calibration of the horizontal scale. Second, the uneven shading across the graph enhances our depth perception by making foreground darker than background, but it ruins our focus on the widening gap, which is the purpose of the graph and article.

The lower graph represents the same data in a simple two-dimensional filled line chart. The fill area is dark enough to contrast strongly with the background. Vertical lines in the graph segment the trend so that year to year differences are clearly visible. We have induced a possible figure-ground effect in the lower graph. That is, we could focus on the central dark portion as the figure against a light background, or we could view the white bars as figures against a dark background. This effect does not interfere with the perception of the widening gap, however.

2.9 Pseudo perspective line graph vs. filled line graph

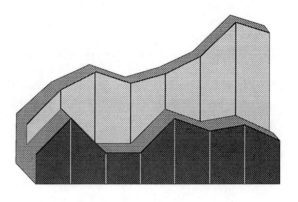

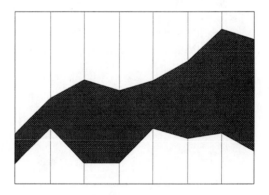

Perspective pie charts

Pie charts are among the most abused graphics icons. A favorite among business packages is the three-dimensional pie chart. These floating platters frequently appear in newspapers, TV graphics, and textbooks. They incorporate nearly every visual illusion we have discussed. Figure 2.10 shows an example of a 3-D versus a regular pie chart with the same information. The upper figure includes some of the texturing which is popular in these displays and which further distorts the proportional area information. The shading on the side of the pie makes the area judgments even more difficult. Finally, removing the slice impedes anchoring judgments, in which we must mentally superimpose one slice on another in order to compare their magnitudes. Pulling slices out of 3-D or 2-D pies is never as effective as shading or coloring the slice in its proper place in the pie, as we have done in the lower graph. Coloring and shading pies can enhance their attractiveness, but if you are interested in accurate judgments, keep them empty. Both shading and coloring interfere with size judgments.

2.10 Three-dimensional vs. two-dimensional pie chart

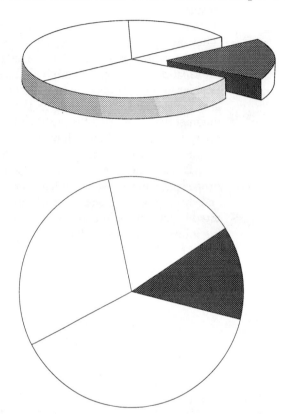

Pie charts have been ridiculed in recent years by many statisticians and graphic designers (e.g. Bertin, 1983; Tufte, 1983). Many studies, going back to the 1920s show that bar charts are more effective than pie charts—even for proportion-of-the-whole judgments.

Information
overload

You can put too much information in a graph intended for a glance.
Tufte (1983) and Bertin (1983) recommend a high ratio of "data" to
"ink" in order to discourage distracting irrelevant features, but this prin-
ciple can backfire if pushed to the extreme. Figure 2.11 shows a graph
we adapted from an advertisement showing off all the bells and whistles
of a new computer graphics package. The graph was being used in a
slide presentation. A composite graph of this sort is like "integrated"
software—the pieces work tolerably but the whole is an intimidating
mess. In trying to cram too much information into a single panel of a
display, the designer of this graph compromised the individual choices.
We haven't got an effective alternative to this graph. Several independent graphs would be the logical choice.

2.11 An excessively complicated graph

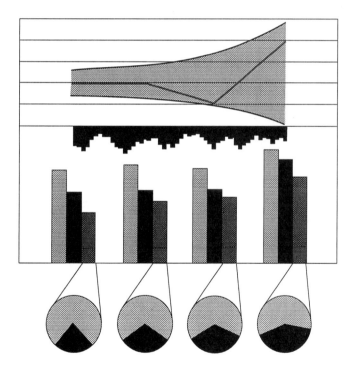

There are times when a complex graph can be appropriate—even in a slide presentation. Earlier in this chapter, we mentioned that we can "chunk" complex information in short-term memory if we can find simple rules and analogies for processing it. Memory experts do this when they memorize thousands of digits of random numbers. For graphs, the best way to facilitate chunking is to integrate the components in an ordered arrangement. You can see the **Icon** and **SPLOM** chapters for examples of complex graphs that can nevertheless be memorized after careful viewing.

3 Overview

Overview   3

No other computer graphics package can produce all the graphs in SYGRAPH. Instead of having numerous separate menus, however, SYGRAPH groups displays under a few common types. This chapter shows you these groupings so that you can produce specific graphs quickly and easily.

Graph menu   Here is the main menu for all the graphics routines:

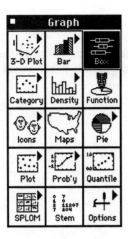

The chapters in this volume cover each selection in this menu. The menu is organized alphabetically, but the chapters are organized by task. Here is a summary of the chapter contents:

Bar   Bar graphs, which are displays of counts or means and other measures against a categorical variable.

Category   Category plots, which are similar to bar graphs, except the tops of bars are designated by symbols and the bars are omitted. Often, these symbols are connected by lines.

Pie   Pie graphs, which represent proportions of wholes by wedges of a disk.

Box   Box-and-whisker (schematic) plots, which are displays of the medians and other quantiles of a continuous variable. These can be plotted for separate subgroups on a common scale.

Density   Density plots, which portray the distribution of a continuous variable. The most common density display is a histogram.

Stem   Stem-and-leaf plots, which display the distribution and significant digits of a continuous variable.

Plot | Bivariate scatterplots, which display the joint distribution of two continuous variables. Numerous enhancements, such as display of subgroups, smoothing, and superimposing additional variables, are available.

3-D Plot | Three dimensional data plots, which display the distribution of three continuous variables. Numerous enhancements, similar to those for 2-D plots, are available.

SPLOM | Scatterplot matrices, which are matrices of bivariate scatterplots. All the enhancements for bivariate scatterplots are available in SPLOMs.

Function | Function plots, which are 2-D and 3-D plots of mathematical functions. Since there are no data involved, you simply type the equation to be plotted.

Probability | Probability plots, which compare observed data values to one of several theoretical probability distributions.

Quantile | Quantile plots, which compare observed data values to their percentiles (Q plot) or compare the percentiles of one variable against those of another (Q-Q plot).

Icon | Icon plots, which are multidimensional icons whose features depend on the variation within many variables. The most popular varieties are Chernoff faces, star plots, Fourier blobs, and weathervanes.

Map | Maps, which are two dimensional representations of geographic or other data.

A taxonomy of graphs | Graphical data are usually of two types, continuous and categorical. Continuous data come from a scale of values that can be any real number from minus to plus infinity. Categorical data may be numerals or characters, but their distinguishing feature is that they fall into a relatively small number of unordered discrete categories. You may plot continuous data on categorical graphs in SYGRAPH, but if there are too many values, the graphs will be messy. Doing a bar chart of income, for example, would be impractical unless you split income into a small number of separate categories.

The following table summarizes the types of graphs available for various combinations of these types of data. There is no best graph for every purpose, but you should try the recommended graphs first.

VARIABLES

DATA	One	Two	Many
Categorical	Bar Category Pie		
Continuous	Box Density Map Probability Quantile Stem	Map Plot Quantile SPLOM	Icon Map Plot Quantile SPLOM
Mixed		Bar Box Category Pie	Bar Category

Many popular writers overlook the duplications in this table. They always recommend a line graph for financial data, for example. You should try several alternatives when there are duplicates, however, especially **Bar, Category (Line)**, and **Pie**. The following pages show typical graphs for each.

Bar

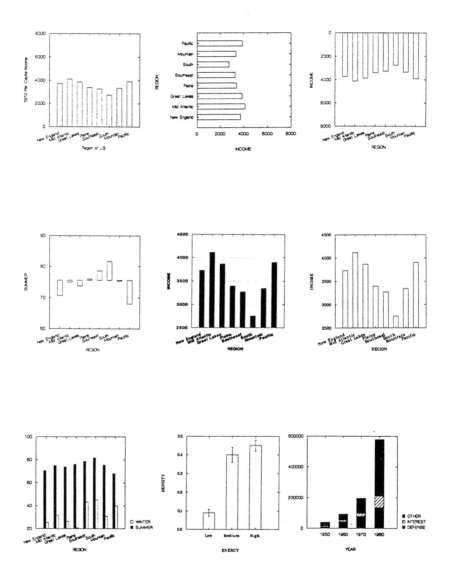

Overview

Category

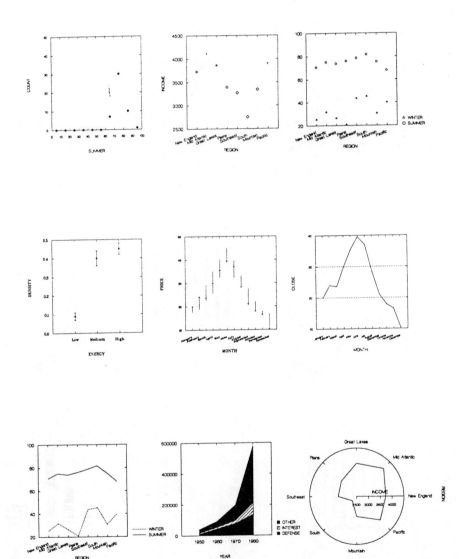

Pie

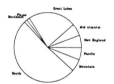

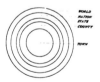

Box

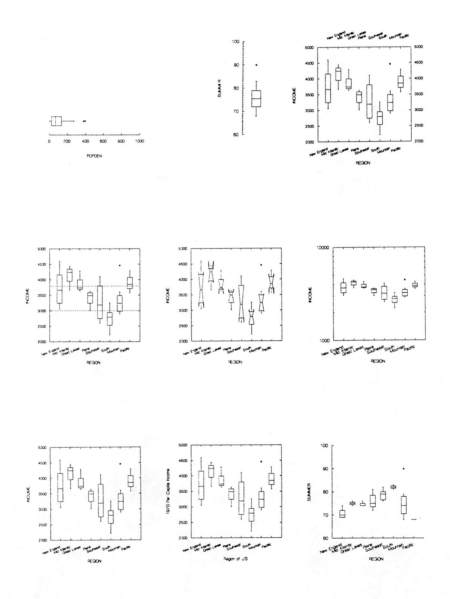

Density

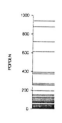
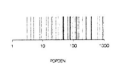
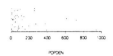

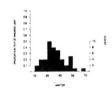
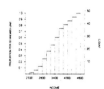

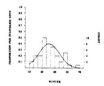
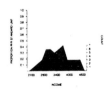
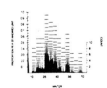

Overview

Stem

```
0    0000000111
0H   222333
0    444455
0M   667777
0    8889
1H   01
1H   22
1    45
1
1    9
2
2
2    55
2    7
     ---OUTSIDE VALUES---
3    79
6    1
7    1
8    7
9    4
```

```
68    0000
69    000
70    000
71    0
72H   00
73    00
74    0000
75M   00000
76    0000
77    00
78    00
79H   00000
80
81    000
82    00000
83    00
      ---OUTSIDE VALUES---
90    0
```

Plot

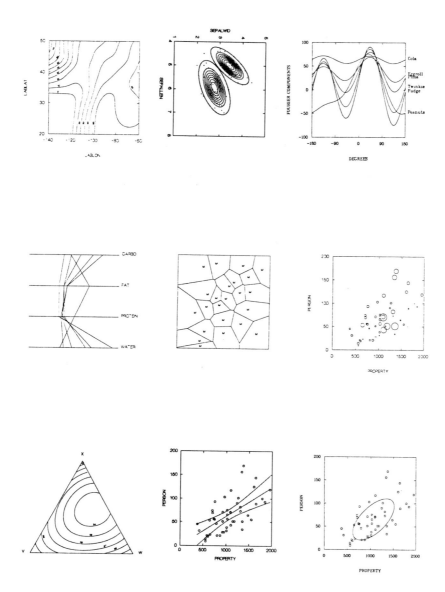

Overview

3-D Plot

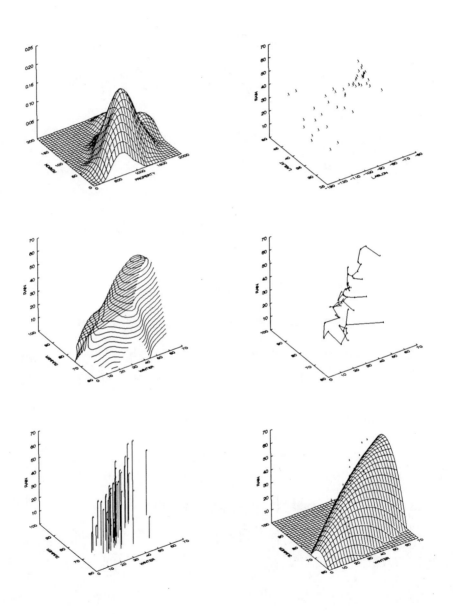

SPLOM

 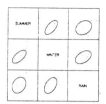 

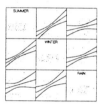  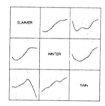

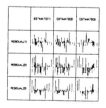 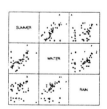 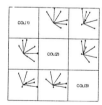

Overview

Function

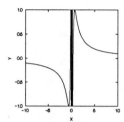 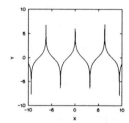 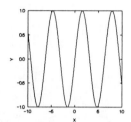

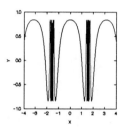 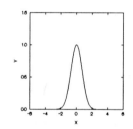 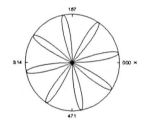

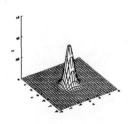 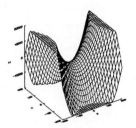 

Probability

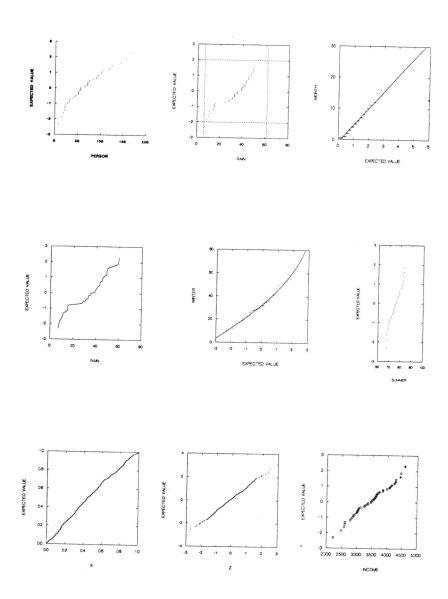

Overview

Quantile

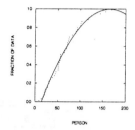

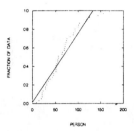

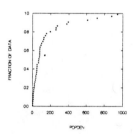

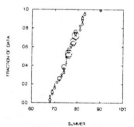

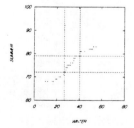

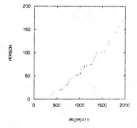

Icon

Socio-Demo-Metero-Mumbo-Jumbo

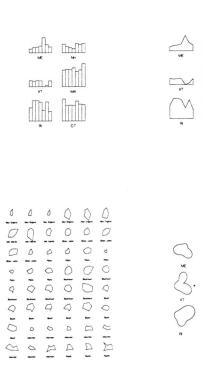

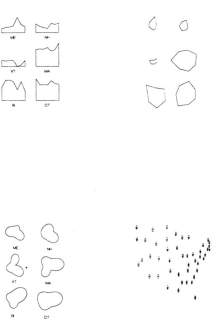

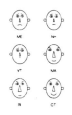

Overview

Map

Common
options

The next chapter covers common options that allow you to customize each graph. These options include controlling features such as axes, scale values, tick marks, symbols, titles, and so on.

Embellishment

You should examine other tools such as drawing tools (in the **Window** menu), the sizing window (available by clicking the ruler in any menu), and fonts (in **Graph/Options...**) for other ways to embellish your graph.

Programming

SYGRAPH contains a general graphics programming language. You can produce almost any graph or part of a graph using this language. The programming language is particularly appropriate for producing automated graphs for industrial control, batch processing, and other repeated graphing tasks on large batches of data. See the **Using SYGRAPH commands** chapter at the end of this volume for further information.

4

Common options

Common options   4

Usage

The options documented in this chapter are those that appear in the dialog boxes for many types of graphs. Note that the icons for the options vary from one type of plot to the next, but the options work the same.

Some options present a dialog box for you to make various decisions. Other options just toggle between "on" and "off."

Common options

Adjusting size and position with the ruler

A tiny ruler appears in every graphics dialog box. Use the ruler to adjust the size and origin of a graph.

- Click the ruler icon
- Specify size and origin by typing in the boxes or resizing and moving the marquee
- Click OK

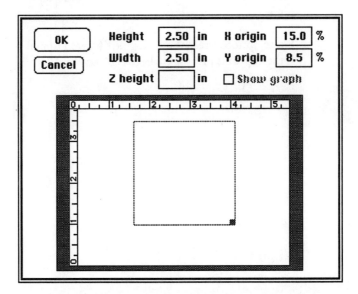

If you have a graph in the View window, you may click [Show graph] to see that graph in the screen. This can be useful, for instance, for placing a box plot beside a graph; you can click [Show graph] to see a mini graph, and then move the marquee around and resize it to suit the graph.

Height and width are expressed in inches. The default [Height] and [Width] are the same as for the default graph axes. Thus, if you two plots without using the ruler option, the new plot will exactly overlap the previous one.

Specify a [Z height] for a three-dimensional graph in perspective. Remember, [Z height] is specified in real units, but the actual physical height of the object depends on the [Eye] setting in **Options/Formats....** Many three-dimensional perspective options appear in the **Using SYGRAPH commands** chapter.

Options with
dialog boxes

Most options present a dialog box when you click them. You make various choices and then click OK to return to the main dialog box for the plot. You will then notice that a button has appeared in the upper right corner of the icon.

For example, suppose you are working on a bar chart and you click [Axes] and make some choices. After you click OK and return to the main dialog box, the [Axes] icon has a *button* :

Before   *After*

The [Axes] choices you made will remain in effect until you click [Axes] again and change the dialog box. You could click [Axes] again right away and change everything around. Or, you could draw a bar chart and come back to **Bar** to do another plot with the same choices. If you clicked "Axes" again you would see that your choices would still be there. You can turn them "off" by clicking the little button in the corner. Your choices remain in the dialog box, but the defaults are used instead.

Defaults   *Your choices*

To return to using your choices, just click the [Axes] option and click OK. The button will be back.

Common options

Options that are on or off

Some options, like [Sort], do *not* present a dialog box. When you click those options, you just turn them on or off. The little button means the option is "on." For example:

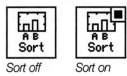

Sort off   Sort on

[Sort] and [T'pose] are the only common options that toggle between on and off.

4.1
Basic bar chart

In this chapter, we will experiment with a basic bar chart. Before we start adjusting things and changing options, let's see the way SYGRAPH draws it by default. We are using the US data file.

- Select **Bar/Bar** from the **Graph** menu
- Select the Y variable: INCOME
- Select the X variable: REGION$
- Click OK

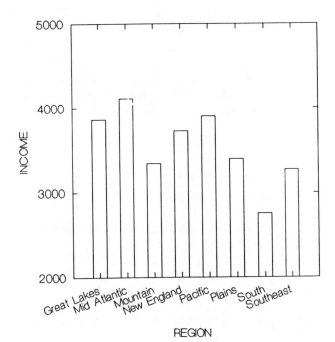

© 1989, SYSTAT, Inc.

Axes

[Axes] lets you control the appearance (and presence) of axes on a graph. To control axis features, click the [Axis] icon in the dialog box for the type of graph you are drawing.

- Click [Axes]
- Choose the options you want
- Click OK

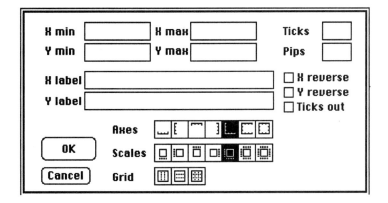

The [Axes] dialog box differs slightly for three-dimensional graphs, which add a Z axis:

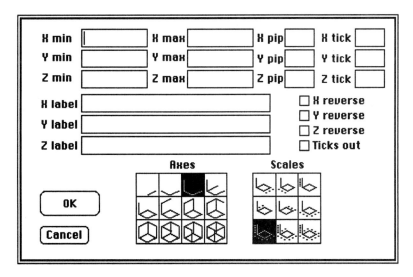

4.2
Data limits

Notice that our bar graph has a minimum income of $2500 and a maximum of $4500. SYGRAPH chooses this range based on the data. It searches for round numbers below and above the minimum and maximum values in the data, respectively. You can set [X min], [X max], [Y min] and [Y max] to modify these values to standardize your graph on a different scale. Points outside of the axes limits you set are treated as missing in all computations involved in your graph.

The horizontal axis is called X and the vertical axis is called Y, unless you have transposed the graph by clicking [T'pose], discussed below.

Here we set [Y min] to 0 for the INCOME axis. Since we have not specified YMAX, the maximum value for the scale is chosen from the data.

- Select **Bar/Bar** from the **Graph** menu
- Select the Y variable: INCOME
- Select the X variable: REGION$
- Click [Axes]
  - Specify 0 for [Y min]
- Click OK

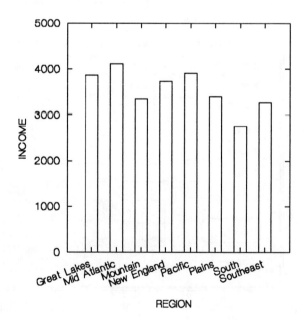

Ticks

SYGRAPH chooses a number of tick marks that produces round scale numbers and a pleasing display. Sometimes you might want fewer or more tick marks. You can change the number of tick marks on a graph with [X tick] and [Y tick].

Usually, it is difficult to choose a number of tick marks that produces a better display than SYGRAPH does by default, but this option can be helpful when you have unusual data. There is no limit to the number of ticks, but if you choose too many, the scale values overlap.

Ticks out

Click [Ticks out] to place the tick marks outside the graph frame.

4.3
Pips

You can also make finer tick marks between those with scale values. These are called "pip marks." You can choose any number of pip marks for any axis. For example, if you want to divide each segment between tick marks on the X axis into fifths, set [X pip] to 5.

Here we request 4 tick marks and 4 pip marks for the Y axis. Because we also set [Y min] to 0, the ticks divide INCOME into $2000 intervals, and the pips into $500 intervals.

- Select **Bar/Bar** from the **Graph** menu
- Select the Y variable: INCOME
- Select the X variable: REGION$
- Click [Axes]
  - Set [Y min] to 0
  - Set [Ticks] to 4
  - Set [Pips] to 4
- Click OK

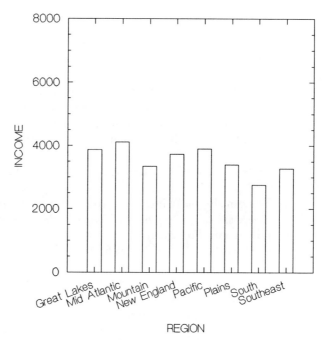

4.4
Labeling axes

You may not always want to label axes with variable names. Sometimes longer labels are necessary to make a clear graph. You can specify your own axis labels by typing them in the boxes for [X label] and [Y label].

We choose to delete our [Y min], [Ticks] and [Pips] settings.

- Select **Bar/Bar** from the **Graph** menu
- Select the Y variable: INCOME
- Select the X variable: REGION$
- Click [Axes]
  - Type the [X label]: Census Region
  - Type the [Y label]: Income
- Click OK

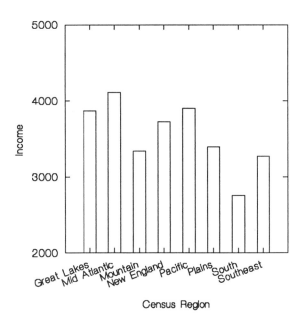

Census Region

4.5
Control limits

For most SYGRAPH plots, you can add dashed lines to mark limits on any numerical axis. Quality control charts, for example, mark upper and lower limits on an axis to indicate permissible bounds for a production process. Axis limits can be used in other applications to mark simultaneous standard errors.

For most plots, you must specify two numbers (upper and lower) for the limit. They need not be in order. Limits will not be plotted for numbers outside the extremes of the specified axes. Thus, if you want to plot only one limit (dashed line) on your axis, specify something like "2, –9999." In addition, SYGRAPH can automatically compute three-sigma limits for bar charts and category plots. To draw three-sigma limits on a bar chart, select [Limit] but do not specify any values. To draw three-sigma limits on a category plot, check [Sigma limits] in the [Axes] dialog box.

Common options

Here is our bar graph with automatic three-sigma limits. (We deleted our [X label] and [Y label] settings).

- Select **Bar/Bar** from the **Graph** menu
- Select the Y variable: INCOME
- Select the X variable: REGION$
- Click [Limit] but leave the box blank
- Click OK

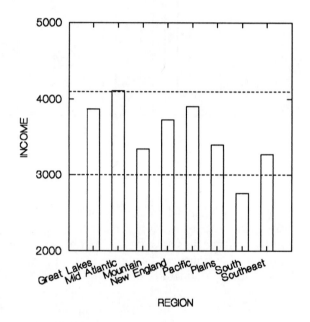

4.6
Axes

You may not want four axes, like a box, around your graph. You can choose from the combinations shown for between 0 and four axes. Here we choose only the lower X axis. (We deleted our limits).

- Select **Bar/Bar** from the **Graph** menu
- Select the Y variable: INCOME
- Select the X variable: REGION$
- Click [Axes]
  - Choose the first [Axes] icon: lower X axis only
- Click OK

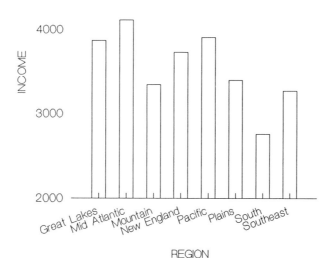

4.7
Scales

You may have noticed that the scale values for INCOME were shown even though its axes were omitted. You can choose from the combinations shown. Here is the same graph with no axes and two scales:

- Select **Bar/Bar** from the **Graph** menu
- Select the Y variable: INCOME
- Select the X variable: REGION$
- Click [Axes]
  - Click off the [Axes] icon
  - Choose the L-shaped [Scales] icon
- Click OK

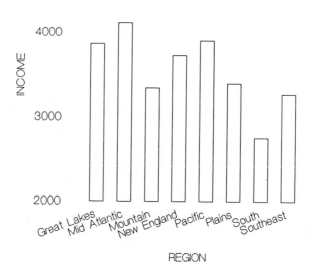

4.8
Grids

You can add grid marks by clicking one of the three [Grids] icons. You can choose from horizontal, vertical, or horizontal and vertical grid lines. (We put [Axes] and [Scales] back to the defaults).

- Select **Bar/Bar** from the **Graph** menu
- Select the Y variable: INCOME
- Select the X variable: REGION$
- Click [Axes]
  - Choose the square "Axes" icon
  - Choose the third [Grids] icon
- Click OK

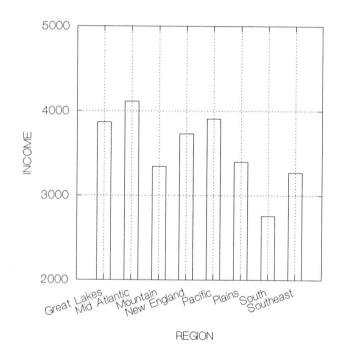

4.9
Reversing scales

You can reverse the scale on any axis. Below, we reverse the Y scale to make an upside-down bar chart.

Why would you want to do this? Maybe you like upside-down graphs. You can transpose an upside-down bar graph to make back-to-back or dual bar graphs. In the **Two dimensional plots** chapter, you can see some more reasons for reversing scales. (We clicked off the [Grids] icon.)

- Select **Bar/Bar** from the **Graph** menu
- Select the Y variable: INCOME
- Select the X variable: REGION$
- Click [Axes]
  - Click [Y reverse]
- Click OK

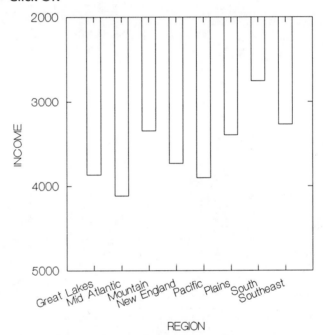

Colors

Two options control colors of a graph. The [Colors] option that appears in most dialog boxes controls the plotting elements: the boxes in a box plot, the bars of a bar chart, the wedges in a pie chart, the curve in a function plot, etc.

Options/Color... controls global coloring: the background, foreground, graph, and labels of every graph. You use it to set up the general details of how you want graphs colored. We discuss **Color...** near the end of the chapter with the other **Options** items.

These color features are only available if you have equipment capable of producing color output. If you have a color printing device, you can print in color even if your monitor is not capable of color display.

Colors

The [Colors] option colors plotting elements of a graph. You can choose color by name or wavelength. Black, white, red, green, blue, cyan, magenta, and yellow are available by name. Some colors and their approximate nanometer wavelengths are: Red (615), Orange (590), Yellow (575), Green (505), Blue (480), and Violet (450).

- Click the [Colors] option
- Choose a color for the plotting element, or specify a wavelength, or specify a variable name
- Click OK

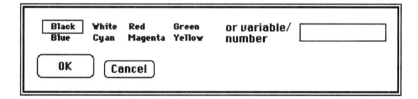

4.10
Colored bars

You may click one of the basic colors, type an exact wavelength in the [or variable/number] box, or type a variable name. That variable should be either a character variable containing color names or a numeric variable containing wavelengths.

For example, we can draw a bar chart with green bars. (We also clicked off the [Axes] option so SYGRAPH would return to its defaults.)

- Select **Bar/Bar** from the **Graph** menu
- Select the Y variable: INCOME
- Select the X variable: REGION$
- Click [Colors]
  - Click [Green]
- Click OK

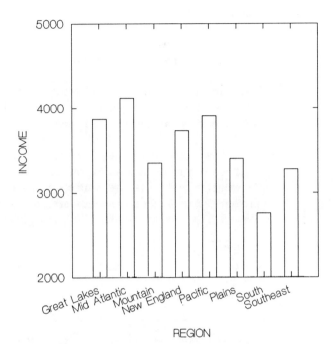

**4.11
Solid colored
bars**

If you want solid green bars, you also have to select a solid [Fill], which is discussed in more detail later.

- Select **Bar/Bar** from the **Graph** menu
- Select the Y variable: INCOME
- Select the X variable: REGION$
- Click [Colors]
  - Click [Green]
- Click [Fill]
  - Click the solid option
- Click OK

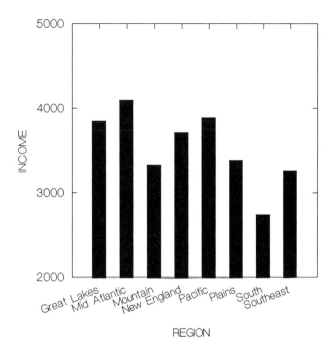

For graphs with more than one Y variable, you may specify several color names in the [or variable/number] box. For instance, a bar chart of INCOME and SUMMER by REGION$ could have colors [Red, Green]. The bars for INCOME would be red and those for SUMMER green.

Fill

You can fill bars, symbols, and other fillable features in a graph with the [Fill] option.

- Click [Fill]
- Choose a fill pattern by number or by clicking
- Click OK

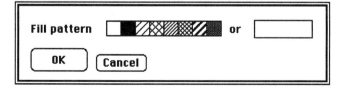

4.12
Filled bars

If you specify a number between 0 and 1, you get an even gradation of shading between empty and solid (white and black, unless you have chosen another color). You can also refer to the patterns shown by numbers 0, 1, 2, ..., 7.

Here is the bar chart with 50% black bars. (We clicked off [Colors].)

- Select **Bar/Bar** from the **Graph** menu
- Select the Y variable: INCOME
- Select the X variable: REGION$
- Click [Fill]
  - Type .5 in the box
- Click OK

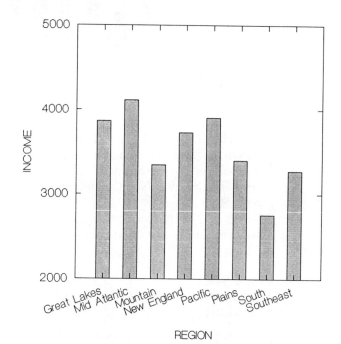

4.13
Two-variable bar chart

Here's a two-variable bar chart of average summer and winter temperatures, with the summer bars black and the winter bars shaded.

- Select **Bar/Bar** from the **Graph** menu
- Select the Y variables: SUMMER, WINTER
- Select the X variable: REGION$
- Click [Fill]
  - Type 1,7 in the box
- Click OK

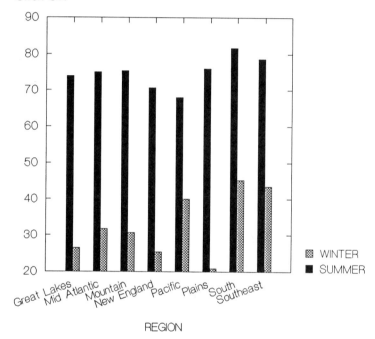

Legend

For **Bar, Category,** and **Plot,** you can add a legend to label the various plotting symbols and fills when you have more than one Y variable. The legend provides a key to the symbols or fills that you choose to distinguish several independent variables.

You get legends automatically for any **Bar**, **Category**, or **Plot** when you've chosen more than one Y (independent, or vertical) variable. By default, SYGRAPH shows the symbol (or fill) used to plot each variable alongside the variable names. You only need to use the [Legend] option if you want some text other than the variable names or if you want to place the legend elsewhere than at the graph's lower right (the default).

- Click [Legend]
- Type the text for each Y variable, in the same order you selected the variables
- Specify the X and Y coordinates for the origin (lower left corner) of the legend in percentage, inches (IN), or centimeters (CM)
- Click OK

#1	
#2	
#3	
#4	
#5	

Origin for legend

OK   X

Cancel Y

Notice that the dialog box only allows for five labels (for five Y variables). If you need to show and label more than five variables in a single plot—and we caution you *not* to overload your graphs this way—you can use the LEGEND command in the command interface to specify more. See the **Command reference** chapter.

Line

Line

The [Line] option connects plotting symbols with a line. You can choose from various types of lines.

- Click [Line]
- Choose the type of line, or specify line/s by number
- Click OK

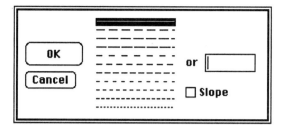

You may specify lines by typing a number(s) between 1 and 11 in the box or by clicking the line type to the left if there is only one. If you are plotting more than one dependent variable for **3-D** or **Plot**, or more than one variable for **Category**, you must specify as many lines as variables. For example, if you are drawing a **Category** plot of three variables, you must specify three line types, e.g. 1,2,7. You can, however, use the same line type for each, e.g. 1,1,1.

4.14 Category plot with line

Here is a **Category** plot with a dotted line connecting the points.

- Select **Category/Category** from the Graph menu
- Select the Y variable: INCOME
- Select the X variable: REGION$
- Click [Line]
  - Choose the dotted line at the bottom
  - Click OK
- Click OK

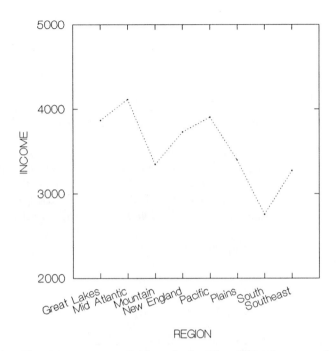

Slope

The [Slope] option is available only for **Plot**. [Slope] automatically scales line graphs for data such as time series. It adjusts the height and width of the graph so that the median absolute physical slope of the plotted line segments is one, following theory and experiments of Cleveland. It is highly recommended for time series plots.

Log

You may log the scales of your graphs. Transform the X axis with the [X log] option, the Y axis with [Y log], and the Z axis with [Z log]. Specify the base for the logarithm in the corresponding box. The default is base e for natural logarithms (ln, or $\log_e$).

Of course, you can also log your data in the Editor. Then your scales would be in log units. The advantage of logging within a plot is that the scales are displayed in original data units.

- Click [Log]
- Click [X log], [Y log], and [Z log] to log the corresponding axis
- Specify a base for each logarithm; the default is e
- Click OK

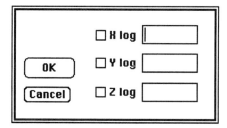

For some types of graphs, like **Pie**, there is only one "axis" that you can log, so the dialog box looks different.

A button appears in the upper right corner of the [Log] icon to remind you that scales are being logged. To turn logging off, click off the button.

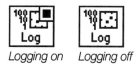

Logging on *Logging off*

Log tick marks are evenly spaced. Sometimes you wish to have unevenly spaced tick marks with nice scale values. You may do this by setting **Log scale spacing** in the global **Options/Formats...** menu at the lower right corner of the Graph menu.

**4.15
Logged bar chart**

Here we draw the familiar bar chart with the vertical axis logged (base 10 logarithms). The vertical axis values will be logged means of temperature.

- Select **Bar/Bar** from the **Graph** menu
- Select the Y variables: SUMMER, WINTER
- Select the X variable: REGION$
- Click [Log]
    - Specify base 10 for [Log]
- Click OK

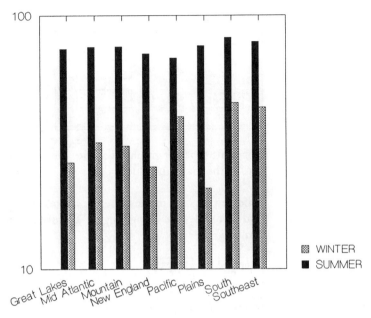

Polar coordinates

Polar coordinates translate rectangular (Cartesian) coordinates into a circular arrangement. Each point is given by its distance (r) from the origin and the angle (θ) between the positive X-axis and the vector from the origin to the point. You may want to trace a square plotting frame before drawing plots in polar coordinates, so that the r scale remains the same for any θ.

Polar coordinates are most often used where direction and extent are the most meaningful expression of the relation between two variables. More generally, however, polar coordinates are a mathematical transformation of the expression of an image. In SYGRAPH, the [Polar] option is available for almost every type of graph, but it is most frequently applicable to plots and category plots. In **Category...**, the [Polar] option appears in its own icon. In **Plot...**, the polar option appears in a [Coord] icon together with triangular coordinates.

Power

You may power the scales of your graphs. Transform the X axis with the [X power] option, the Y axis with [Y power], and the Z axis with [Z power]. Specify the exponent for the power in the corresponding box. The default is exponent .5, which square roots the scale. To return to the default, delete your specifications from the boxes.

- Click [Power]
  - Click [X power], [Y power], and [Z power] to power the corresponding axis
  - Specify an exponent for each; the default is .5
- Click OK

OK	☐ **X power** _____
	☐ **Y power** _____
Cancel	☐ **Z power** _____

A button appears in the upper right corner of the [Power] icon to remind you that scales are being powered. To turn powering off, click off the button.

Project

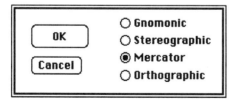

Project

Projections are transformations of spherical to rectangular coordinates. Think of them as mathematical methods for taking an orange peel and stretching it to lie flat on a table.

All maps must be projected from a sphere to a plane unless you live in Flatland. If you want to overlay a **Plot** or a **Surface** on a map, you should use the same projection as your map so the two plots coincide properly.

- Click [Project]
- Choose [Gnomic], [Stereographic], [Mercator], or [Orthographic] projection
- Click OK

OK	○ **Gnomonic**
	○ **Stereographic**
Cancel	◉ **Mercator**
	○ **Orthographic**

Some examples of projections appear in the **Map** chapter.

As with other options, a button appears in the upper right corner of the [Project] icon to remind you that you have chosen a projection. Click off the button if you want to return to the default (Mercator) without changing the choice in the dialog box.

Project off   *Project on*

Sort

[Sort] lets you plot levels of a categorical variable in ascending numeric or character (alphabetical) order. **Bar, Category,** and **Pie** can plot counts of categorical variables (that is, if you select only a categorical variable, you get a plot of how many cases are in each group or level of that variable) or continuous data against a categorical variable.

By default, SYGRAPH turns sorting on, for plots ordered (alphabetized) according to the categories. You might prefer to have the categories *not* sorted but rather shown in the same order as they first appear in the data file. For instance, it probably makes more sense not to sort the REGION$ categories, since they are ordered geographically in the file.

As with other options, a button appears in the upper right corner of the [Sort] icon to tell you that sorting is "on." Click the button to turn sorting "off."

[Sort] has no dialog box—it's either on or off.

Sort off   *Sort on*

4.16
Unsorted bars

Let's draw the bars unsorted.

- Select **Bar/Bar** from the **Graph** menu
- Select the Y variables: SUMMER, WINTER
- Select the X variable: REGION$
- Click off [Sort]
- Click OK

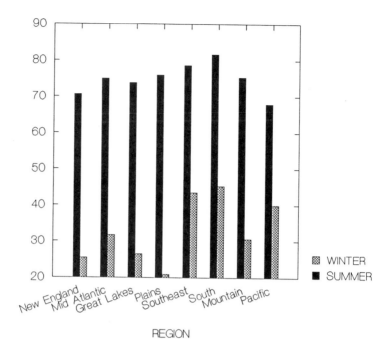

Symb'l

Most of the graphical procedures allow special symbols. You can select any of six different symbols if you are printing with an ImageWriter, or any of 21 symbols with a LaserWriter or for the screen. For these symbols, you have your choice of size, fill, and color.

You may also specify numeric variables to govern [Fill], [Size], and [Color], or character variables for [Label]. Check the index for these other approaches to differentiating data points.

- Click [Symbol]
- Make the choices you want
- Click OK

Choosing a symbol

You may specify symbols by number. The symbols are numbered from left to right in the rows of choices for LaserWriter—the star, for example, is 9, and the female symbol is 21.

If you are plotting several variables (or, for **Plot**, several dependent variables), you *must* specify a symbol for each variable, e.g. 1,3 to use little squares for the first variable selected and triangles for the second.

You can also specify characters to be used as plotting symbols. You must enclose characters (which could include numbers) in single or double quotation marks and separate them with commas or spaces. For example, 'A','*' plots the first variable with A's and the second with asterisks.

Finally, you can specify a character variable. If you do this, the first letter for the value of the character variable is used as the plotting symbol.

Label symbols with variable names

After choosing one of the ImageWriter or LaserWriter symbols, you may use the [Label symbols with variable name(s)] option. Specify a character variable. The first letter of that variable's value for a given case is placed near the plotting symbol in the graph.

4.16 Filled symbols

You may specify fills by number (the patterns are numbered left to right). Just as with symbols, you must specify as many fills as variables.

You may specify a variable for [Fill]. The variable must be a numeric variable with fill pattern numbers (1–7) for values. If you do this, each plotting symbol is filled with the pattern indicated for that case.

Here's a **Category** plot with female zebras for the plotting symbols.

- Select **Category/Category** from the **Graph** menu
- Select the Y variable: INCOME
- Select the X variable: REGION$
- Click [Symb'l]
  - Click the female symbol (the last in the LaserWriter set)
  - Click the striped fill pattern (second to last)
- Click OK

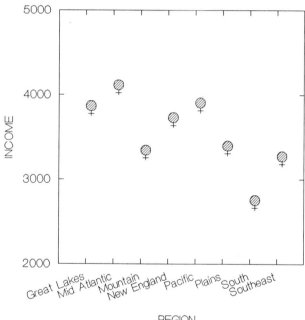

Size

You may scale sizes by positive numbers; the default (smallest) symbol size is multiplied by the number you specify. For example, to make the symbols half the size as the default, type .5. Just as with symbols and fills, you must specify as many sizes as variables.

You may specify a variable for [Size]. The variable must be a numeric variable with positive values. If you do this, each plotting symbol is scaled by the number given by the variable for that case. You can produce bubble plots with this option.

If you want to plot with no symbols, just set [Size] to 0 to make the symbols invisible. This is handy for line plots and contour plots, for example, where you don't want to see the actual data points.

Color

You may specify symbol colors by wavelength in nanometers or by name in the box..

You may specify a variable for color. The variable should either be a character variable with color names for values or a numeric variable with wavelengths for values. If you do this, the color for each plotting symbol is determined by the value of the variable for that case.

Title

Use the [Title] option to place a title or caption above the graph.

- Click [Title]
- Type the text of the title
- Click OK

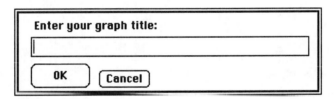

4.18
Titled bar chart

Here we add a title to our INCOME bar chart. (We clicked off [Fill].)

- Select **Bar/Bar** from the **Graph** menu
- Select the Y variable: INCOME
- Select the X variable: REGION$
- Click [Title]
  - Type the title: Income within Region
- Click OK

© 1989, SYSTAT, Inc.

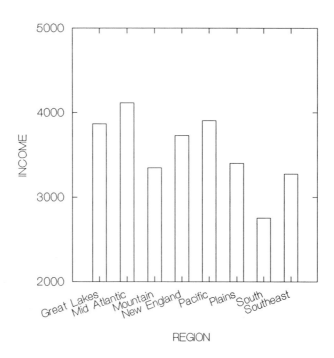

Income within Region

T'pose

The [T'pose] option reverses the X and Y axes. Use [T'pose] to get sideways plots, bar charts, etc.

[T'pose] is a toggle option: it's either on or off. When a button appears in the upper right corner, the plot will be drawn sideways.

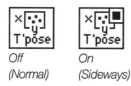

Off   On
(Normal)   (Sideways)

**4.19
Transposed bar
chart**

Here we flip the bar chart sideways. (We clicked off [Title])

• Select **Bar/Bar** from the **Graph** menu
• Select the Y variable: INCOME
• Select the X variable: REGION$
• Click [T'pose]
• Click OK

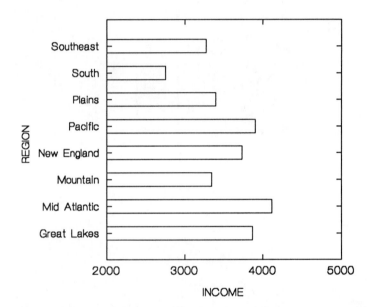

Color...

Options has three subitems that effect global changes—changes that affect all subsequent graphs and that stay in effect until you turn them off or alter them. These changes are saved when you quit SYSTAT. To return to the defaults, drag the "SYSTAT prefs" file (stored in your "SYSTAT Work" folder) to the Trash.

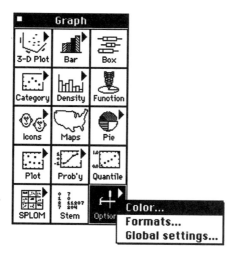

With **Options/Color...**, you can choose the color settings to be used for all subsequent plots.

You can choose a color for the [Background], for the [Foreground], for the [Graph] (axes and scales), and for the [Labels]. [Background] sets the color of the View window before you draw a graph, [Graph] sets the color of the lines and points and shapes that SYGRAPH draws, and [Foreground] sets the color of the View window inside the boundaries of the graph.

- Select **Options/Color...** from the **Graph** menu
- Choose colors for each element
- Click OK

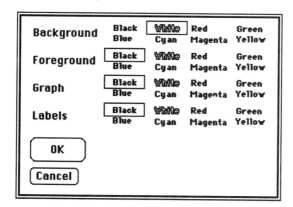

Common options

Formats...   With **Options/Formats...**, you can choose various settings used for all
subsequent plots.

- Select **Options/Formats...** from the **Graph** menu
- Choose the options you need
- Click OK

```
┌─────────────────────────────────────────────────────┐
│ ┌─────────────────────────────────────────────────┐ │
│ │                                                   │ │
│ │  Depth  [        ]      Eye   [    ][    ][    ]  │ │
│ │                                                   │ │
│ │  Facet ☒ Off [    ]     Scale [    ][    ]        │ │
│ │                                                   │ │
│ │  Separate [        ]    Thickness  ☐ │ │ │ ▮     │ │
│ │                                                   │ │
│ │  Size     [        ]    Log ticks ◉ Log ☐ Indent │ │
│ │                                             ○ Equal│ │
│ │  Decimal Places [0][▼]                            │ │
│ │                                                   │ │
│ │  Low-resolution font                              │ │
│ │     [ Monaco    ▼][9][▼][ Bold      ▼]            │ │
│ │                                                   │ │
│ │  High-resolution font                             │ │
│ │     [ Stroke  ▼][ Plain ▼]                        │ │
│ │                                                   │ │
│ │      (     OK     )        ( Cancel )             │ │
│ │                                                   │ │
│ └─────────────────────────────────────────────────┘ │
└─────────────────────────────────────────────────────┘
```

[Depth], [Facet], and [Eye], control positioning in three dimensions.
[Scale] rescales graphs, usually by a percentage. [Thickness] and [Size]
enlarge the lines and characters in graphs, respectively.

The lower half of the dialog box controls fonts. With **Options/Global
settings...** you can choose [High resolution] output. If you do so,
SYGRAPH uses its own special fonts for all graph text. If you do not
choose [High resolution], SYGRAPH uses the regular Macintosh fonts,
and you can choose from the fonts, sizes, and styles listed in the [Low-
resolution font] pop-up boxes.

Depth   The [Depth] option controls the position of a plane along a facet (see
below). The depth of a plane is normally set at the rear of the usual 3-D
plotting frame, which is equivalent to specifying a depth of 50. You can
move the plane to any other position by specifying a positive distance d,
where d is a distance in inches (e.g. "3in"), centimeters (e.g. "3.7cm") or
percentage of the display window (e.g. "50" or "50%").

© 1989, SYSTAT, Inc.

To return to the default depth, use the Delete key to remove your specifications from the box.

Facet

Two-dimensional graphs are plotted inside a unit square; three-dimensional graphs are plotted inside a unit cube. You can place in two-dimensional graph in 3-D perspective by specifying a [Facet].

Ordinarily, you would use [Facet] to produce complex three-dimensional graphics by overlaying several 2-D plots in perspective. Use this feature sparingly and wisely! For almost every 3-D graph, there is a clearer, simpler 2-D graph of the same data.

To specify a facet, you must first click [Off] and then type the name of the facet on which you want to draw in the box. To return to the usual two-dimensional placement, click [Off].

Eye

The [Eye] option sets the point of view for 3-D plots. Think of a 3-D plot as a cube floating in three dimensional space. Each edge of the cube is one unit long. The lower left corner of the cube is the origin. The viewing coordinates of your eye as you float in space looking at the cube are specified by the [Eye] option.

If you specify –1,–1,1, for example, you will look at the cube from the southwest upper corner. The default setting is –8, –12, 8.

You can set your point of view anywhere, but in some positions you get curious results. For example, if you put your eye inside the cube (.5,.5,.5), you see your data distorted from inside. If you put your eye under the cube (–1,–1,–6), some axis labels are backwards in true perspective.

To return to the default setting, use the Delete key to remove your specifications from the box. The Spinning window shows [Eye] settings for whatever data rotation you choose. This way, you can plot data in 3-D, spin them, and then produce a high resolution presentation graph from the same point of view.

4.20
Looking up at a
surface

Let's plot a function while looking from underneath the surface.

- Select **Options/Formats...** from the Graph menu
- Specify –.5, –2, –1 for [Eye]
- Click OK

- Select **Options/Global settings...** from the **Graph** menu
- Check [High resolution] on
- Click OK

- Select **Function** from the **Graph** menu
- Specify the function: Z=X^2–Y^2
- Click [Hide]
- Click OK

Here is the result.

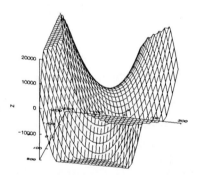

Scale

The [Scale] option rescales graphs to a specified size or percentage of the window; it is similar to the [Reduce or Enlarge] option in **File/Page Setup...** except that you can scale the vertical and horizontal dimensions separately.

The usual [Scale] setting is 100 in both boxes (100% on both the X and Y axes). You can specify a size in inches (IN) and centimeters (CM), but percentages are easier. For example, typing 50 in both boxes halves both dimensions.

Scaling affects all features of the graph, including lettering. Consequently, you should usually specify the same number in both boxes. If you want rectangular plots, use the ruler which lets you change the size and shape of graphs by tracing a marquee with the mouse in the View window. This is discussed in *Getting Started*.

Size

The [Size] option sets the size of characters (text) used in all subsequent graphs. The default is 1. Setting [Size] to 2, for example, makes characters twice as large as usual in graphs, scales, and labels.

[Size] only affects the high-resolution SYGRAPH fonts (British, Greek, etc.). It lies dormant if you are using the standard Macintosh fonts; instead, use the point size option.

Note to users of previous versions of SYGRAPH: the [Thickness] option used to control character size. This is no longer true. Now you can control characters and lines separately.

Separate

You can plot color separations (where you print the different colored elements of a graph separately, one color per page, so a printer can expose separate films for each color ink). Just specify the color you want and then plot the graph (sending output to your printing device). Then, return to **Global settings...** and name the next color, plot the graph again, and so on, until you have all the colors printed.

Note that you must choose axes and labels to be black and do a black separation. Otherwise, the black elements are included in every separation.

4.21
Thickness

You can choose a thickness for lines in a graph. The thinnest is the default. If you want to make graphics for slides or overhead projectors, you might want to use thicker lines. If you choose very thick lines, SYGRAPH scales labels and scale values automatically to keep them in proportion to line widths. If you use a thick enough line, you can make a graph that looks like the ones you did in kindergarten with a thick crayon.

- Select **Options/Formats...** from the **Graph** menu
- Choose the thickest line
- Set [Size] to 5
- Delete all the settings from the last example and click faceting [Off]
- Click OK

- Select **Bar/Bar** from the **Graph** menu
- Select the Y variables: SUMMER, WINTER
- Select the X variable: REGION$
- Click OK

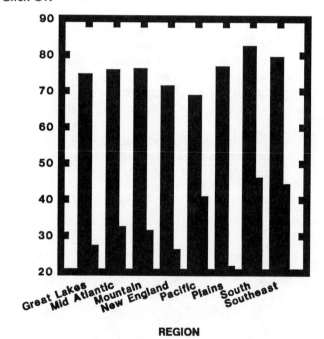

REGION

Log tick spacing

Usually, ticks for logarithmic scales are equally spaced. If you wish logarithmically spaced tick marks, choose [Log] spacing.

Fonts, styles, and sizes

You may choose from the usual Macintosh assortment of fonts and styles. The fonts that appear in the selection list are those that you have installed in your System or in Suitcases. You can choose various styles and sizes.

If you have chosen [High-resolution] output in **Options/Global settings...**, you may choose from the [High-res fonts] list. The [High-res] fonts are fonts designed especially for SYGRAPH. You may check [Italic] for any of the fonts to get oblique versions of the fonts.

The [Size] option controls the size of [High-res fonts]. If you are using the standard Macintosh fonts, the [Size] option lies dormant.

Global settings...

Global settings offers three toggles (on-off switches) controlling the features of all subsequent graphs.

- Select **Options/Global settings...** from the **Graph** menu
- Choose the options you want
- Click OK

```
┌─────────────────────────────────────────┐
│  ┌─────────────────────────────────────┐ │
│  │  ☒ Automatic graph font scaling     │ │
│  │  ☐ Graph scales as editable text    │ │
│  │  ☐ High-resolution (LaserWriter only)│ │
│  │  ┌──────────┐                        │ │
│  │  │    OK    │                        │ │
│  │  └──────────┘                        │ │
│  │  ┌──────────┐                        │ │
│  │  │  Cancel  │                        │ │
│  │  └──────────┘                        │ │
│  └─────────────────────────────────────┘ │
└─────────────────────────────────────────┘
```

Automatic graph font scaling

By default, [Automatic graph font scaling] is on. This option automatically resizes text in graphs when you resize the graph itself: if you make the graph bigger, SYGRAPH prints the text bigger to match, and vice versa. If you click the option off, all text is printed at exactly the point size or [Size] you have chosen in **Options/Formats...**

Graph scales as editable text

Usually, you cannot alter elements of a graph with the **Plot tools**. (This is so you won't accidentally distort the information in your graph.) If you want to be able to edit the scales and variable labels using the tools, click [Graph scales as editable text] on.

High-resolution

By default, SYGRAPH draws all graphs with Quickdraw commands, which operate with a resolution of 72 dpi (dots per inch). If you print such graphs (the default), you still get 72 dpi resolution, even if you are using a higher resolution device such as a 300 dpi LaserWriter. At 72 dpi lines are somewhat thick (about pixel-size) and curves are somewhat jagged.

For best results, if you have a LaserWriter or a similar high-resolution printing device, click [High-resolution]. This changes SYGRAPH output to PostScript commands, which are device independent, meaning your graphs are printed at whatever resolution your screen and printing device can handle. If you have a 300 dpi LaserWriter, you will get finer, smoother lines and characters.

You also get the special high-resolution SYGRAPH fonts when you choose [High resolution] output.

Either way, you can save graphs as PICT files or **Cut** and **Paste** them to other applications. However, [High-resolution] graphs are slower and more cumbersome than the usual screen-quality graphs. For this reason, you will probably want to leave [High-resolution] off until you have a final graph that you want to print. Or, if you are pasting the graphs into a word-processing application for a report, you might want to wait until you're almost done before you paste the graphics, because many graphs will slow down your word processor.

5   Bar

Bar

5

Overview

A bar graph displays a bar for each category of a variable, where the height of the bar represents:

- the count in that category
- the mean of the cases in that category
- the percent of cases in that category
- some other measurement or statistic input for that category

You may include several variables in one display with their respective bars laid out side-by-side within each category or stacked on top of one another. You may define categories using either the discrete values of a character or numeric variable or by equal intervals of a continuous numeric variable.

Data for **Bar** may be in cases-by-variables form (several records per bar), or aggregated with counts (one record per bar). Either data layout may contain an additional variable which is the measure for determining heights of bars. If there is one record per category, this measure determines the height directly. If there are several records per category, the measure is averaged within category to determine height.

Bar offers three types of bar charts. **Bar/Bar** produces simple bar charts. **Bar/Percent** draws percentage bar charts, where each bar shows the percentage of the whole that is held by that group of the categorical variable. **Bar/Range** plots the interval between two continuous variables.

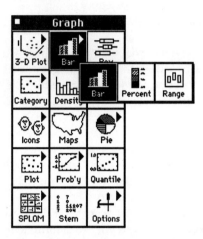

First, press and hold the mouse button on **Bar**. A submenu pops up offering **Bar, Range,** or **Percent**. Select the item you want and release the mouse button. All three items present the same dialog box and work the same.

- Select **Bar/Bar, Range,** or **Percent** from the **Graph** menu
- Select one or more continuous variables from the list on the left
- Select a categorical variable from the list on the right
- Click OK

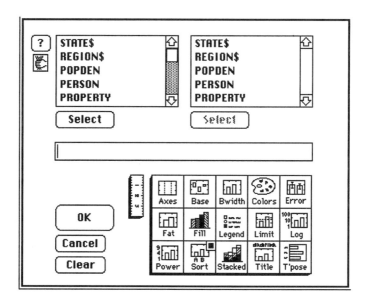

SYGRAPH automatically prints bar labels at a slant if there is not enough room to print the labels horizontally. Furthermore, if there are more than 10 categories on the horizontal axis, SYGRAPH shrinks the size of the lettering to fit the labels on the scale.

You can use character or numeric variables to specify categories. With numeric variables, however, the values of the categories will be displayed as numbers—that is, the bars are labeled with numbers rather than words. You can do a bar graph on up to 256 categories, but you will need an ultra high resolution device to display the labels clearly for that many categories.

Common options

See the **Common options** chapter for information on using [Axes], [Colors], [Fill], [Legend], [Limit], [Log], [Power], [Sort], [Title], and [T'pose].

A *rootogram* is a histogram with square roots of frequencies on the vertical axis (Velleman & Hoaglin, 1981). You can produce a rootogram with **Bar** and [Power]. Square rooting frequencies this way equalized expected standard errors of the bars for large samples.

The remaining options, [Base], [Bwidth], [Error], [Fat], and [Stacked] are discussed at the end of this chapter.

Bar

Bar/Bar produces bar charts of counts (if you choose a categorical variable from the left selection list) or of means (if you choose a measure from the left selection list and a category from the right).

5.1
Bar chart of
counts

Bar produces a bar graph of counts in categories by a simple command. To tally counts of states in each census region from the US file, for example:

- Select **Bar/Bar** from the **Graph** menu
- Select a categorical variable: REGION$
- Click off [Sort]
- Click OK

We click off [Sort] because we want the regions to remain in geographical order; if we had left [Sort] on they would be sorted alphabetically. SYGRAPH reads the file and tallies duplicate values. The bar graph shows the counts of cases for each region in the file.

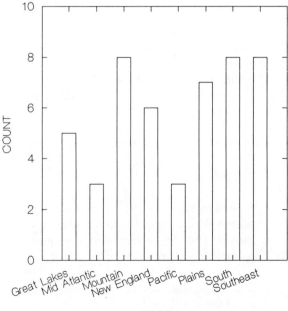

5.2
Using a count
variable

If you have already tallied a variable, you can produce a bar chart directly from the counts. Suppose your file looks like the following. Instead of 48 cases with duplicates, you have only 8 cases with a COUNT variable indicating duplicates.

REGION$	COUNT
New England	6
Mid Atlantic	3
Great Lakes	5
Plains	7
Southeast	8
South	8
Mountain	8
Pacific	3

To produce the same bar chart, weight the dataset:

• Select **Weight** from the **Data** menu
• Select a weight variable: COUNT
• Click OK

• Select **Bar/Bar** from the **Graph** menu
• Select a categorical variable: REGION$
• Click off [Sort]
• Click OK

5.3
Bar chart of
means

Here we plot the average summer temperatures for each region.

- Select **Bar/Bar** from the **Graph** menu
- Select a continuous variable: SUMMER
- Select a categorical variable: REGION$
- Click off [Sort]
- Set [Y min] to 0 in the [Axes] dialog box
- Click OK

We set [Y min] to zero because the vertical scale of the bar graph is most useful when it is anchored at zero. If you do not wish to anchor the scale, you probably should consider a **Cplot** instead of **Bar** chart. SYGRAPH ordinarily draws a bar graph without anchoring the bars at zero, but you should not allow this unless you have a good reason.

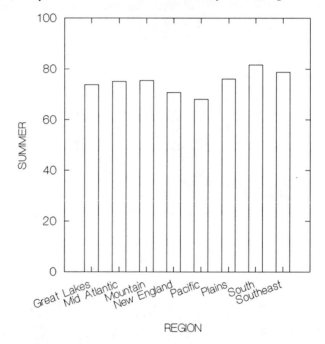

We could have produced the same bar graph by inputting the means directly:

REGION$	SUMMER
New England	70.7
Mid Atlantic	75.0
Great Lakes	73.8
Plains	76.0
Southeast	78.6
South	81.6
Mountain	75.4
Pacific	68.0

Since there is only one case per category, the means are the same as the measures. With this form of file input, you can display *any* statistic (e.g. minimum temperature per region) in a bar graph.

**5.4
Multi-variable
bar chart**

If you select more than one continuous variable, more bars are drawn for each group. You can tabulate up to twelve continuous variables against a categorical variable. As with single bars, SYGRAPH computes the mean of each continuous variable within subgroups of the categorical variable. Each variable in the left selection list is placed on a common vertical scale against the categories on the horizontal scale.

In the following example, SYGRAPH computes the average summer and winter temperatures for each region in the US dataset:

REGION$	SUMMER	WINTER
New England	70.7	25.3
Mid Atlantic	75.0	31.7
Great Lakes	73.8	26.4
Plains	76.0	20.9
Southeast	78.6	43.5
South	81.6	45.3
Mountain	75.4	30.6
Pacific	68.0	40.0

We use two different fills to distinguish the summer and winter bars. The left bar in each pair is filled with pattern number 7 and the right with number 4. We also add YMIN=0 to force a zero minimum on the vertical scale. Since the temperatures are Fahrenheit, however, you might object. Should we use 32 degrees? Perhaps a category plot might be more appropriate.

- Select **Bar/Bar** from the **Graph** menu
- Select continuous variables from the left selection list: SUMMER, WINTER
- Select a categorical variable from the right selection list: REGION$
- Set [Y min] to 0 in the [Axes] dialog box
- Specify "7,4" for [Fill]
- Click off [Sort]
- Click OK

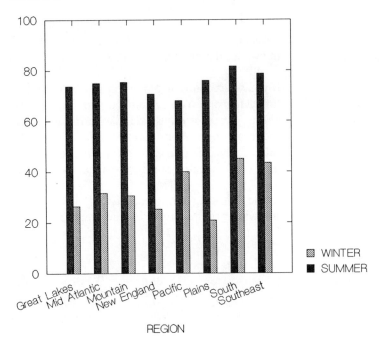

REGION

**5.5
Creating
categories from a
continuous
variable**

If you want a bar graph to display counts for each interval of a continuous variable (like INCOME), you can use the [Bwidth] option to break the variable at evenly spaced cutpoints. In this case, **Bar** does not plot a single bar for each separate data value. Instead, the data on the continuous variable are binned into separate bars defined by equally spaced cutpoints on the continuous variable. This works for when the bars represent counts or means.

- Click [Bwidth]
- Specify the width of the bar intervals
- Click OK

You may specify any number greater than zero.

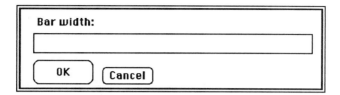

You must specify the minimum value ([X min]) for the bars with [Axes]. You can use [X max] to align your scale or force the bars to any position on the range. See the **Common options** chapter for further information about [Axes].

When you use the [Bwidth] option, the bars are squeezed together because the scale is continuous. In other words, [Fat] is assumed if you specify [Bwidth]. (See the [Fat] option later in this chapter for more information.)

The following collects the 48 states in the US dataset into temperature groups at each 10 degree increment:

- Select **Bar/Bar** from the **Graph** menu
- Select a continuous variable: SUMMER
- Specify width of bar intervals for [Bwidth]: 10
- Set [X min] to 0 in the [Axes] dialog box
- Click OK

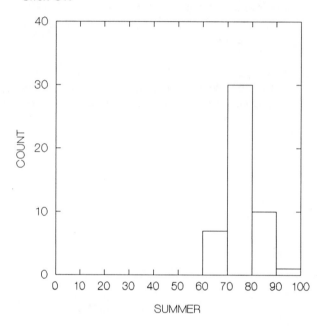

Percent

If you have data that are percents of wholes, you can use a pie or ring chart (see the **Pie** chapter). Or, you can do a divided bar chart. We're not sure which chart is better, since the experimental evidence favoring one or the other is scant and mixed (e.g., Simkin and Hastie, 1987). In any case, the divided bar graph is like unrolling a pie chart into a soldier's service bars.

As with the pie graph, the percentage bar graph can be produced several ways. If you select only a categorical variable, SYGRAPH tallies the instances of each separate value of the variable, sums the tallies, and finally divides the bar according to the proportions of tallies.

If you select a continuous variable and a categorical variable, SYGRAPH computes the mean value of the continuous variable within each separate level or category of the categorical variable. It then sums these means and divides the bar according to the proportions of the sum.

Multi-variable percentage graphs

If you have more than one variable to apportion in a percentage bar graph, you can do it in a multi-variable percentage graph. This graph is like placing several divided bar graphs next to each other. Almost always, you want to use the [Stacked] option also (discussed later). Otherwise, the percentages are placed alongside one another instead of dividing a single bar.

As with the pie graph, the multi-variable percentage bar graph can be produced several ways. If you select one or more categorical variables, SYGRAPH tallies the instances of each separate value of the variables, sums the tallies, and finally divides the bars according to the proportions of tallies.

If you select one or more continuous variables and a categorical variable, SYGRAPH computes the mean value of the continuous variables within each separate level or category of the categorical variable. It then sums these means and divides the bar according to the proportions of the sum.

5.6
Divided bar
graph

Here is a divided bar graph of INCOME by REGION$.

- Select **Bar/Percent** from the **Graph** menu
- Select a continuous variable: INCOME
- Select a categorical variable: REGION$
- Click off [Sort]
- Click OK

Southeast

South

Plains

Pacific

New England

Mountain

Mid Atlantic

Great Lakes

5.7
Multi-variable
divided bar graph

These data are U.S. expenditures in millions of dollars for defense, interest on public debt, and all other.

YEAR$	DEFENSE	INTEREST	OTHER
1950	9919	5750	23875
1960	43969	9180	39075
1970	78368	19304	98972
1980	136138	74860	368013

The percentage bar graph would be useful for these data if we were interested primarily in the percentages of outlays in each year rather than the absolute amount. Since inflation has changed the meaning of these dollars in this period, percentages make some sense.

Here is a divided bar graph of these data. Compare this graph to the graph of the same data using **Bar/Bar** in Example 5.12, "Stacked percentage chart." You may also want to consider the [Fat] option for this graph. We use different fills to distinguish the areas.

- Select **Bar/Percent** from the **Graph** menu
- Select continuous variables: DEFENSE, INTEREST, OTHER
- Select a categorical variable: YEAR$
- Click [Stacked] to stack the bars
- Specify 1,2,7 for [Fill]
- Click OK

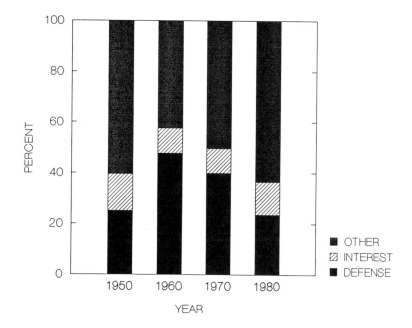

Range

Range

You can use **Bar/Range** to plot the interval between two continuous variables against a categorical variable. You can select the two variables in either order. You must use only two variables to define a low and high value.

5.8
Range chart

The following data consist of record low and high July temperatures for eight U.S. cities in 1983. We can plot the range of temperatures by city with **Bar/Range**.

CITY$	HIGH	LOW
Los Angeles	86	62
Miami	90	71
New York	91	59
Seattle	91	50
Denver	97	55
Chicago	99	47
Dallas	104	64
Phoenix	112	68

- Select **Bar/Range** from the **Graph** menu
- Select two variables: LOW, HIGH
- Select a categorical variable: CITY$
- Click OK

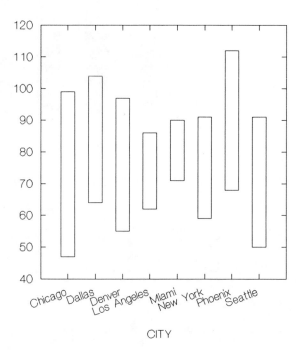

© 1989, SYSTAT, Inc.

Anchored bars

The [Base] option anchors bars at a selected level. This feature is useful for profit-loss charts and other graphs which compare a variable against a standard level.

- Click [Base]
- Specify the base value
- Click OK

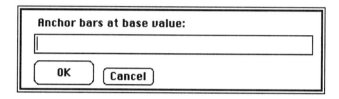

**5.9
Anchored bar
chart**

We have already seen a bar chart of average SUMMER temperatures by REGION$ in Example 5.2. We can use the [Base] option to compare each of these regions against the average summer temperature for the whole United States, which we computed with **Stats** (75.6 degrees Fahrenheit).

- Select **Bar/Bar** from the **Graph** menu
- Select a continuous variable: SUMMER
- Select a categorical variable: REGION$
- Specify 75.6 for [Base]
- Click off [Sort]
- Click OK

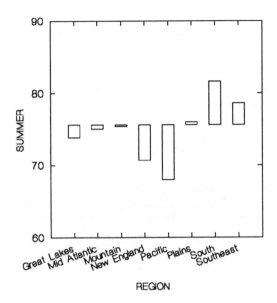

If you want to draw a horizontal line at the reference point, you can use [Limit] (see the **Common options** chapter) or use **Draw**. Because the bars themselves create a subjective contour, this is usually unnecessary.

Bar width

The [Bwidth] option cuts a continuous variable into equally spaced intervals Bwidth units wide. See Example 5.5 to see [Bwidth] used.

Error bars

You can add error bars to your bar graph with the [Error] option. You can specify a variable that determines the length of the error bars, or you can request that SYGRAPH automatically compute error bars from the standard error of the mean or standard deviation of the dependent variables.

- Click [Error]
- Specify the error variable (or leave the box blank for automatic error bars)
- Click [One way] for one-sided error bars
- Click [SError] for error bars computed from the standard error of the dependent variables
- Click OK

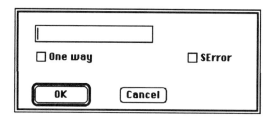

You can draw one-sided error bars by clicking [One way]. If the error variable is positive, the error bar faces upward. If it is negative, the bar faces downward. If you do not specify a variable, error bars are automatically computed from the standard deviation of the dependent variable(s). If you click [SError], they are automatically computed from the standard error of the mean of the dependent variable(s).

**5.10
Automatic error bars**

Here's the INCOME by REGION$ bar graph with automatic error bars.

- Select **Bar/Bar** from the **Graph** menu
- Select a continuous variable: INCOME
- Select a categorical variable: REGION$
- Click [Error] but do not specify a variable
- Click OK

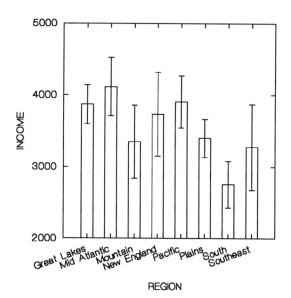

Fat bars

Bar graphs are easiest to discern when the bars are separated by a space. Occasionally, however, you may want to squeeze them together. This is done with the [Fat] option.

5.11
Fat bars

Here is the SUMMER by REGION$ chart with fat bars.

- Select **Bar/Bar** from the **Graph** menu
- Select a continuous variable: SUMMER
- Select a categorical variable: REGION$
- Click [Fat]
- Click off [Sort]
- Click OK

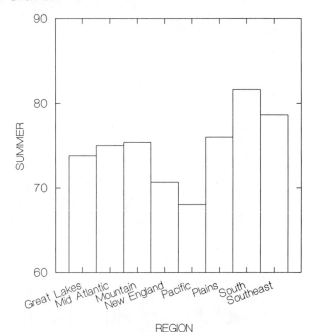

Stacked bars

A stacked bar chart works like a multi-variable bar chart (see Example 5.4) except that the bars for each category are stacked on top of each other rather than placed side by side. As with the multi-variable charts, you can stack up to 12 different variables. These charts are most useful for comparing segments of a single variable over several categories, such as budget information.

5.12
Stacked
percentage chart

We used the EXPEND dataset for Example 5.7, "Multi-variable divided bar graph". The variables are millions of dollars in U.S. budget outlays.

We can represent these percentages in a stacked bar graph. The height of each stacked bar represents the total dollars spent in the given year. The segments delineate the relative portions for each category.

Here is the stacked bar graph for these data. We use three different fill patterns. You may want to try using colors instead if your equipment allows it.

- Select **Bar/Bar** from the **Graph** menu
- Select one or more continuous variables: DEFENSE, INTEREST, OTHER
- Select a categorical variable: YEAR$
- Click [Stack]
- Specify 1,2,7 for [Fill]
- Click OK

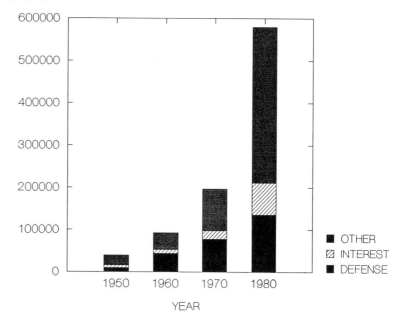

Compare this to the percentage version of the graph in Example 5.7.

6 Category

Category 6

Overview **Category** plots counts of categories and plots means of continuous variables against categorical variables. Many of the displays look like those produced by **Plot**, which plots continuous against continuous variables. **Category**, however, works more like **Bar**; a simple categorical plot tallies the counts of the different categories of a variable and a multi-way categorical plot computes and plots the averages of one or more continuous variables within the categories of a categorical variable. That is, **Category** omits the bar and simply plots the point where the top of the bar would have been.

Several popular graphs are in fact special instances of the category plot. Line graphs are category plots with the plotting symbols connected by line segments. High-low-close plots are category plots with vertical line segments. Star plots are polar category plots. To make these plots more accessible, **Category** includes separate icons for these plots.

Category offers four types of category plots. **Category/Category** produces simple category plots. **Category/High-low** draws high-low-close plots, which show the high, low, and closing values for, say, stock data. **Line** draws line plots, where the points are connected by lines, and **Star** draws star plots, which are line plots in polar coordinates.

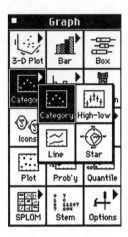

Press and hold the mouse button on **Category**. A submenu pops up offering **Category, High-low, Line,** and **Star**. Select the item you want and release the mouse button. All three buttons present the same dialog box and work the same.

- Select **Category/Category**, **High-low**, **Line** or **Star** from the **Graph** menu
- Select one or more continuous variables from the list on the left
- Select one categorical variable from the list on the right
- Click OK

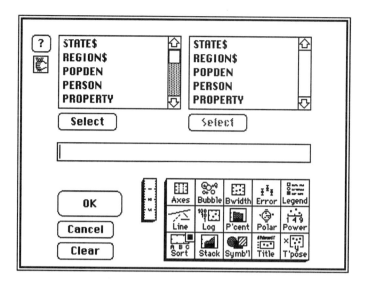

The categorical variable can be either character or numeric, with SYGRAPH displaying the corresponding categories as character strings or numbers, respectively.

SYGRAPH automatically prints labels for categories at a slant if there is not enough room to print them horizontally. Furthermore, if there are more than 10 categories, SYGRAPH shrinks the size of the lettering to fit the labels on the scale. You can do a category plot on up to 200 categories, but you will need an ultra high resolution device to display the labels clearly for that many categories.

Common options

See the **Common options** chapter for information on using [Axes], [Legend], [Line], [Log], [Power], [Sort], [Symbol], [Title], and [T'pose]. The remaining options, [Bubble], [Bwidth], [Error], [P'cent], [Polar], and [Stack], are discussed at the end of this chapter.

Types of plots

Category

The **Category** option produces category plots of counts or means.

6.1
Category plot of
counts

Here we use **Category/Category** to tally counts of states in each census region of the US file.

- Select **Category/Category** from the **Graph** menu
- Select a categorical variable: REGION$
- Click OK

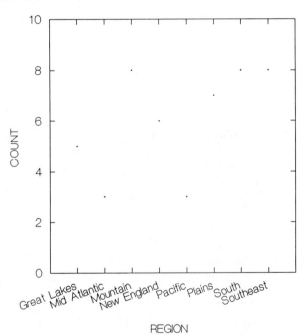

We click off [Sort] so that the regions remain in geographical order; if we had left [Sort] on, the regions would be sorted alphabetically. You might notice that a bar graph of these data (shown as Example 5.1 in the **Bar** chapter) might be preferable. **Bar** and **Category** work similarly; both plot continuous against categorical data. In general, you should use **Bar** when the origin of the vertical scale is zero and **Category** when the origin is arbitrary. In plain terms, bars are like houses. They should have a good foundation at ground zero (as in this example). Do not build your house on sand.

6.2
Using a count
variable

If you have already tallied a variable, you can produce a category plot directly from the counts. Suppose your file looks like the following. Instead of 48 cases with duplicates, you have only 8 cases with a COUNT variable indicating duplicates.

REGION$	COUNT
New England	6
Mid Atlantic	3
Great Lakes	5
Plains	7
Southeast	8
South	8
Mountain	8
Pacific	3

To produce the same plot as in Example 6.1, just use weighting.

- Select **Weight** from the **Data** menu
- Select a weight variable: COUNT
- Click OK

- Select **Category/Category** from the **Graph** menu
- Select a categorical variable: REGION$
- Click off [Sort]
- Click OK

**6.3
Category plot of
means**

Here, SYGRAPH computes and plots the average summer temperatures
in 1970 for each region in the US dataset.

- Select **Category/Category** from the **Graph** menu
- Select the continuous variable: SUMMER
- Select the categorical variable: REGION$
- Click off [Sort]
- Click OK

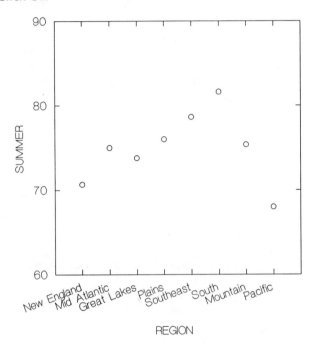

**6.4
Multi-variable
category plot**

You can produce a category plot of a several continuous variables
against a categorical variable. SYGRAPH plots the average value of each
continuous variable, excluding missing values, for each subgroup of the
categorical variable. You can plot up to 12 continuous variables against a
categorical variable. Each variable in the left selection list is placed on a
common vertical scale against the categories on the horizontal scale.

In this example, SYGRAPH computes and plots the average summer and winter temperatures in 1970 for each region in the US dataset.

- Select **Category/Category** from the **Graph** menu
- Select the continuous variables: SUMMER, WINTER
- Select the categorical variable: REGION$
- Specify 2,3 for [Symbol]
- Click off [Sort]
- Click OK

Compare this plot with the corresponding bar chart: Example 5.4, "Multivariable bar chart."

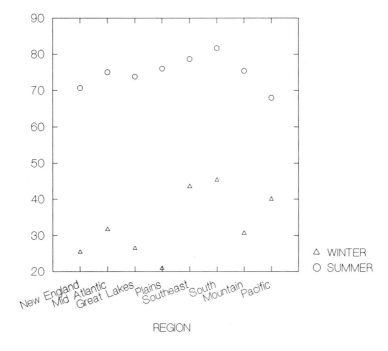

6.5
Creating
categories from a
continuous
variable

To plot a category plot of a continuous variable (like INCOME), use the [Bwidth] option to break the variable at evenly spaced cutpoints. In this case, **Category** does not plot a single symbol for each separate data value. Instead, the data on the continuous variable are binned into separate categories defined by cutpoints on the continuous variable. This works when plotting counts or means.

You must specify the minimum value ([X min]) for the categories. The Bwidth can be any number greater than zero.

For example, the following instructions collect the 48 states in the US dataset into temperature groups at 10 degree increments:

- Select **Category/Category** from the **Graph** menu
- Select the continuous variable: SUMMER
- Specify 10 for [Bwidth]
- Set [X min] to 0 in the [Axes] dialog box
- Click OK

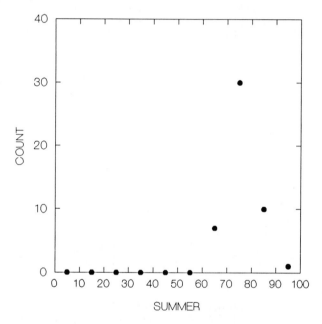

High-low

Stock market daily, weekly, or monthly statistics are often plotted as a set of ranges between *high* and *low* prices with a marker for the *closing* price at each period. This is the way most newspapers plot the market.

Category/High-low produces this plot. You must select three continuous variables for the high, low, and close, and one categorical variable.

The high-low-close plot has other applications. Use it for asymmetrical error bars, for example. You can also do one-sided error bars by making the low (or high) the same value as the close variable. These can be superimposed on bar and line graphs as well. Finally, compare this to the [Range] option. The range bar graph plots only highs and lows (no close).

**6.6
High-low-close
plot**

Here are some typical data on a stock. They are in the file HILO.

MONTH$	MONTH	HIGH	LOW	CLOSE
January	1	20.1	17.5	20.0
February	2	24.5	18.8	24.0
March	3	29.3	22.5	23.6
April	4	35.1	25.6	29.9
May	5	40.2	32.3	35.5
June	6	45.1	38.8	39.5
July	7	39.6	32.3	37.1
August	8	33.1	28.3	28.3
September	9	27.8	20.5	21.1
October	10	22.1	17.8	17.9
November	11	17.9	16.1	16.5
December	12	16.8	10.2	10.3

We can draw a high-low-close plot of these data using the month character variable as the horizontal variable.

- Select **Category/High-low** from the **Graph** menu
- Select the continuous variables: HIGH, LOW, CLOSE
- Select the categorical variable: MONTH$
- Select the horizontal line (12th) symbol in the [Symbol] dialog box
- Specify the [Y label]: PRICE in the [Axes] dialog box
- Click OK

We used a horizontal line to mark the close. You can use any other symbol you wish. Compare this plot to the same graph in the **Plot** chapter (Example 11.8). The only difference between the two is that this one is plotted against a (possibly unordered) category variable and the other is plotted against a numerical variable.

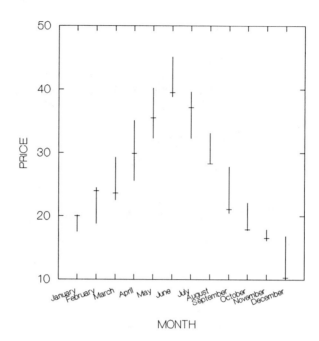

Line

Connecting symbols with a line in a category plot can highlight trends or elevations. The line connects the centers of any symbols you draw. This is sometimes called a *profile plot*.

You can do line plots two ways. Either use **Category/Category** and click the [Line] option to turn line drawing on and to pick a line type, or use **Category/Line**. **Category/Line** draws a line automatically, and you only need to use the [Line] option if you want to use a line type other than the default (a solid line).

6.7
Profile plot

Here is a profile plot of INCOME by REGION$.

- Select **Category/Line** from the **Graph** menu
- Select the continuous variable: INCOME
- Select the categorical variable: REGION$
- Click off [Sort]
- Click OK

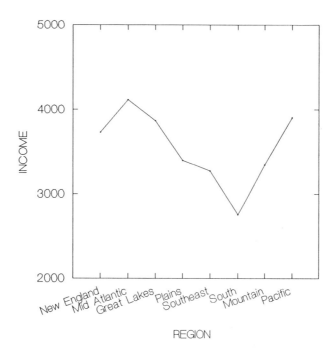

6.8
Multi-variable
profile plot

You can do category plots with a different type of line connecting the values of several continuous variables. Here is a category (profile) plot of summer and winter temperatures against region. SYGRAPH computes and plots the average temperatures for each region in the US dataset

Each profile is drawn with a different line. Remember, if you do a multi-variable category plot, you must specify as many line types in the [Line] option as you have continuous variables, even if you are using the same line type for each variable (e.g. 2,2). We set the symbol [Size] to 0 because we only want to see the line connecting the points, not the points themselves.

- Select **Category/Line** from the **Graph** menu
- Select the continuous variables: SUMMER, WINTER
- Select the categorical variables: REGION$
- Specify 1,10 for [Line]
- Set [Size] to 0 in the [Symbol] dialog box
- Click off [Sort]
- Click OK

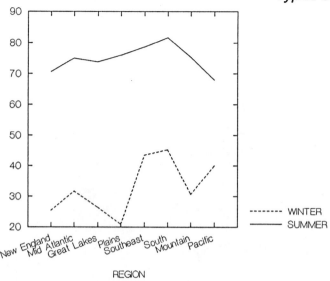

**6.9
Multi-variable
divided line plot**

If you want to apportion several variables in a line graph, you can do it in a multi-variable percentage graph by clicking [P'cent]. This graph divides the vertical axis (denoting 100 percent) among several categories or variables. You need to use the [Stack] option (discussed at the end of this chapter) to divide the vertical axis this way. Otherwise, the percentages are not summed on the vertical axis.

The multi-variable percentage line graph is exactly like connecting the tops of the bars in a multi-variable percentage bar graph. Look at the [Percent] option in the **Bar** chapter to compare the two.

The EXPEND data in the **Bar** chapter illustrate the multi-variable percentage bar graph. They are U.S. expenditures in millions of dollars for defense, interest on public debt, and all other.

The percentage line graph is useful for these data if we are interested primarily in percentages of annual outlays rather than absolute amounts. Since inflation has changed the meaning of these dollars in this period, percentages make some sense.

Here is a percentage line graph of these data. Compare this graph to the graph of the same data using the [Stack] option without [Percent] in Example 6.12. We use different fills to distinguish the areas. Again, we suppress the plotting symbols by setting [Size] to 0. We use [Ticks out] so we can still see the ticks for the years.

- Select **Category/Line** from the **Graph** menu
- Select the continuous variables: DEFENSE, INTEREST, OTHER
- Select the categorical variable: YEAR$
- Click [Stack]
- Click [Percent]
- Specify 1,2,7 for [Fill] in the [Symbol] dialog box
- Set [Size] to 0 in the [Symbol] dialog box
- Select [Ticks out] in the [Axes] dialog box
- Click OK

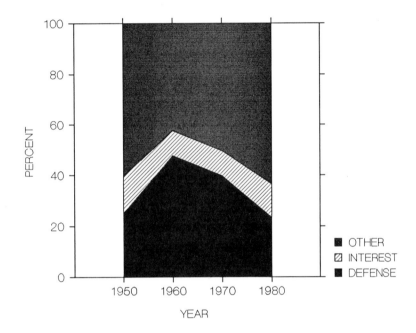

Star

You can do category plots in polar coordinates. This may seem strange at first, but this is a way to produce what are sometimes called *star*, *snowflake*, or *radar plots*. For frills, you can add grid marks inside the frame. You can fiddle with the other options (e.g. tick marks, error bars, axes, minima and maxima, etc.) to produce variants.

Icon contains a star icon plot which is a close relative of the polar category plot. The star icon, however, plots each case in a file as a separate star and each variable as a point. The polar category plot makes each case a point and each variable a star.

6.10
Star plot

Here is an example of a polar category plot.

- Select **Category/Star** from the **Graph** menu
- Select the continuous variable: INCOME
- Select the categorical variable: REGION$
- Click off [Sort]
- Click OK

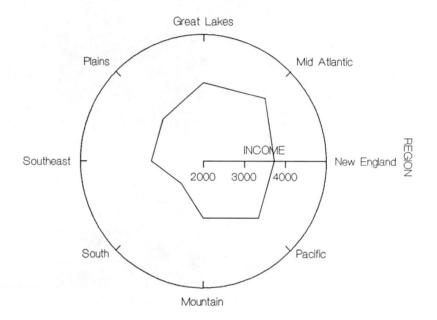

© 1989, SYSTAT, Inc.

Bubble plots

You can use the value of a variable in your file to control the size of a plotting symbol. This is especially useful for representing a third variable against two others in a two-way plot.

- Click [Bubble]
- Specify the variable to be used: DEN
- Click OK

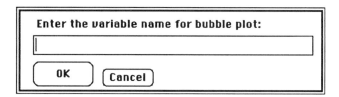

One caution: the size of the plotting symbols is taken directly from the values in your value. There is no upper or lower limit. If the variable you specify has a value as small as .001 or a negative value, the point will be invisible; if it has a value as large as 100, the symbol will fill the entire plot. If your sizing variable does not lie in this range, you should rescale it. Finally, you should usually use empty symbols with this type of plot, since filled ones can occlude each other and make the plot difficult to interpret.

These plots are sometimes called **bubble plots**, for obvious reasons.

Cleveland, Kleiner, McRae, and Warner (1976) used open circles to represent levels of pollution on a map of New England. You can use other symbols. Bickel, Hammel, and O'Connell (1975) used open squares to represent the size of university departments in plotting admissions data at the University of California-Berkeley.

Category width

The [Bwidth] option cuts a continuous variable into equally spaced intervals Bwidth units wide. See Example 6.5 for its use.

Error bars

Error

You can add error bars to your category plot with the [Error] option. You can specify a variable that determines the length of the error bars, or you can request that SYGRAPH automatically compute the error bars from the standard error of the mean or standard deviation of the dependent variable(s).

You can draw one-sided error bars by clicking [One way]. If the error variable is positive, the error bar faces upward. If it is negative, the bar faces downward. If you do not specify a variable, error bars are automatically computed from the standard deviation of the dependent variable(s). If you click [SError], they are automatically computed from the standard error of the mean of the dependent variable(s).

6.11
Automatic error bars

Here is a category plot with automatic error bars. We use solid triangles to make the plot more visible.

- Select **Category/Category** from the **Graph** menu
- Select the continuous variable: INCOME
- Select the categorical variable: REGION$
- Click [Error] but do not specify a variable
- Select the triangle (3rd) symbol and the solid fill in the [Symb'l] dialog box
- Click off [Sort]
- Click OK

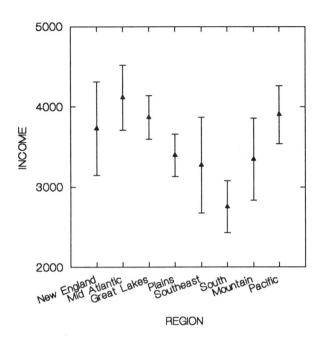

Percentage category plots

The [P'cent] option produces percentage category plots. See Example 6.9 for an example.

Stacked or cumulative line plots

A stacked line graph works like a multi-variable line graph (see Example 6.8) except that the lines are cumulative at each value of the *x* or horizontal axis. As with the multi-variable line graphs, you can stack up to 12 different variables. These charts are most useful for comparing segments of a single variable over several categories, such as budget information.

6.12
Stacked line plot

We used the EXPEND data to illustrate the [Percent] option for Example 6.9. They are U.S. budget outlays in millions of dollars.

We can represent these percentages in a stacked line graph. The height of the top line at each year represents the total dollars spent in the given year. The segments delineate the relative portions for each category.

Here is the stacked line graph for these data. We use three different fill patterns. You may want to use colors instead if your equipment allows it.

- Select **Category/Line** from the **Graph** menu
- Select the continuous variables: DEFENSE, INTEREST, OTHER
- Select the categorical variable: YEAR$
- Click the [Stack] option
- Specify 1,2,7 for [Fill]
- Set [Size] to 0 in the [Symbol] dialog box
- Set [Ymin] to 0 and [Ymax] to 600000 in the [Axes] dialog box
- Click OK

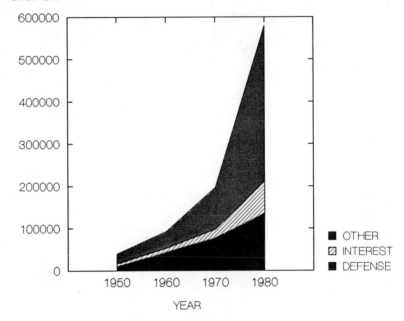

Compare this graph with the [Percent] version in Example 6.9.

7   Pie

Pie

7

Overview

A pie chart displays proportions of either counts or measures within categories. It is particularly suited for displaying portions of wholes. Although many statisticians and graphic designers have attacked the pie chart, recent studies (e.g., Simkin & Hastie, 1987) show it to be effective in some situations. SYGRAPH produces a variety of pie charts.

Pie offers two types of charts. **Pie/Pie** produces simple pie charts. **Pie/Ring** produces ring charts, also known as donut charts or attention maps.

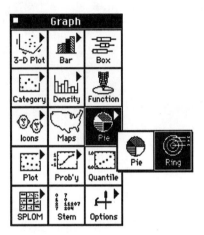

Press and hold the mouse button on **Pie**. A submenu pops up offering **Pie** and **Ring**. Slide the pointer to the item you want and release the mouse button. Both buttons present the same dialog box and work the same.

- Select **Pie/Pie** or **Ring** from the **Graph** menu
○ Select a continuous variable from the list on the left
- Select a categorical variable from the list on the right
- Click OK

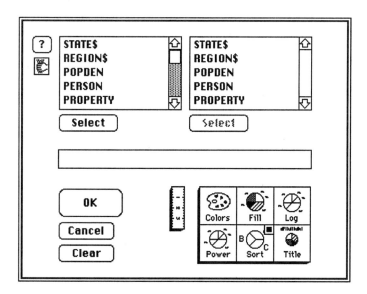

The categorical variable can be either character or numeric, with SYGRAPH displaying the corresponding categories as character strings or numbers, respectively.

Common options

See the **Common options** chapter for information on using [Colors], [Fill], [Log], [Power], [Sort], and [Title].

Pie

Pie

The **Pie** option produces pie charts showing proportions of counts (if you choose a categorical variable from the left selection list) or of means (if you choose a measure from the left selection list and a category from the right). For counts, SYGRAPH tallies the number of cases in each category, converts each count to a proportion of the total count, and shows that proportion with a wedge. For measures, SYGRAPH computes a mean for each category, converts each mean to a proportion of the sum of the means, and shows that proportion as a wedge of the whole.

7.1
Pie chart of
counts

Here we use **Pie** to tally counts of states in each census region of the US file. We click off [Sort] because we want the regions to remain in geographical order; if we had left [Sort] on they would be sorted alphabetically.

- Select **Pie** from the **Graph** menu
- Select a categorical variable: REGION$
- Click OK

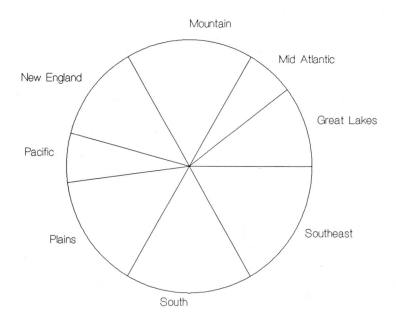

© 1989, SYSTAT, Inc.

7.2
Using a count variable

If you have already tallied a variable, you can produce a pie chart directly from the counts. Suppose your file looks like the following. Instead of 48 cases with duplicates, you have only 8 cases with a COUNT variable indicating duplicates.

REGION$	COUNT
New England	6
Mid Atlantic	3
Great Lakes	5
Plains	7
Southeast	8
South	8
Mountain	8
Pacific	3

To produce the same pie chart, just use weighting.

- Select **Weight** from the **Data** menu
- Select a weight variable: COUNT
- Click OK

- Select **Pie/Pie** from the **Graph** menu
- Select a categorical variable: REGION$
- Click off [Sort]
- Click OK

7.3
Pie chart of
means

Assume, for example, that we have the following sales data by region.
SALES contains percentages that total to 100.

REGION$	SALES
New England	10
Mid Atlantic	10
Great Lakes	20
Plains	5
Southeast	5
South	30
Mountain	10
Pacific	10

- Select **Options/Formats…** from the **Graph** menu
- Choose [British] from the [High-res fonts] list
- Click OK

- Select **Options/Global settings…** from the **Graph** menu
- Choose [High resolution] fonts
- Click OK

- Select **Pie/Pie** from the **Graph** menu
- Select a continuous variable: SALES
- Select a categorical variable: REGION$
- Click off [Sort]
- Click OK

To compute portions of the pie for each category, SYGRAPH divides
SALES by its total across all categories. In this case, the total is 100, so
each percentage is converted to a proportion. Normally, you feed
SYGRAPH data like these, but you get the same result if you feed proportions instead of percents. If you feed it some other kind of numbers,
remember the pie will represent proportions of the total of your numbers.

One more thing. If you feed **Pie** a dataset with more than one value per
category (e.g., several states in each REGION$ as in the US dataset),
SYGRAPH first averages the numbers in each category, totals the averages, and finally divides each average by the total of the averages. If you
have an application for this sort of thing, don't call SYSTAT. Feel free
to make a million dollars on it yourself.

Here is the pie chart of our nifty sales data.

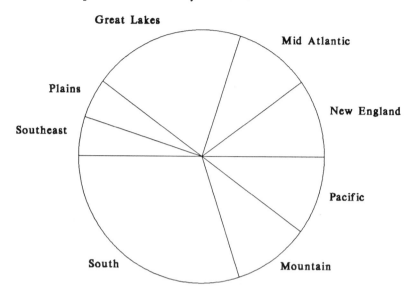

Ring

Let's make donuts instead of pies. Imagine the categories of a pie ordered from inside to outside. The *ring plot*, or *attention map*, draws a set of concentric rings beginning with a smallest ring for the first category. The radius of each ring is the sum of the previous radii plus the amount due to the corresponding category. This plot is sometimes used by newspapers as an attention map showing a paper's relative rates of reporting from local to international news.

Pie/Ring produces the donut chart. We decided to make it a subitem of **Pie** because both are baked goods and consistency in human-computer interfaces is important.

7.4
Attention map

For this type of chart, it's best to have an ordered scale of categories. Here are some typical attention data from *The Cape Codder*, a salty local paper. We have expressed the attention values as percents. If we hadn't, SYGRAPH would add them together and compute percents before drawing the map, just as it does with pies. The results would have been the same.

LOCUS$	PERCENT
TOWN	40
COUNTY	20
STATE	10
NATION	16
WORLD	14

- Select **Options/Formats...** from the **Graph** menu
- Choose [British] from the [High-res fonts] list
- Click [Italic]
- Click OK

- Select **Options/Global settings...** from the **Graph** menu
- Choose [High resolution] fonts
- Click OK

- Select **Pie/Ring** from the **Graph** menu
- Select the continuous variable: PERCENT
- Select the categorical variable: LOCUS$
- Click off [Sort]
- Click OK

Here is the attention map for these data. As an alternative to this map (other than pie), take a look at the percentage bar chart (see the [Percent] option for **Bar**).

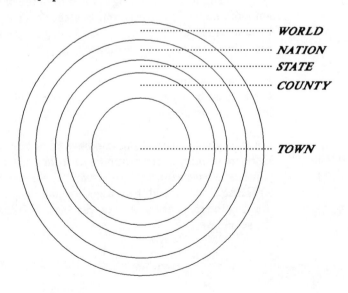

Options

Logging data

Why would you log data for a pie chart? Don't ask us. The procedures in SYGRAPH are orthogonal, however. This means that **Pie** is designed to plot continuous against categorical data and there is no good reason why the procedures that work in this context shouldn't work for **Pie**. Besides, some biochemist in Arizona is going to call up SYSTAT with the perfect application for logged pie charts and we're going to send her a free T-shirt when she does.

[Log] works with any form of pie chart. The following example logs frequencies.

7.5 Logged data pie chart

We log the SALES data from our previous example before plotting:

REGION$	SALES	SALESMAN
New England	10	Leah
Mid Atlantic	10	Ruth
Great Lakes	20	Lydia
Plains	5	Susan
Southeast	5	Eve
South	30	Harry
Mountain	10	Dorothy
Pacific	10	Michelle

- Select **Options/Formats...** from the **Graph** menu
- Choose [Stroke] from the [High-res fonts] list
- Click [Italic]
- Click OK

- Select **Options/Global settings...** from the **Graph** menu
- Choose [High resolution] fonts
- Click OK

- Select **Pie** from the **Graph** menu
- Select the continuous variable: SALES
- Select the categorical variable: REGION$
- Specify base for [Log]: 10
- Click off [Sort]
- Click OK

Notice how logging smooths out differences between regions. If you want to downplay Harry's performance in the South, use log pie charts. Just a matter of emphasis, isn't it? Hey, whose job is on the line?

© 1989, SYSTAT, Inc.

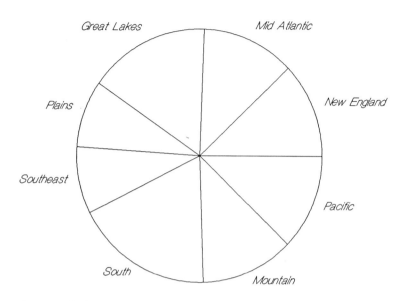

Powering data

If we can do log pie charts, why not power pie charts? These are for power users. [Power] is implemented in SYGRAPH only for positive data, however; negative values are deleted.

[Power] works with any form of pie chart. The following example transforms frequencies.

**7.6
Powered data pie chart**

Let's examine our SALES data with a power pie chart.

REGION$	SALES	SALESMAN
New England	10	Leah
Mid Atlantic	10	Ruth
Great Lakes	20	Lydia
Plains	5	Susan
Southeast	5	Eve
South	30	Harry
Mountain	10	Dorothy
Pacific	10	Michelle

The previous example downplayed Harry's sales in the South. Here is Harry's revenge pie chart :

- Select **Options/Formats...** from the **Graph** menu
- Choose [Hershey] from the [High-res fonts] list
- Click OK

- Select **Options/Global settings...** from the **Graph** menu
- Choose [High resolution] fonts
- Click OK

- Select **Pie** from the **Graph** menu
- Select the continuous variable: SALES
- Select the categorical variable: REGION$
- Specify base for [Power]: 2
- Click off [Sort]
- Click OK

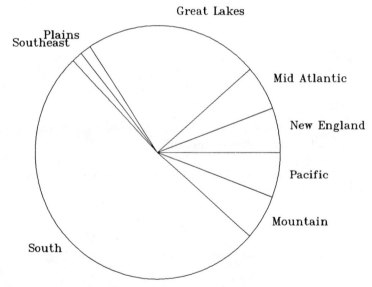

Isn't lying with statistics fun?

8   Box

Box

8

Overview

Box plots provide a simple graphical summary of a batch of data. Tukey (1977) originally presented them as schematic plots. Velleman and Hoaglin (1981) introduced them to non-technical users and demonstrated their power for a range of data.

Some programs produce plots that resemble the schematic plots invented by John Tukey and produced by SYGRAPH. The most common alternatives to box plots are displays that show 5th, 25th, 50th, 75th, and 95th percentiles as boxes with whiskers. While these displays are simpler to compute, they are not box plots and should not be called so at the risk of confusing data analysts. See the Definitions section below for further information.

SYGRAPH offers both single and within group box plots. Single plots display the distribution of a single variable and grouped plots show the distribution of a single variable stratified across the levels of a grouping variable. The latter are especially useful for illustrating the results of an experiment or survey data on multiple groups. As in other SYGRAPH procedures, **Box** offers numerous options for scaling and annotating box plots for presentation graphics.

Box

If you select one continuous variable, **Box** produces a single box plot aligned on a scale. If you select one variable and one grouping variable, **Box** produces separate boxes for each category, all aligned on a common scale.

If you select several continuous variables, separate plots or grouped plots are drawn for each. You can only select one grouping variable at a time.

- Select **Box** from the **Graph** menu
- Select one or more continuous variables from the list on the left
○ Select one grouping variable from the list on the right
- Click OK

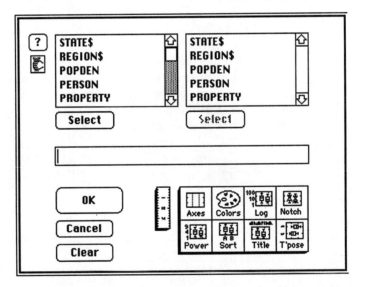

The values of the grouping variable appear along the horizontal axis. If you use a numerical grouping variable, only integers are printed.

The median of the batch is marked by the center vertical line. The lower and upper hinges comprise the edges of the central box. The median splits the ordered batch of numbers in half, and the hinges split the remaining halves in half again.

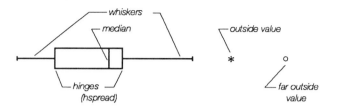

Definitions

To understand the remainder of the box plot, we need some definitions. *Hspread* is comparable to the interquartile range or midrange. It is the absolute value of the difference between the values of the two hinges.

The *inner fences* are defined as follows:

> lower fence = lower hinge – (1.5Hspread)
> upper fence = upper hinge + (1.5Hspread)

The *outer fences* are defined as follows:

> lower fence = lower hinge – (3Hspread)
> upper fence = upper hinge + (3Hspread)

Values outside the inner fences are plotted with asterisks. Values outside the outer fences are plotted with empty circles.

You can use the [Axes] options to control the scale on which the boxes are plotted. This is handy when several different variables are measured on the same scale.

Common options

See the **Common options** chapter for information on using [Axes], [Colors], [Log], [Power], [Sort], [Title], and [T'pose]. The specific option [Notch] is described below.

Box

If you select one continuous variable, **Box** produces a single box plot aligned on a scale. If you select several continuous variables, separate plots are drawn for each. If you select a grouping variable, **Box** produces a separate box for each category aligned on a common scale.

8.1
Box plot

Here is a simple box plot of POPDEN (population density per square mile) from the US dataset.

- Select **Box** from the **Graph** menu
- Select the continuous variable: POPDEN
- Click OK

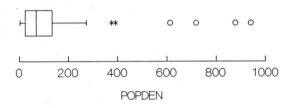

© 1989, SYSTAT, Inc.

8.2
Grouped box
plot

To plot several box plots against a common vertical scale, select a grouping variable. Here is an example:

- Select **Box** from the **Graph** menu
- Select the continuous variable: INCOME
- Select the grouping variable: REGION$
- Click OK

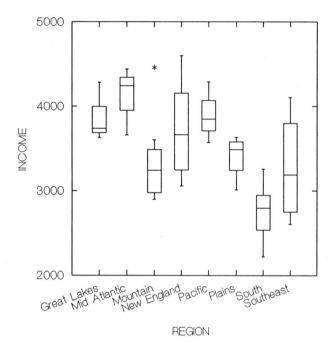

See the **Density** chapter for similar grouped plots using dots and stripes. These plots can be overlaid on box plots to reveal more details of the sample distribution.

Notched box plots

Notch

McGill, Tukey, and Larsen (1978) implemented confidence intervals on the median of several groups in a box plot. If the intervals around two medians do not overlap, you can be confident at about the 95% level that the two population medians are different. You can do this plot in SYGRAPH by clicking [Notch].

Example 8.3 shows a notched box plot of INCOME (per-capita income) by REGION for the 1970 US dataset. The boxes are notched at the median and return to full width at the lower and upper confidence interval values. Notice that some of the outer confidence limits extend beyond the hinges (the horizontal lines on either side of the narrow median line). This is unaesthetic but adheres to Tukey and McGill's original standard for the plot.

Notches are especially handy for judging differences between groups. Note, for example, that the South had a significantly lower income than New England, but not significantly lower than the Mountain states.

8.3
Notched box plot

Here is a notched plot of INCOME by REGION$.

- Select **Box** from the **Graph** menu
- Select the continuous variable: INCOME
- Select the grouping variable: REGION$
- Click the [Notch] option
- Click OK

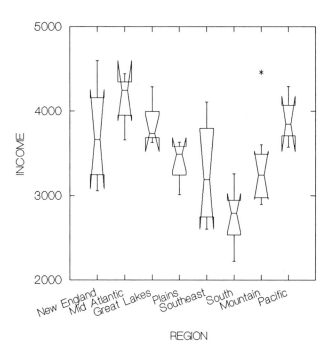

9   Density

Density 9

Overview

The density of a sample is the relative concentration of data points at different sections of the scale on which the data are measured. Graphically representing the density of measurements on a variable is not a trivial problem. Most introductory statistics texts use a histogram, which is a crude density estimator. It is crude because the shape of a histogram depends on the choice of the number of bars. Most other graphical density estimation methods rest on more or less subjective choices of parameters or settings as well, which is one reason the general field of density estimation is rather controversial among statisticians (Wegman, 1982).

Density offers several ways to represent a density. **Hist** produces garden variety histograms. **Cum'tive** produces cumulative histograms. The [Poly] option produces cumulative frequency polygons. **Fuzzy** produces fuzzygrams, which are probability enhanced histograms. **Jitter** produces jittered sample densities. **Polygon** produces frequency polygons. **Stripe** produces vertical density stripes. **Dot** produces dot density plots. **Dit** produces dot plots which look like histograms.

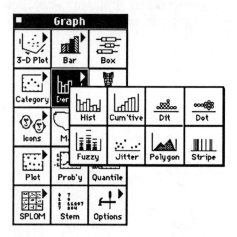

- Select **Density/Hist, Cum'tive, Fuzzy, Jitter, Polygon, Dot, Dit,** or **Stripe** from the **Graph** menu
- Select one or more variables
- Click OK

You can use a numeric or character grouping variable with **Jitter, Dot, Dit,** or **Stripe.** This produces two-way densities which look like grouped box plots (see the **Box** chapter).

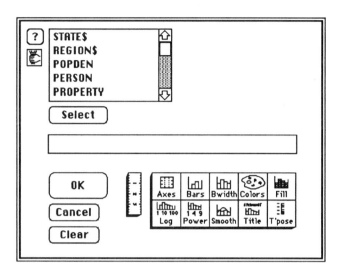

Common options

See the **Common options** chapter for information on [Axes], [Colors], [Fill], [Log], [Power], [Title], and [T'pose]. Additional options, [Bars], [Bwidth], and [Smooth], are discussed below.

Types of plots

Histograms

A histogram displays the sample density of a numerical variable. The word comes from a Greek word (*histos*) for a straight standing beam, like a mast or loom frame, and a word for "picture" that derives from the word for "writing." Thus, a histogram is a display of bars standing vertically.

Unlike bar charts, however, histograms in statistics are based on continuous variables. The bars are ordered along a continuum and the cutpoints between the bars are chosen to make the shape of the histogram particularly revealing of the distribution of a variable.

We mention this background to highlight the use of histograms to display the shape of data. Many people use histograms to count data values. This is a misuse of the display. If you want to examine actual data values, you should use **Bar** or **Stem**.

SYGRAPH uses initial estimates and a heuristic strategy to pick the number of bars and scale values to produce an aesthetic histogram (Sturges, 1926; Doane, 1976; Scott, 1979). If there are too many empty bars (more than half), the program reduces the number. If some bars are too tall, the program increases the number. Several options let you adjust the values selected by the program.

9.1
Histogram

This is a histogram of INCOME (per capita income) from the US file.

- Select **Density/Hist** from the **Graph** menu
- Select the continuous variable: INCOME
- Click OK

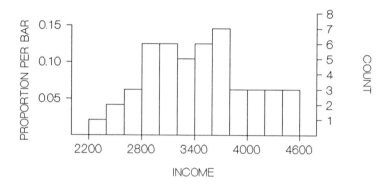

The scale on the right (COUNT) helps to show the number of cases in each bar. The scale on the left (PROPORTION PER BAR) is the proportion of the sample in each bar. The horizontal scale is chosen to provide very round numbers.

See [Bwidth] below and [Axes], and [Scale] in the General Options chapter for more information on how to control the number of bars and scale values. We should warn you, however, that the number of bars chosen by SYGRAPH is taken from an optimal statistical estimator, and you are unlikely to do better.

Cumulative histograms

Density/Cum'tive draws cumulative histograms. In a cumulative histogram, each bar's area is the sum of the preceding bar's areas plus its own incremental area. This makes a cumulative histogram correspond to a cumulative frequency distribution or, for continuous data, a distribution function. Keep in mind that you can use other options to produce more complex histograms.

9.2
Cumulative
histogram

Here is the cumulative version of the INCOME histogram.

- Select Density/Cum'tive from the Graph menu
- Select the continuous variable: INCOME
- Click OK

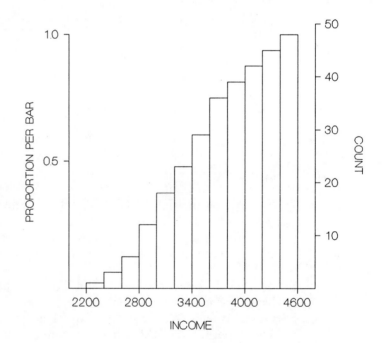

　　　　　　　　　　　　　　　　　　　　© 1989, SYSTAT, Inc.

Fuzzygrams

Fuzzy

Wilkinson (1983) devised a variation of the histogram that superimposes a probability distribution on each bar. The purpose of this display is to make the bars for histograms based on small samples fuzzier than the bars for large sample histograms. This way, when we examine sample histograms to see if they plausibly represent a population distribution, we will not place too much faith in small sample variations or features.

Basically, it works like this. Let

$$p_i = \frac{n_i}{n}$$

be the sample estimate of π_i, the expected proportion of a sample of n values from a continuous distribution to fall in the ith of k histogram bars ($i = 1, k$). Assume k is selected such that $0 < \pi_i < 1$. A fuzzygram is a histogram with bars represented by a gray scale distribution on
$P_i = P(p_i > \pi_i)$. That is, the more likely p_i is greater than π_i, the lighter the bar.

The program computes the gray scale assuming that the joint distribution of the counts in the bars is multinomial. Using an arcsine transformation of the square root of the p_i it chooses the gaps between successive stripes in the bar from a normal variate with variance $1/4n$. This distribution is adjusted for the number of bars in the display using an approximation to Bonferroni deviates. Haber and Wilkinson (1982) discuss perceptual issues in viewing the fuzzygram. A vertical line in the center of each bar reveals the height of the bar in the sample. If the sample size is small, the graph will be very blurred. If large, the bars are sharp. Finally, if we fit a curve through the bars with a normal smooth (discussed later in this chapter), we should expect the curve to follow cleanly through the fuzzy part of the graph (i.e., the expected part).

9.3
Fuzzygram

Here is a fuzzygram on the WINTER temperature data.

- Select **Density/Fuzzy** from the **Graph** menu
- Select the continuous variable: WINTER
- Click OK

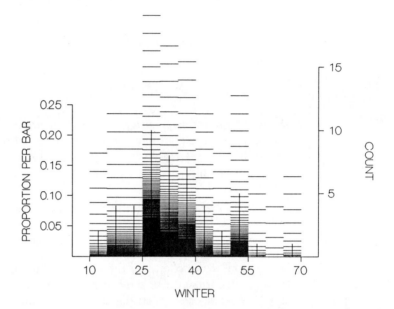

Jitter

A jittered density places points along a horizontal data scale at the locations of data values. To keep points from colliding, they are located randomly on a short vertical axis. Unlike histograms, no binning into bars is required. Unlike density stripes (see below in this chapter), jittered densities work well with large samples because points do not overlap. Jittering is less appropriate for small samples, however, because the quantity of points is usually not sufficient to indicate a density in a given region.

9.4
Jittered density

Here is a jittered plot of POPDEN (population density). This sample is a bit too small for jittering. Compare it to Example 9.6, which reveals the density better.

- Select **Options/Formats...** from the **Graph** menu
- Choose [British] from the [High-res fonts] list
- Click OK

- Select **Options/Global settings...** from the **Graph** menu
- Choose [High resolution] fonts
- Click OK
- Select **Density/Jitter** from the **Graph** menu
- Select the continuous variable: POPDEN
- Click OK

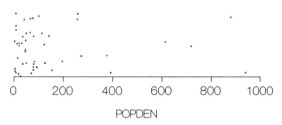

Polygon

Polygon

Frequency polygons can be produced by connecting the tops of the bars of a histogram with a line and then removing the bars. If we are thinking of a histogram as a sample density estimator, then a frequency polygon does a better job because it smooths the square edges of the bars.

Remember, the shape of the polygon depends on the number of bars or cutpoints chosen. You may want to experiment with [Bars] to see the differences.

9.5
Frequency
polygon

Here is a frequency polygon of the INCOME variable (per-capita income) from the US dataset. We've added a gray fill pattern to highlight the density.

- Select **Options/Formats...** from the **Graph** menu
- Choose [Hershey] from the [High-res fonts] list
- Click OK

- Select **Options/Global settings...** from the **Graph** menu
- Choose [High resolution] fonts
- Click OK

- Select **Density/Polygon** from the **Graph** menu
- Select the continuous variable: INCOME
- Choose the last fill pattern
- Click OK

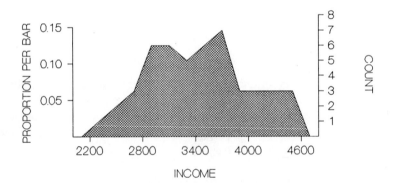

Stripe

Density stripes are vertical lines placed at the location of data values on a horizontal data scale. Unlike histograms, no binning into bars is required, so density stripes are especially suited for small to moderate sized samples of continuous data.

For larger datasets, stripes tend to overlap and produce black bars. In these cases, you should consider **Jitter**.

9.6
Stripe plot

Here is a density stripe plot of POPDEN (population density).

- Select **Density/Stripe** from the **Graph** menu
- Select the continuous variable: POPDEN
- Click OK

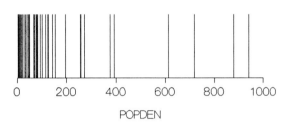

Dot and Dit

Dit plots look like histograms. Unlike histograms, dit plots represent every observation with a unique symbol, so they are especially suited for small to moderate sized samples of continuous data. The resolution of the graph is controlled by the size of the plotting symbol. Dit plots also resemble stem-and-leaf diagrams without the stems and substituting circle symbols for the leaves.

Dot plots are symmetric dit plots. See Example 9.8 for an example of a grouped dot plot.

9.7
Dit plot

Here is a dit plot of SUMMER (summer temperature).

- Select **Density/Dit** from the **Graph** menu
- Select the continuous variable: SUMMER
- Click OK

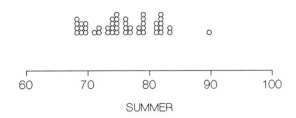

9.8
Grouped Dot
plot

Here is a grouped dot plot of INCOME against REGION. You can
do the same type of plot with **Jitter, Dot, Dit,** or **Stripe**. Compare
this result with the same data in the **Box** chapter, Example 8.2. It
sometimes is valuable to superimpose a dot plot on a box plot to
show the fine grained distribution of the data.

- Select **Density/Dot** from the **Graph** menu
- Select the continuous variable: SUMMER
- Select the grouping variable: REGION$
- Click OK

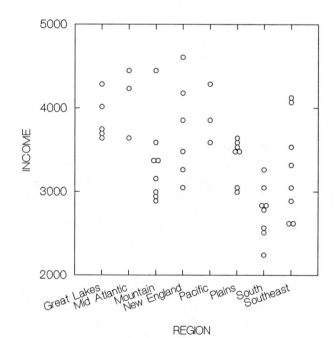

© 1989, SYSTAT, Inc.

Options

Number of bars

[Bars] controls the number of bars drawn in a histogram. SYGRAPH usually chooses an optimal number of bars via a statistical algorithm based on the binary log of the number of cases and other factors. You can force a different number of bars with the [Bars] option.

This leaves SYGRAPH with the choice of scale values (cutpoints). To manipulate the cutpoints as well, use [Bwidth], discussed next.

9.9
More bars

Here we plot a histogram with 15 bars. Because SYGRAPH chooses even cutpoints, the upper three bars are left empty and we are forced back to the same shape we had in 9.1.

- Select **Options/Formats...** from the **Graph** menu
- Choose the Hershey [High-res] typeface
- Click OK

- Select **Options/Global settings...** from the **Graph** menu
- Click [High resolution]
- Click OK

- Select **Density/Hist** from the **Graph** menu
- Select the continuous variable: INCOME
- Specify 15 for [Bars]
- Click OK

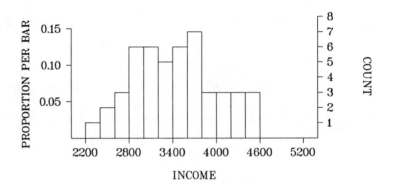

Bar widths

[Bwidth] controls the width of bars drawn in a histogram. Normally, SYGRAPH chooses the cutpoint interval (bar width), number of bars, and scale values with an optimization algorithm. You can modify the chosen bar width with the [Bwidth] option. Usually, you should set [Min] (in the [Axes] dialog box) when you set [Bwidth]. Otherwise, the SYGRAPH optimization algorithm may not give you the minimum values you wish.

9.10
Choosing bar widths

Here, we completely override the optimization algorithm by specifying both the width of the bars and the minimum value.

- Select **Density/Hist** from the **Graph** menu
- Select the continuous variable: INCOME
- Set [Min] to 2000 in the [Axes] dialog box
- Specify 150 for [Bwidth]
- Click OK

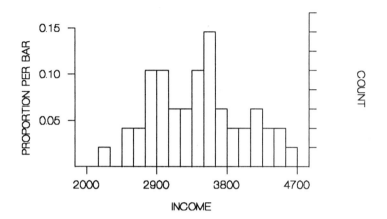

Smoothing

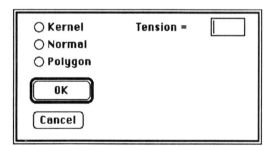

You can superimpose a kernel, normal, or polygon smoothing on histograms. You can eliminate the histogram but keep the smoothing by clicking [Plot smooth only].

- Click [Smooth]
- Choose type of smoothing
- Click OK

○ **Kernel**   **Tension =** ☐
○ **Normal**
○ **Polygon**

[**OK**]

[Cancel]

Kernel

Kernel smoothing is new with this version of SYGRAPH. It lets you superimpose a univariate nonparametric kernel density estimator. The estimator shows areas where the data are most concentrated in the sample. This smoothing method uses the Epanechnikov kernel; see Silverman (1986) for more information.

Normal

If data are sampled from a normal distribution, then their histogram should tend to have a normal shape. We can examine this possibility by using the sample mean and standard deviation to superimpose a normal curve on a histogram. If you are doing a cumulative histogram, then the cumulative normal curve is used.

Polygon

[Polygon] produces a polygon smoothed histogram.

**9.11
Histogram
smoothed with
normal density**

This example shows a normal smooth through the WINTER temperature data from the US file. The lower tail in the graph is a bit short, probably because we are not sampling temperatures as far north as south, given the geographic distribution of the continental U.S.

- Select **Options/Formats...** from the **Graph** menu
- Choose the British [High-res] typeface
- Click OK

- Select **Options/Global settings...** from the **Graph** menu
- Click [High resolution]
- Click OK

- Select **Density/Hist** from the **Graph** menu
- Select the continuous variable: WINTER
- Choose [Normal] for [Smooth]
- Click OK

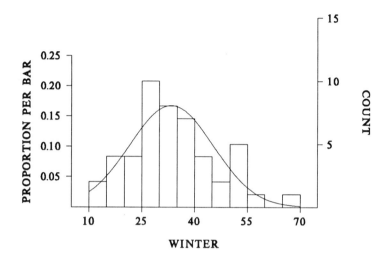

10

Stem

Stem

Overview

The stem-and-leaf display looks like a sideways histogram or tally. Unlike the histogram, however, the stem-and-leaf display shows the numerical values of the variable. The stems are printed on the left side. These are the most significant digits in which variation occurs. The leaves—the next digits after each stem—are printed to the right. The leaves are not rounded, so the original data can be recovered to the precision of the leaves. For more information, consult Tukey (1977) or Velleman and Hoaglin (1981).

A stem-and-leaf diagram is similar to a histogram, except that individual values of the variables are retained and can be accessed at a glance. The digits of each numeric value are separated into a *stem* and a *leaf*. For the number 1,398.4, possible stems and leaves are as follows:

Stem	Leaf
1	3
13	9
139	8
1398	4
13984	0

Choosing which stem and corresponding leaf to use depends on the resolution desired, the number of values to display, and the distribution of the sample batch of values.

For most batches of numbers, each stem has several values for leaves. The leaves are the next digit to the right of the stem. For example, the numbers 1398.4 and 1397.0 and 1391.2 can share a stem as follows:

Stem	Leaves
139	8 7 1

The stem-and-leaf diagram is assembled by listing all stems vertically in order, followed by their leaves in order as well.

Stem also prints medians, hinges, and minima and maxima of variables.

Stem

Stem produces stem-and-leaf displays.

- Select **Stem** from the **Graph** menu
- Select the variable to be analyzed
- Click OK

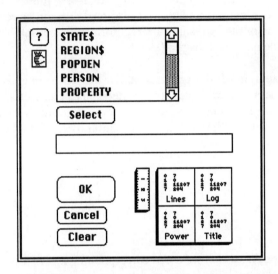

SYGRAPH constructs the display in an heuristic manner similar to that for histograms. It first chooses a number of lines based on the number of cases in the dataset. Then it picks a stem (digit of significant variation, displayed on the left) that allows roughly the number of lines chosen for the display. The difference between adjacent stems is a very round number $\{1,2,5\}*10^n$, where n is an integer.

Next, the next digits after the stem for each case are displayed as leaves (the numbers on the right). The leaf for each case is written on the line corresponding to the stem for the observation and leaves for other cases with the same stem are written next to each other on the same line.

If there are more leaves than can fit on one line, an asterisk is printed at the end of the line to indicate the overflow. This should rarely happen, however, since more lines are used when there are more data values.

SYGRAPH prints the median (M) and the hinges or quartiles (H) in the margin between the stems and leaves. (See the **Box** chapter for more information on these statistics.) Any values outside the inner fences are printed on additional lines separated from the inner values by the label "***OUTSIDE VALUES***."

If you use the [Facet] together with **Stem**, you will have the world's only three-dimensional stem-and-leaf diagram. We will send a SYSTAT watch to anyone who manages to get such a monstrosity past the editors of a reputable scientific journal and into print.

You will notice that **Stem** adjusts the height and width of numerals to make the entire plot fit the usual plotting frame. The left edge of the "leaves" is set at the left edge of the usual frame. This can sometimes cause squished-looking diagrams. You can cure this by adjusting the graph size. In addition, height is adjusted only for the values inside the inner fences. If you have a lot of outliers, you need to make additional adjustments.

Common options

See the **Common options** chapter for information on the [Log], [Power], and [Title] options. The [Lines] option is discussed below.

Stem and leaf diagrams
10.1
Stem-and-leaf
display

Here is an example from the US data. This one is black on white. If you want a color stem-and-leaf diagram (blasphemy!), use **Options/Color...**

- Select **Stem** from the **Graph** menu
- Select a variable: INCOME
- Click OK

```
2   2
2   45
2   667
2   888899
3H  000001
3   22333
3M  444555
3H  6666667
3   889
4   011
4   222
4   445
```

Options

Number of lines

If your diagram is too coarse, you can increase the number of lines with the [Lines] option.

It may take you several tries to set the number of lines correctly. If you set too many lines, your stem-and-leaf diagram will look long and stringy. If too few, it will be too coarse.

10.2
More lines

Here is the same stem-and-leaf diagram as in Example 10.1 but with more lines. Notice that you do not necessarily get the exact number you specify. SYGRAPH has to back and fill to cover all the values and come as close as it can to the number you request. You may need to adjust the height and width of the graph to get a nice display.

- Select **Stem** from the **Graph** menu
- Select a variable: INCOME
- Specify Lines=30
- Click OK

```
22  1
23
24  8
25  8
26  00
27  8
28  0489
29  59
30H 12457
31  3
32  45
33  057
34M 578
35  247
36  003358
37H 3
38  45
39  9
40  7
41  05
42  489
43
44  45
45  9
```

11   Plot

Plot

11

Overview

Plot produces two-way scatterplots and other types of plots of continuous variables against each other. See the **Function** chapter and the **3-D data plots** chapter for other types of related plots (which, incidentally, are produced by the same PLOT command in SYGRAPH). Also, see the **Splom** chapter for information on scatterplot matrices, i.e. matrices of scatterplots.

Plot offers eight types of scatterplots. **Plot** draws X-Y plots. **Border** draws X-Y plots with density plot borders. **Contour** draws X-Y plots with data contours. **Fourier** draws Fourier plots of data. **High-low** draws high-low-close plots for depicting ranges of stock prices and other statistics. **Influence** draws influence plots, where the size of each plotting symbol reflects the amount of influence that case has on the Pearson correlation coefficient. **Parallel** plots in parallel coordinates. **Voronoi** draws Voronoi tesselations.

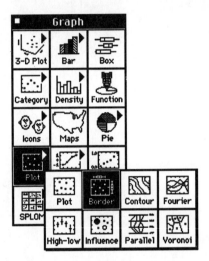

To select a plot, press and hold the mouse button on **Plot**. A submenu pops up offering **Plot, Contour, Border, Fourier, High-low, Influence, Parallel,** and **Voronoi**. Select the item you want and release the mouse button.

In general, you will do the following to draw a plot:

- Select **Plot** from the **Graph** menu
- Select one or more Y variables from the selection list on the left
- Select one X variable from the list on the right
- Click OK

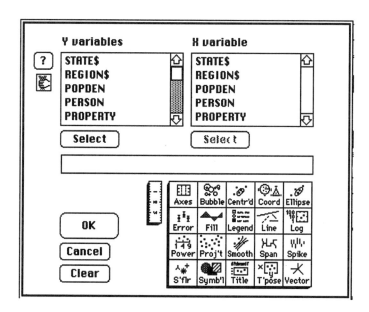

To plot several variables against another variable on the same graph, select several Y variables. When you do this, it is usually a good idea to use a different symbol (see [Symbol] in the **Common options** chapter) for each vertical axis variable. Although SYGRAPH can plot up to 12 variables on the vertical axis against one on the horizontal, it is not a good idea to do more than two or three.

Common options

See the **Common options** chapter for information on how to use [Axes], [Fill], [Legend], [Line], [Log], [Power], [Proj't], [Symb'l], [Title], and [T'pose]. The [Bubble], [Centroid], [Coord], [Ellipse], [Error], [Smooth], [Span], [Spike], [Sunflower], and [Vector] options are discussed below.

Note that you can use **Plot** with [Limit] (in the [Axes] dialog box) to produce *Shewhart charts* or *control charts*. Shewhart charts mark upper and lower limits on one axis to indicate permissible bounds for a production process. Axis limits can be used in other applications to mark standard errors that you compute with **Stats/Statistics...**

Types of plots

Scatterplots

Plot

Plot/Plot produces X-Y scatterplots of continuous variables. The Y variables are the vertical axis variables, and X is the horizontal. See the [Symbol] option in the **Common options** chapter for more information on how to produce scatterplots with different symbols for each subgroup or different labels for each point.

11.1
Scatterplot

Here is a plot of SUMMER (summer temperatures) against LABLAT (latitude) using the US file.

- Select **Options/Formats...** from the **Graph** menu
- Choose [British] from the [High-res fonts] list
- Click OK

- Select **Options/Global settings...** from the **Graph** menu
- Choose [High resolution] fonts
- Click OK

- Select **Plot** from the **Graph** menu
- Select the Y variable: SUMMER
- Select the X variable: LABLAT
- Click OK

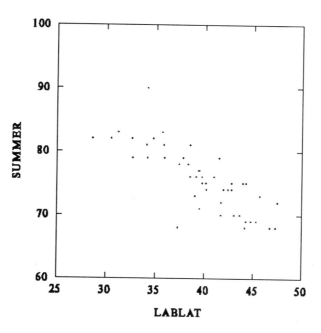

11.2
Multiple Y
variable
scatterplot

The next example shows SUMMER and WINTER values plotted
against LABLAT using circles and triangles for the points.

- Select **Plot/Plot** from the **Graph** menu
- Select the Y variables: SUMMER, WINTER
- Select the X variable: LABLAT
- Specify symbols: 2,3 in the [Symb'l] dialog box
- Click OK

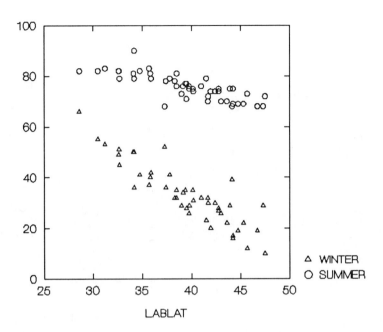

Bordered scatterplots

You can do scatterplots bordered by box plots, jitter plots, and stripe plots with **Borders.** The default is [Box]; click [Jitter] or [Stripe] if you prefer.

If you specify several Y variables, the density plot is drawn for the first Y variable.

11.3
Scatterplot with box plots

Here is an example using our U.S. data. You might want to substitute density stripes or jitter plots for the box plots.

- Select **Plot/Border** from the **Graph** menu
- Select the Y variable: RAIN
- Select the X variable: SUMMER
- Click OK

© 1989, SYSTAT, Inc.

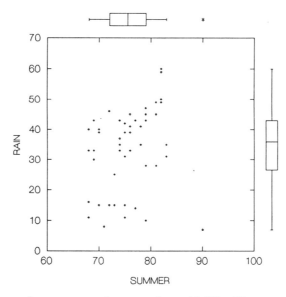

Contour plots

You can produce contoured scatterplots with **Plot/Contour.** Contours show a third dimension with contours on a two-dimensional scatterplot. You should select three variables (Z, Y, and X) in order, and type asterisks in between. The contour variable is Z. For [Kernel], just select Y and X variables as usual; density values are represented as the third (contoured) dimension.

For contouring data from a file, you must use one of the [Smooth] options, discussed later in this chapter. **Contour** uses [Nexpo] smoothing if you don't choose one yourself. All of the smoothing options work with regularly or irregularly spaced points. You need not input a regular grid to produce contours.

Note: Only [DWLS], [Inverse], [Kernel], [Linear], [Nexpo], and [Quadratic] are available with **Contour.** [LOWESS], [Log], [Power], [Spline], and [Step] are dimmed in the [Smooth] dialog box.

SYGRAPH first computes its own square grid of interpolated or directly estimated values. From this grid, contours are followed using the method of Lodwick and Whittle (1970) combined with linear interpolation. This method is guaranteed to find proper contours if the grid is fine enough. The standard grid is 30 by 30. To increase this resolution, use the [Cut] option in [Smooth] to add up to 100 grid cuts. For rough contours, you can reduce computing time by setting cuts below 30.

SYGRAPH automatically determines the number of contours to draw so that the surface is delineated and the contour labels are round numbers. If you wish to modify this number, use [Z tick] (in the [Axes] dialog box), which determines the number of tick marks on the third axis, and thus the number of contours to be drawn.

**11.4
Contour plot with lines**

Here is a contour plot of RAIN (average annual rainfall) against latitude and longitude from the US file. We have used distance weighted least squares smoothing to interpolate the rainfall surface, assuming that the estimate of rain at the state centroids contains measurement error.

- Select **Plot/Contour** from the **Graph** menu
- Select the variables: RAIN*LABLAT*LABLON
- Choose [DWLS] smoothing
- Specify [Z tick] as 10 in the [Axes] dialog box
- Click OK

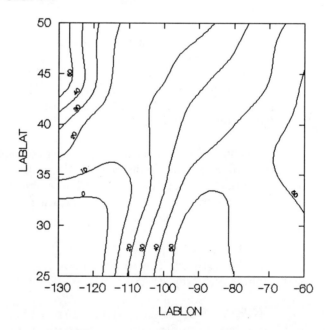

**11.5
Contour plot with shading**

You can produce shaded contour plots of functions and smoothed surfaces with the [Fill] option. Instead of lines, this method uses fill patterns from empty (white) to full (black) in even gradations that are determined by the height of the function at a given pixel (grid square).

© 1989, SYSTAT, Inc.

Here is a filled version of the previous contour plot.

- Select **Plot/Contour** from the **Graph** menu
- Select the variables: RAIN*LABLAT*LABLON
- Choose [DWLS] smoothing
- Specify [Z tick] as 10 in the [Axes] dialog box
- Click [Fill]
- Click OK

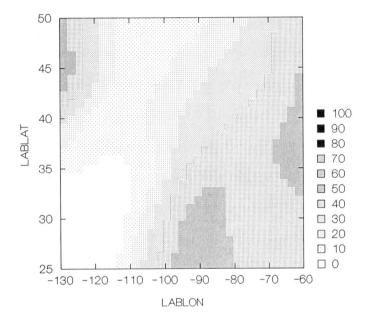

11.6
Contour plot with color

You can produce color contour plots of smoothed surfaces by using the [Color] option. Instead of lines, this method uses fill patterns from blue to red in even perceptual gradations that are determined by the height of the function at a given grid square.

Here is how you would produce a color contour plot of the rainfall plot. Since this is a two-color manual, it wouldn't make much sense to try to show the plot here.

- Select **Plot/Contour** from the **Graph** menu
- Select the variables: RAIN*LABLAT*LABLON
- Choose [DWLS] smoothing and click [Color]
- Specify [Z tick] as 10 in the [Axes] dialog box
- Click [Colors]
- Click OK

Some graphics devices, including color displays that represent fewer than 256 colors at the same time, cannot produce this plot. Pen plotters give a fair approximation because SYGRAPH selects the pen with the closest color appearance, provided the pens are ordered properly in the carousel.

**Andrews'
Fourier plots**

Fourier

A particularly powerful method for identifying clusters of cases in a multivariate dataset is to plot their Fourier components. Andrews (1972) developed these plots. Fourier functions have the following form:

$$f(t) = \frac{y_1}{\sqrt{2}} + y_2\sin(t) + y_3\cos(t) + y_4\sin(2t) + y_5\cos(2t) + \ldots$$

where y is a p dimensional variate and t varies from -3.14 to 3.14 (π radians on either side of zero). The result of this transformation is a set of waveforms made up of sine and cosine components. Each waveform corresponds to one case in the dataset. Cases that have similar values across all variables will have overlapping waveforms in the plot. Cases with different patterns of variation will have contrasting waveforms.

To use **Fourier**, you select all the variables from a single selection list All numeric variables in the file are used by default.

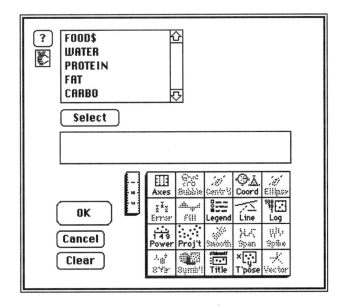

When using Fourier plots, you should be sure all the variables are on the same scale. Otherwise, variables with large values tend to dominate the Fourier plot.

11.7
Fourier plot

The NUTRIENTS data are the percentages of selected nutrients in a typical computer programmer's diet, estimated from figures supplied by the U.S. Department of Agriculture.

FOOD$	WATER	PROTEIN	FAT	CARBO
Twinkie	22.0	5.4	13.6	57.0
Eggroll	55.0	6.2	8.2	20.0
Cola	90.0	0.0	0.0	8.0
Pizza	45.0	9.3	8.0	35.8
Fudge	8.0	3.5	13.8	72.7
Peanuts	2.0	26.1	50.8	19.1

Here is a Fourier plot of these data. Notice that we do not need to select any variables, since the default (all numeric variables) is what we want.

The Fourier plot reveals the four essential nutrition groups: beverage (Cola), entree (Eggroll, Pizza), dessert (Twinkie, Fudge), and snack (Peanuts). Compare **Fourier** with the **Parallel** axes plot (see Example 11.10). Also compare **Fourier** to **Icon** blobs and **Parallel** to **Icon** stars. Blob and star plots are polar coordinate versions of Fourier and parallel coordinate plots, respectively.

- Select **Options/Formats...** from the **Graph** menu
- Choose [Hershey] from the [High-res fonts] list
- Click OK

- Select **Options/Global settings...** from the **Graph** menu
- Choose [High resolution] fonts
- Click OK

- Select **Plot/Fourier** from the **Graph** menu
- Specify FOOD$ for symbol labels
- Click OK

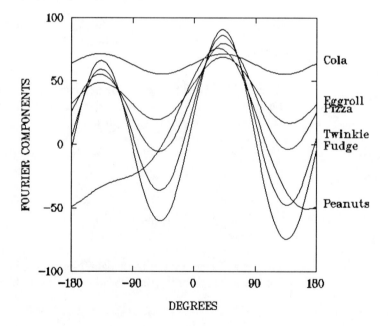

© 1989, SYSTAT, Inc.

High-low-close plots

Stock market daily, weekly, or monthly statistics are often most effectively plotted as a set of ranges between high and low prices with a marker for the closing price at each period. This is the way most newspapers plot the market. **High-low** produces this plot.

The high-low-close plot has other applications. You should consider it for asymmetrical error bars, for example. You can also do one-sided error bars by making the low (or high) the same value as the close variable.

To use **High-low**, select three continuous variables for the high, low, and close from the [Y variables] list and one (horizontal) variable from the [X variables] list.

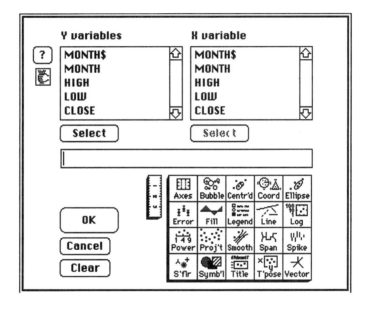

11.8
High-low-close
plot

Here are some typical data on a stock. These data, which we also use in the **Category** chapter, are in the file HILO.

MONTH	MONTH	HIGH	LOW	CLOSE
January	1	20.1	17.5	20.0
February	2	24.5	18.8	24.0
March	3	29.3	22.5	23.6
April	4	35.1	25.6	29.9
May	5	40.2	32.3	35.5
June	6	45.1	38.8	39.5
July	7	39.6	32.3	37.1
August	8	33.1	28.3	28.3
September	9	27.8	20.5	21.1
October	10	22.1	17.8	17.9
November	11	17.9	16.1	16.5
December	12	16.8	10.2	10.3

Here is a high-low-close plot of these data using the index of the month as the horizontal variable. We have used a horizontal line to mark the close. You can use any other you wish.

- Select **Plot/High-low** from the **Graph** menu
- Select the Y variables: HIGH, LOW, CLOSE
- Select the X variable: MONTH
- Choose the horizontal line (12th in the LaserWriter list) in the [Symb'l] dialog box
- Click OK

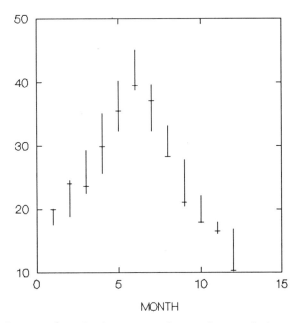

MONTH

Influence plots

The influence of a point in a scatterplot on the correlation coefficient is the amount the correlation would change if that point were deleted. Plotting influences can help us determine whether a linear fit to the scatterplot is relatively robust or is dependent on just a few points. **Plot/Influence** makes the size of the plotting symbol represent the extent of influence of each point on the Pearson correlation coefficient. A scale to the right of the plot helps us judge the extent of the influence. If any large points appear in the plot, we should scrutinize them before we draw any conclusions concerning the correlation.

You can use any symbol for influence plots, although circles are standard. Positive influences are represented by hollow symbols and negative influences by filled.

Other types of influences or leverages on statistical estimators can be represented in SYGRAPH by using statistics computed in SYSTAT. For example, MGLH saves Mahalanobis distances (distances weighted by a covariance matrix) into a file when you do a discriminant analysis or save scores when testing hypotheses. You could specify the DISTANCE variable for [Size] in the [Symbol] dialog box. See Gnanadesikan (1977) for further information.

11.9
Influence plot

Here is an influence plot of RAIN (annual average inches of rainfall) on SUMMER (average summer temperature). One point (corresponding to Arizona) has a large negative influence. Its summer temperature is extremely high, yet it has little rainfall. This point is shown on the plot with a large filled plotting symbol. Hollow symbols (some appear in the upper right and lower left) have positive influence. That is, their presence increases the correlation.

- Select **Options/Formats...** from the **Graph** menu
- Choose [Hershey] from the [High-res fonts] list
- Click OK

- Select **Options/Global settings...** from the **Graph** menu
- Choose [High resolution] fonts
- Click OK

- Select **Plot/Influence** from the **Graph** menu
- Select a Y variable: RAIN
- Select an X variable: SUMMER
- Click OK

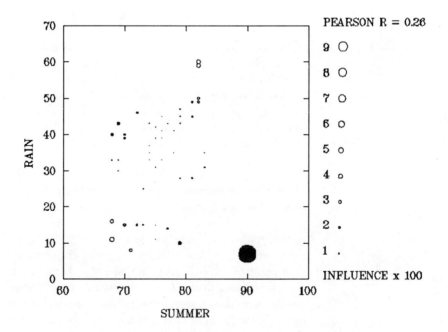

© 1989, SYSTAT, Inc.

Parallel coordinate plots

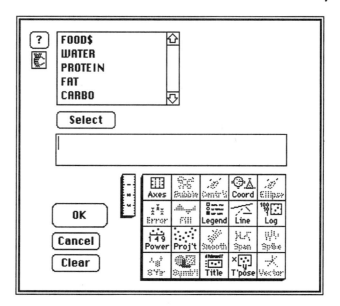

Cartesian coordinates are computed on perpendicular axes. This works fine for two and three dimensional plots. Higher dimensions, however, would be difficult to visualize. Inselberg (1985) proposed making coordinate axes parallel for these higher dimensional plots. Each case is represented by a point on each of several parallel scales, one for each variable on which the case is measured. The points on these scales are joined by line segments to represent the case. See Wegman (1986) and Curtis, Burton & Campbell (1987) for further information. Parallel coordinate plots are sometimes called *profile plots*.

To use **Parallel**, like **Fourier**, you select all the variables from a single selection lists. All numeric variables in the file are used by default.

Parallel and **Fourier** coordinates provide alternative representations of the same data. The advantage of Fourier coordinates is that variables are reduced to a smaller number of features in the plot. The advantage of parallel coordinates is that the plotting parameters are the raw variables themselves, which facilitates interpretation.

When you do a parallel coordinates plot, be sure that the data are on comparable scales. If not, they should be standardized before producing the plot.

11.10
Profile plot

Here is a parallel coordinate plot of the junk food data (NUTRIENTS) used in the Fourier plot, Example 11.7. As with that example, we do not need to select variables, since all numerical variables in the file are to be included.

Compare the **Parallel** plot to **Icon** stars in the **Icon** chapter. Star plots are polar coordinate versions of the parallel coordinate, or profile plot.

- Select **Plot/Parallel** from the **Graph** menu
- Click OK

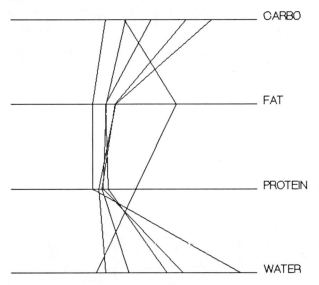

Voronoi tesselations

This is the cutest plot in the whole package. It takes a long time to compute, on the order of the square of the number of points. There are faster algorithms than SYSTAT's for large datasets (e.g. Green and Sibson, 1978; Preparata and Shamos, 1985), but they require much more storage and code.

The Voronoi tesselation is also known as the Dirichlet tesselation or the Thiessen diagram. Imagine placing little balls of hot roll dough at irregular spacings in a baking pan. After letting them rise, you notice that the boundaries between rolls are straight and approximately half way between the points where you placed the balls. The same thing happens with colonies of yeast irregularly spaced on a Petri dish or grass fires started at different points on a plain or cats establishing their turf in the city. These boundaries appear in diverse physical phenomena: geography (Rhynsburger, 1973), hydrology (Croley and Hartmann, 1985), ecology (Ripley, 1981), crystallography (Gilbert, 1962), physics (Miles, 1974), psychology (Coombs, 1964), and others.

As with the [Span] option, which draws a minimum spanning tree (see below in this chapter), **Voronoi** presumes you have equivalent distances on the X and Y axis. If your scales differ, resize the plot to make its dimensions reflect the true scale values. For example, if your vertical scale runs from 0 to 50 and the horizontal from 0 to 100, make the physical width twice the height.

11.11
Voronoi plot

The following figure shows the location of McDonald's restaurants in Memphis, Tennessee. Because we used a street map instead of latitude and longitude, the scales of the location variables are arbitrary.

We have suppressed scales and axes in the figure to highlight the structure. Notice that the smallest polygons are in the center of the map, where population densities are highest. The McDonald's people obviously planned carefully to insure an adequate supply of customers for each restaurant. If you are thinking of opening a chain of stores or restaurants in a uniformly dense area, the Thiessen polygons should be relatively compact instead of elongated to provide maximum access to your customers.

Here are the choices needed to produce the map. Try one with some data of your own.

- Select **Plot/Voronoi** from the **Graph** menu
- Select the Y variable: Y
- Select the X variable: X
- Click [Axes]
  - Specify ' ' for [X label] and [Y label]
  - Click off the axis and scale choices
- Click OK

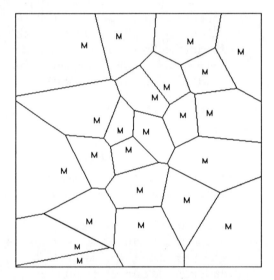

If you live in Memphis and are looking for the nearest McDonald's from your home (as the crow flies), just find the one inside the polygon containing your house. Every point within a polygon is closer to its corresponding McDonald's than to any other. This is true even when the McDonald's is not at the center of the polygon.

Bubble plots

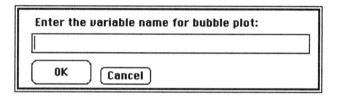

You can use the value of a variable in your file to control the size of a plotting symbol. This is especially useful for representing a third variable against two others in a two-way plot.

- Click [Bubble]
- Specify the variable to be used: DEN
- Click OK

Enter the variable name for bubble plot:

| |

(**OK**)   [**Cancel**]

One caution: the size of the plotting symbols is taken directly from the values in your value. There is no upper or lower limit. If the variable you specify has a value as small as .001 or a negative value, the point will be invisible; if it has a value as large as 100, the symbol will fill the entire plot. Try a range between 0 and 10. If your sizing variable does not lie in this range, you should rescale it. Finally, you should usually use empty symbols with this type of plot, since filled ones can occlude each other and make the plot difficult to interpret.

These plots are sometimes called **bubble plots**, for obvious reasons.

Cleveland, Kleiner, McRae, and Warner (1976) used open circles to represent levels of pollution on a map of New England. You can use other symbols. Bickel, Hammel, and O'Connell (1975) used open squares to represent the size of university departments in plotting admissions data at the University of California-Berkeley.

11.12
Bubble plot

We want to plot PERSON against PROPERTY from the US dataset, using bubbles to show population density. First, let's make a new variable using POPDEN.

- Select **Math...** from the **Data** menu
- Fill in the Let statement: Let DEN = 4*SQR(POPDEN/1000)
- Click OK

By this transformation, we have made a variable DEN in the range of 0 to 4 because 1000 is the maximum value of POPDEN in the file. We used square root, because we want the area of the symbols (not their diameter) to be proportional to the value of POPDEN. Now we can use this variable to determine the size of a plotting symbol.

- Select **Plot/Plot** from the **Graph** menu
- Select the Y variable: PERSON
- Select the X variable: PROPERTY
- Specify DEN for [Bubble]
- Choose the open circle for [Symb'l]
- Click OK

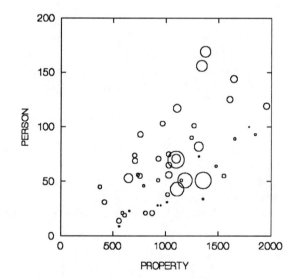

© 1989, SYSTAT, Inc.

Notice that the large circles (high population density) are not all at the upper right of the plot. Higher crime rates do not necessarily correspond to higher population densities.

Confidence intervals on bivariate centroids

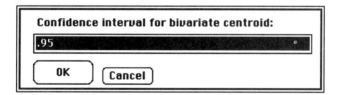

You can draw Gaussian bivariate confidence intervals on centroids with the [Centr'd] option. As with the [Ellipse] option (see directly below), the ellipse produced is centered on the sample means of the X and Y variables. Its major axes are determined by the unbiased sample standard deviations of X and Y and its orientation is determined by the sample covariance between X and Y. You choose the size of the ellipse by specifying a probability value between 0 and 1, e.g. .95 for 95%. This size is adjusted by the sample size so that the ellipse will always be smaller than that produced by the [Ellipse] option. The default value is .95.

- Click [Centr'd]
- Specify a probability value
- Click OK

Confidence interval for bivariate centroid:
.95
OK   Cancel

11.13
Scatterplot with
bivariate
confidence
interval

Here is an ellipse superimposed on the plot of PERSON (person crimes) against PROPERTY (property crimes). We use a 95 percent confidence region on the centroid.

- Select **Options/Formats...** from the **Graph** menu
- Choose [Hershey] from the [High-res fonts] list
- Click OK

- Select **Options/Global settings...** from the **Graph** menu
- Choose [High resolution] fonts
- Click OK

- Select **Plot/Plot** from the **Graph** menu
- Select the Y variable: PERSON
- Select the X variable: PROPERTY
- Click [Centr'd]
- Choose the open circle for [Symb'l]
- Click OK

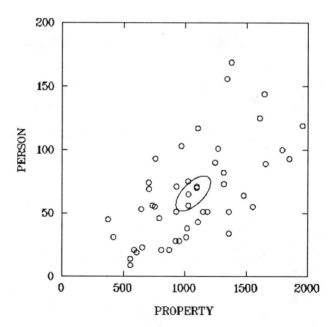

© 1989, SYSTAT, Inc.

Bivariate ellipses

You can draw bivariate ellipses on scatterplots assuming a Gaussian (normal) bivariate distribution for your data. The ellipse produced is centered on the sample means of the X and Y variables. Its major axes are determined by the unbiased sample standard deviations of X and Y and its orientation is determined by the sample covariance between X and Y. You choose the size of the ellipse by specifying a probability value between 0 and 1, e.g. .95. If you make an extremely large ellipse (e.g. .999), it may extend beyond the axes of your plot. The default value is .5.

Remember, these ellipses are always larger than the confidence ellipses (see previous), because these are for the total sample and the previous are for the centroid of the sample. The difference is analogous to the standard deviation versus the standard error of the mean.

- Click [Ellipse]
○ Specify a probability value
- Click OK

If you have two or more samples, such as in a discriminant analysis, you can draw separate ellipses by superimposing them on the same plot. Be sure to keep your variable ranges the same by using [X min], [X max], [Y min], and [Y max] in the [Axes] dialog box. You can plot ellipses without the data by clicking off the [Symbol] choice.

11.14
Scatterplot with
ellipse

Here is an ellipse superimposed on the plot of PERSON (person crimes) against PROPERTY (property crimes). We have used a 50 percent confidence region on the data values (the default). If the data were bivariate normal, then we would expect to find half the data points inside the ellipse. This is approximately the case.

- Select **Options/Formats...** from the **Graph** menu
- Choose [Hershey] from the [High-res fonts] list
- Click OK

- Select **Options/Global settings...** from the **Graph** menu
- Choose [High resolution]
- Click OK

- Select **Plot/Plot** from the **Graph** menu
- Select the Y variable: PERSON
- Select the X variable: PROPERTY
- Click [Ellipse]
- Choose the open circle for [Symb'l]
- Click OK

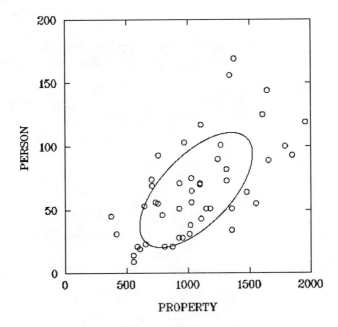

Polar and triangular coordinates

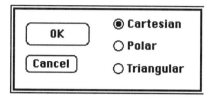

Ordinarily, you draw plots in Cartesian coordinates—the X-Y(-Z) axis system. You can also plot in polar or triangular coordinates. The [Coord] option lets you pick a coordinate system.

OK	● **Cartesian**
	○ **Polar**
Cancel	○ **Triangular**

The default is [Cartesian].

Polar coordinates

Polar coordinates translate Cartesian coordinates into a circular arrangement. Each point is given by its distance (r) from the origin and the angle (θ) of the positive X-axis and the vector from the origin to the point. Polar coordinates may seem confusing in some contexts but they are handy for representing many mathematical equations and data profiles.

SYGRAPH automatically scales polar graphs as well as rectangular graphs. The units printed on the scales are those of the data. You may alter these scales with [Axes]. Use [Y min] and [Y max] for the r axis (distance) and [X min] and [X max] for the θ axis (angle). [Y min] is always at the center of the circle and [Y max] at its periphery. [X min] and [X max] always coincide at the right edge (0 radians).

If the data collide with the axes, you can eliminate the axes by clicking off the [Axes] choice in the [Axes] dialog box. If you choose one axis, you get only the circle, omitting the radial axis. If you choose two or more axes, you get both the r and θ axes.

All the other **Plot** options work in polar coordinates. Use them intelligently, however, or you will get bizarre graphs.

Triangular coordinates

You can plot three variables in two dimensions with triangular coordinates. Consider the figure below. The graph on the left shows a perspective plot of three variables. If we assume that all points in this plot (X1,X2,X3) sum to a constant (SYGRAPH makes them sum to 1), then they fall on a plane, which is represented by the dark triangle in the plot. If we place this plane on the plotting surface, then the original axes correspond to the three vertices of a triangle.

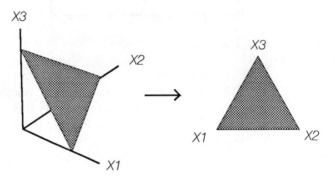

11.15
Polar scatterplot

The following data (in the file POLAR) show the highest frequency (in thousands of cycles per second) perceived by a subject listening to a constant amplitude sine wave generator oriented at various angles relative to the subject. Zero degrees corresponds to straight ahead of the subject.

ANGLE	FREQ
0.0	12.1
20.0	12.4
40.0	12.4
60.0	12.6
80.0	12.9
100.0	12.8
120.0	12.7
140.0	12.4
160.0	12.1
180.0	11.9
200.0	12.0
220.0	12.3
240.0	12.8
260.0	14.1
280.0	14.3
300.0	13.8
320.0	13.4
340.0	12.6
360.0	12.1

Here is the polar plot of these data with the points connected by a spline smooth. Notice that the profile shows hearing impairment in the left ear relative to the right.

- Select **Plot/Plot** from the **Graph** menu
- Select the Y (*r*) variable: FREQ
- Select the X (θ) variable: ANGLE
- Choose [Polar] coordinates
- Choose [Spline] smoothing
- Choose the open circle for [Symb'l]
- Set [X min] to 0 and [X max] to 360 in [Axes]
- Click OK

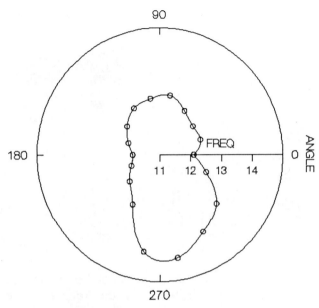

11.16
Triangular
scatterplot

Triangular coordinate plots are usually done on mixture data. For example, we mentioned in the introduction that all color hues can be represented as a mixture of red, green, and blue. Here is an example:

COLOR$	RED	GREEN	BLUE
CANARY	.47	.47	.06
ORANGE	.70	.26	.04
BROWN	.40	.40	.20
WHITE	.33	.33	.33
VIOLET	.49	.02	.49

Here is a triangular plot of these data with each point labeled by its corresponding color. Notice that WHITE is an even mixture of the three colors and is thus in the middle.

You can add grid lines to your triangular plot with [Axes]. All the grid choices produce the same result: a triangular grid. Other **Plot** options work also. The [Smooth] options do not work with triangular plots, however.

- Select **Options/Formats...** from the **Graph** menu
- Choose [Swiss] from the [High-res fonts] list
- Click OK

- Select **Options/Global settings...** from the **Graph** menu
- Choose [High resolution] fonts
- Click OK

- Select **Plot/Plot** from the **Graph** menu
- Select the variables: RED, GREEN, BLUE
- Choose [Triangular] coordinates
- Specify the variable COLOR$ for [Symb'l]
- Click OK

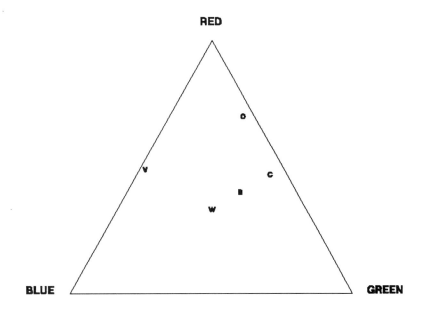

Error bars

Sometimes we want plots that show standard errors around plotted points. For example, each point might represent a group of plants receiving the same dose of a growth hormone. In this case, you can plot the standard error of the mean around the mean for the group. It is up to you whether you choose standard deviations, standard errors of the mean, two times the standard deviation, or some other measure of spread. SYGRAPH takes the values from the variable you specify and plots tick marks on each side of the point by the same amount. As with the [Size] option, you are responsible for insuring that your tick marks fit the graph. If they go outside the axes, you can use [Axes] options to control the scales ([X min], etc.).

- Click [Error]
- Specify an error variable
○ For one-sided error bars, click [One way]
- Click OK

For one sided error bars, click [One way]. If the variable you specify is positive, the error bar faces upward. If it is negative, the bar faces downward.

11.17
Scatterplot with error bars

Here are some data with a one way error variable, in the file ERROR:

DOSE	GROWTH	SE
500	110	5
800	112	6
1000	116	7
1200	118	9
1400	120	13
1700	135	20
1900	140	22
2200	150	24
2900	210	26

Here is the graph for these data. we have used closed circles so that the centers are more visible.

- Select **Plot/Plot** from the **Graph** menu
- Select the Y variable: GROWTH
- Select the X variable: DOSE
- Specify the variable SE for [Error]
- Choose the open circle with black fill for [Symb'l]
- Click OK

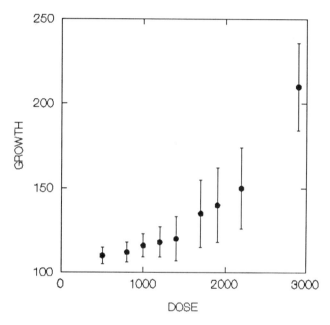

Line graphs

Line

Time series and other data plot best when the points are connected with a line. This is easy to do in SYGRAPH. Just use the [Line] option.

- Click [Line]
- Choose a type of line, or specify one for each Y variable by typing numbers in the box
○ Click [Slope] to adjust the slopes of the lines
- Click OK

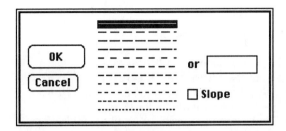

The lines are numbered 1–11 from top to bottom. Specify lines by number in the same order as you selected the dependent variables.

If you do not want to see the symbols that the lines connect, then set [Size] to 0. If you have several Y variables, you *must* specify the same number of lines. You can, however, specify the same type of line several times.

Slope

The [Slope] option automatically scales line graphs for data such as time series. [Slope] adjusts the height and width of the graph so that the median absolute slope of the line segments is one, following theory and experiments of Cleveland. It is highly recommended for time series plots.

11.18
Time series plot

The next figure shows the U.S. adjusted Gross National Product in millions of dollars plotted against year for 100 years. The data are in time order in the file GNP. If the data were in some other order, the lines would connect successive points and produce a messy spider web.

- Select **Plot/Plot** from the **Graph** menu
- Select the Y variable: GNP
- Select the X variable: YEAR
- Click [Slope] in the [Line] dialog box
- Specify [Size] 0 for [Symb'l]
- Click OK

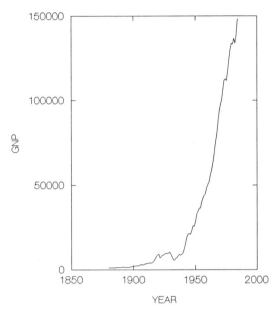

**11.19
Multi-variable
line graph**

You can use a different line for each dependent variable in a multi-variable plot. Here are data on U.S. receipts and expenditures in dollars since 1960, taken from U.S. Treasury annual reports.

YEAR	RECEIPT	EXPENSE
1961	77659424905	81515167453
1962	81409092072	87786766580
1963	86357020251	92589764029
1964	89458664071	97684374794
1965	93071796891	96506904210
1966	106978344155	104727263667
1967	149554815000	153183886000
1968	187792337000	183079841000
1970	193843791000	194968258000

Here are these data plotted with a solid line for receipts and dotted for expenditures. Remember, if you are doing a multi-variable plot (by using more than one variable to the left of the asterisk in the command) then you must specify the same number of line types as you have Y variables, even if you are using the same line type for each variable (e.g. 2,2).

Incidentally, these data push the limits of most graphing packages. SYGRAPH stores numbers in about 17 decimal digits of precision, but it inputs only up to 15 digits. The largest number it can handle is 10^{35}. If the U.S. budget continues to go through the roof, you will have to round the numbers further before inputting them.

- Select **Options/Formats...** from the **Graph** menu
- Choose [Hershey] from the [High-res fonts] list
- Click OK

- Select **Options/Global settings...** from the **Graph** menu
- Choose [High resolution] fonts
- Click OK

- Select **Plot/Plot** from the **Graph** menu
- Select the Y variable: RECEIPT, EXPENSE
- Select the X variable: YEAR
- Specify 1,3 for [Line]
- Specify [Size] 0 for [Symb'l]
- Click OK

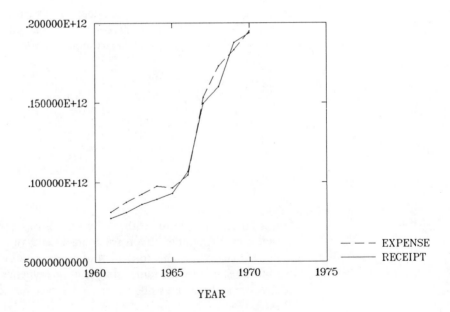

© 1989, SYSTAT, Inc.

11.20
Filled line plot

You can fill a line plot or curve with one of the available fill patterns to highlight its shape. For example, you may want to plot a theoretical probability density with the area under the curve shaded. Or you may wish to reveal the trend across observed data by shading under a line graph. To do this, just use [Fill].

[Fill] fills the area bounded by the line and a straight line connecting the two endpoints of the line. If you want to fill areas under a curve down to the X axis, you have to include data points at the end of the curve that touch the X axis.

Here is an example using a line plot on observed data. The following data were used in Example 11.17 to illustrate error bars. We have added two cases at the beginning and end to bring the line back to the bottom axis. Notice that the data must be sorted on the X variable or the line does not plot in sequence. Here are these data plotted and filled. We set [Y min] to set [Y min] to 0 to anchor the vertical axis at 0.

DOSE	GROWTH
500	0
500	110
800	112
1000	116
1200	118
1400	120
1700	135
1900	140
2200	150
2900	210
2900	0

- Select **Plot/Plot** from the **Graph** menu
- Select the Y variable: GROWTH
- Select the X variable: DOSE
- Click [Slope] in the [Line] dialog box
- Choose the gray pattern (third from right) in the [Fill] dialog box
- Specify [Size] 0 for [Symb'l]
- Specify [Y min] 0 in the [Axes] dialog box
- Click OK

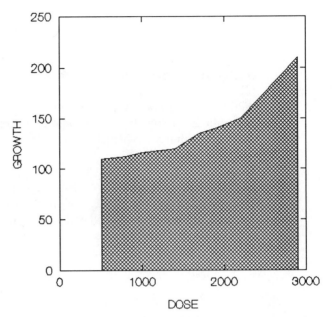

**Geographic
projections**

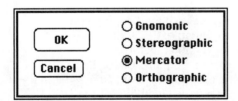

Sometimes you want to plot on top of a map that you have drawn with
Graph/Map. If you used a projection with **Map**, then you will have to
use one with **Plot**. The same projections are available with both commands.

- Click [Proj't]
- Choose a projection
- Click OK

OK	○ **Gnomonic**
	○ **Stereographic**
Cancel	◉ **Mercator**
	○ **Orthographic**

[Gnomonic] is oblique gnomonic projection, [Stereo] is oblique stereographic, [Mercator] is Mercator conformal, and [Orthographic] is
oblique orthographic projection. These projections are documented in
Appendix B of Richardus and Adler (1972)

To make a map and plotted points coincide, you must use common latitudes and longitudes by setting the [Axes] options [X min], [X max], [Y min], and [Y max] in both **Map** and **Plot**. You must use these options if you want [Proj't] to work at all. You should always click off the [Axes] and [Scales] options also, since you will not want to see the messy projection coordinates on your graph. Finally, setting [X label] and [Y label] to blanks (type ' ' in each box) will remove other distracting features from your graph.

**11.21
Map with plot overlaid**

Here is a plot of latitude against longitude of the centers of the states using a gnomonic projection. We have superimposed a map of the U.S. using the same projection. Notice that we have adjusted the height and width of the plot to scale the map correctly. You will have to do this whenever you use the [X min], [X max], [Y min], and [Y max] options to rescale a map.

- Select **Map** from the **Graph** menu
- Specify [X min] –125, [X max] –65, [Y min] 25, and [Y max] 50 in the [Axes] dialog box
- Choose the [Gnomonic] projection
- Click OK

- Select **Plot/Plot** from the **Graph** menu
- Select the Y variable: LABLAT
- Select the X variable: LABLON
- Click [Axes]
  - Specify [X min] –125, [X max] –65, [Y min] 25, and [Y max] 50
  - Click off the current [Axes] and [Scales] choices
  - Specify ' ' for [X label] and [Y label]
- Choose [Gnomonic] projection
- Choose the open circle and specify [Size] 0 for [Symb'l]
- Click OK

Smoothing

The [Smooth] option provides eleven types of smoothing. For [Linear] regression smoothing, it further offers confidence bands.

- Click [Smooth]
- Choose the type of smoothing
- o For [Linear] regression, click [Confidence bands] and specify the confidence level
- o Click [Short] to limit the domain of smoothing to extreme values of the X data
- o Specify your own [Tension] level for [LOWESS], [Spline], or [DWLS] smoothing
- Click OK

```
┌─────────────────────────────────────────────────────┐
│                                                       │
│   ○ DWLS          ☐ Confidence bands ┌──────────┐     │
│   ○ Inverse       ☐ Short            └──────────┘     │
│   ○ Kernel        Tension =          ┌──────────┐     │
│   ○ Linear        Cut =              └──────────┘     │
│   ○ LOWESS                           └──────────┘     │
│   ○ Log                                               │
│   ○ NEXPO          ○ Color                            │
│   ○ Power                                             │
│   ○ Quadratic                                         │
│   ○ Spline                                            │
│   ○ Step                                              │
│   ( OK )   ( Cancel )                                 │
└─────────────────────────────────────────────────────┘
```

The [Color] option is for contouring with color if you are using **Plot/Contour.**

11.22
Linear regression

Regression fits a function to data such that the value predicted by the function at each observed value of X is as close as possible to the observed value of Y at the same value of X. Ordinary linear regression uses a straight line for the function and makes the squared discrepancies between predicted and observed Y values as small as possible. The equation for this function looks like this:

$$Y = a + bX,$$

where a is a constant term and b is a slope coefficient.

You fit this function with the [Linear] option of [Smooth]. This example shows the linear regression of PROPERTY (property crimes) onto LABLON (longitude of the center of each state). It would appear that western states (on the left of the plot) have higher property crime rates. This conclusion is not quite accurate, however. See the LOWESS example below for another analysis of the same data.

- Select **Plot/Plot** from the **Graph** menu
- Select the Y variable: PROPERTY
- Select the X variable: LABLON
- Choose [Linear] smoothing
- Choose the open circle symbol for [Symb'l]
- Click OK

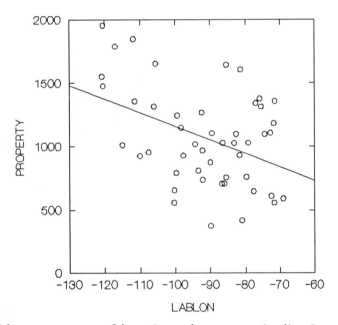

**11.23
Regression with
confidence
intervals**

Often, we want a confidence interval on a regression line. Just check [Confidence] on. You can specify any level you wish for the confidence interval (e.g. .87 for 87% confidence). The default is .95.

Say we specify .90. This will cause SYGRAPH to draw upper and lower hyperbolic bands around the actual fitted line. These bands mean the following: if the discrepancies (residuals) between the fitted and observed values for Y at each X are normally distributed and independent of each other and have the same spread (variance), then 90 times out of a hundred, confidence intervals constructed by SYGRAPH from data sampled in the same way you found these data will cover the true regression line relating Y to X.

The next figure shows the 95 percent confidence intervals on the regression line of WINTER (average winter temperature) on LABLAT (latitude). You must choose [Linear] smoothing to get the confidence line.

- Select **Options/Formats...** from the **Graph** menu
- Choose [Hershey] from the [High-res fonts] list
- Click OK

- Select **Options/Global settings...** from the **Graph** menu
- Choose [High resolution] fonts
- Click OK

- Select **Plot/Plot** from the **Graph** menu
- Select the Y variable: WINTER
- Select the X variable: LABLAT
- Choose [Linear] smoothing and click [Confidence bands]
- Click OK

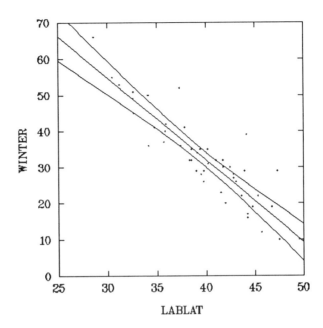

11.24
LOWESS
scatterplot
smoothing

Linear, quadratic and other parametric smoothers presuppose the shape of the function. SYGRAPH offers a LOWESS smoothing method that requires only that the smooth be a function (i.e. unique Y value for every X). This method is called LOWESS (Cleveland, 1979,1981). It produces a smooth by running along the X values and finding predicted values from a weighted average of nearby Y values. Because a lot of computations are involved, the [LOWESS] option can be time consuming for large scatterplots.

The tightness of the LOWESS curve is controlled by a parameter called F, which determines the width of the smoothing window. Normally, F=.5, meaning that half the points are included in each running window. If you increase F, the curve will be stiffer and if you decrease it, the curve will be looser, following local irregularities. F must be between 0 and 1. Use the [Tension] option (discussed soon) to set the value of F.

The next figure shows the result for the regression of PROPERTY (property crime) on LABLON (longitude of center of state) that we used above to illustrate [Linear]. Notice that the fit is distinctly curvilinear, revealing that the eastern states have somewhat higher property crime rates than the midwestern. It is always a good idea to use LOWESS smoothing before fitting a straight line or any other function to data. This way, you can let the data speak for themselves and warn you about whether your model is inappropriate.

- Select **Plot/Plot** from the **Graph** menu
- Select the Y variable: PROPERTY
- Select the X variable: LABLON
- Choose [LOWESS] smoothing
- Choose the open circle symbol for [Symb'l]
- Click OK

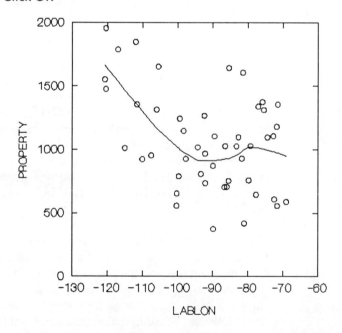

11.25
Negative
exponentially
weighted
smoothing

Negative exponentially weighted smoothing fits a curve through a set of points such that the influence of neighboring points decreases exponentially with distance. It is an alternative to [Spline] smoothing for interpolation. The smoothing algorithm is due to McLain (1974). It is closely related to distance weighted least squares ([DWLS]) regression smoothing.

The following data show output productivity per labor hour in 1977 U.S. dollars for a 15 year period from the U.S. Bureau of Labor Statistics.

YEAR	US	CANADA	JAPAN	GERMANY	ENGLAND
1960	62.2	50.3	23.2	40.3	53.8
1965	76.6	62.7	35.0	54.0	63.9
1970	80.0	76.8	64.8	71.2	77.6
1975	92.9	91.8	87.7	90.1	94.3
1980	101.4	101.9	122.7	108.6	101.2
1985	121.8	115.1	159.9	131.9	129.7

Here is a smooth of the data for ENGLAND. You might want to try cubic splines (with the [Spline] option) on these data for comparison. The primary difference between the two smoothing methods is that negative exponential smoothing is always single valued. For all X, there is a unique Y. Spline smoothing, on the other hand, can produce several Y for a given X in some contexts.

- Select **Plot/Plot** from the **Graph** menu
- Select the Y variable: ENGLAND
- Select the X variable: YEAR
- Choose [NEXPO] smoothing
- Choose the open circle with black fill for [Symb'l]
- Click OK

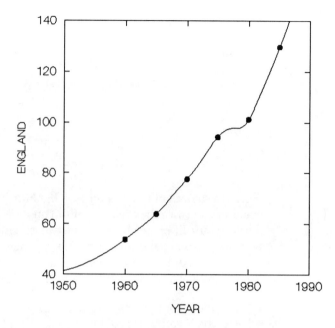

**11.26
Inverse squared
distance
smoothing**

[Inverse] provides inverse squared distance smoothing. It is similar to [NEXPO] except that no regression estimation is used. The height of the curve at a smoothing point is the weighted average of the Y values at X values, where the weights are the squared Euclidean distances from the data points to the smoothing point on the X axis. This is sometimes called Shepard's method of interpolation.

Here is a smooth of the data for ENGLAND, used in the previous example. Notice the rippling effect at each data point. This is a defect of this type of smoothing, which is most pronounced in 2-D examples.

- Select **Plot/Plot** from the **Graph** menu
- Select the Y variable: ENGLAND
- Select the X variable: YEAR
- Choose [Inverse] smoothing
- Choose the open circle with black fill for [Symb'l]
- Click OK

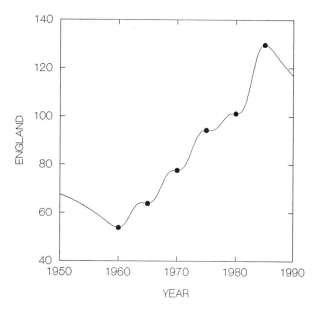

11.27 Quadratic smoothing

You can fit a quadratic regression curve to your data with the [Quadratic] option. This fits the following type of equation to the data:

$$Y = a + bX + cX^2$$

where *a* is a constant and *b* and *c* are slope coefficients.

Here is the quadratic regression of INCOME (per-capita income) onto POPDEN (people per square mile).

- Select **Plot/Plot** from the **Graph** menu
- Select the Y variable: INCOME
- Select the X variable: POPDEN
- Choose [Quadratic] smoothing
- Choose the open circle with [Size] .5 for [Symb'l]
- Click OK

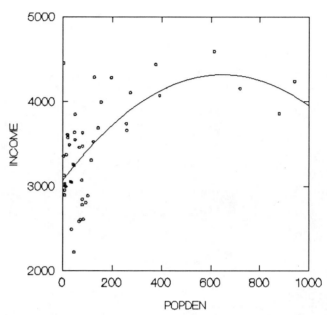

**11.28
Distance
weighted least
squares
smoothing**

[DWLS] (distance weighted least squares) fits a line through a set of points by least squares. Unlike linear or low order polynomial smoothing, however, the surface is allowed to flex locally to fit the data better. The amount of flex is controlled by the [Tension] parameter.

If you use [DWLS] on a two-dimensional plot, be prepared to wait a while, particularly on slow machines. Every point on the smoothed line requires a weighted quadratic multiple regression on all the points. The wait is worth it, however. This method produces a true, locally weighted curve running through the points using an algorithm due to McLain (1974). If you want to do a regression of one variable on another, but are not positive about the shape of the function, we suggest you use DWLS (or LOWESS) first.

Here is a distance weighted least squares smooth of INCOME (per-capita income) on POPDEN (population density per square mile). The line adds some detail to the quadratic smooth in Example 11.27. Compare it, as well, to the smooth of the same data using LOWESS. While not as robust as LOWESS, DWLS produces smoother curves.

- Select **Plot/Plot** from the **Graph** menu
- Select the Y variable: INCOME
- Select the X variable: POPDEN
- Choose [DWLS] smoothing
- Choose the open circle with [Size] .5 for [Symb'l]
- Click OK

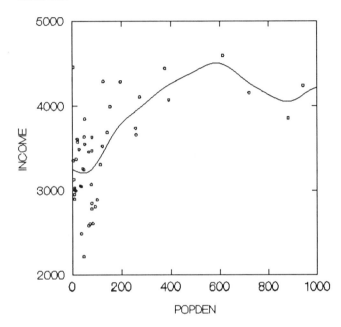

| 11.29
Spline smoothing | You can fit a spline curve to your data with the [Spline] option. Spline smoothing fits a curved line through every point in the plot such that the curve is smooth everywhere. SYGRAPH employs cubic splines (Brodlie, 1980) for smoothing. Cubic splines involve fitting several sections of the curve with cubic equations: |

$$Y = a + bX + cX^2 + dX^3$$

where a is a constant, and b, c, and d are coefficients. These curves are joined smoothly at "knots," which usually coincide with the data points themselves.

         261

Cubic splines are especially useful for interpolation, when you need a computer French curve. This means that you should use splines through the data points only when you believe your data contain no error. Otherwise, you should choose one of the regression methods ([Linear], [Quadratic], [DWLS], or [LOWESS])

The tightness of the spline curve is controlled by a tension parameter, which determines how tightly the curves are pulled between the knots. Normally, the parameter is 2, but you can set it down to 0 to make it looser and up to 10 to make it tighter. We hate to say this is a matter of aesthetics, but you really should try several values on the same data to see what we mean. You can control the tension parameter with the [Tension] option, discussed soon.

The following data were taken from Brodlie (1980). The plot shows a spline smooth through the points. We have used open circle plotting symbols to show the point locations more clearly. In many circumstances, however, you might want to use no symbols and leave only a curve.

X	Y
2.5	6.90
5.0	2.20
10.0	0.80
15.0	0.50
20.0	0.35
25.0	0.25
30.0	0.20
40.0	0.15

- Select **Plot/Plot** from the **Graph** menu
- Select the Y variable: Y
- Select the X variable: X
- Choose [Spline] smoothing
- Choose the open circle with black fill for [Symb'l]
- Click OK

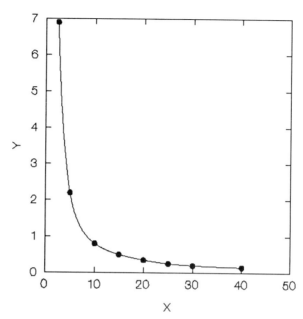

11.30
Step smoothing

You can fit a step function to your data with the [Step] option. The function begins at the point with the smallest X value and drops (or rises) to the point with the next larger X value. If you wish to drop (or rise) immediately from the first point to the second, you need to shift the Y data values one lag down the list for each X in your data.

Here is the step smooth for the data used in the spline example, 11.29.

- Select **Plot/Plot** from the **Graph** menu
- Select the Y variable: Y
- Select the X variable: X
- Choose [Step] smoothing
- Choose the open circle with black fill for [Symb'l]
- Click OK

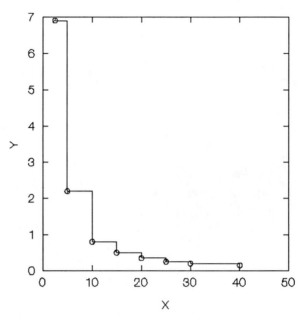

11.31
Log smoothing

[Log] smoothing is a new feature to SYGRAPH. It includes linearizable functions

$$E[Y] = a + b\ln(X)$$

Here is a log smooth of the plot of INCOME (per-capita income) vs. POPDEN (people per square mile), which we used in the quadratic smoothing example. The smooth is not much better than the quadratic method for these data.

- Select **Plot/Plot** from the **Graph** menu
- Select the Y variable: INCOME
- Select the X variable: POPDEN
- Choose [Log] smoothing
- Choose the open circle with [Size] .5 for [Symb'l]
- Click OK

         © 1989, SYSTAT, Inc.

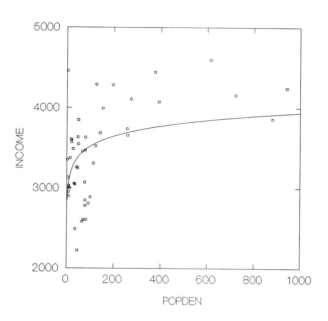

**11.32
Power smoothing**

[Power] smoothing is a new feature to SYGRAPH. It includes linearizable functions

$$E[Y] = aX^b$$

Here is the power function smooth of INCOME (per-capita income) vs. POPDEN (people per square mile), used in the previous examples. The power (this example) and log smooth (previous example) are barely distinguishable because the power exponent is near zero. You can compute it exactly in the **Nonlin** procedure in SYSTAT.

- Select **Plot/Plot** from the **Graph** menu
- Select the Y variable: INCOME
- Select the X variable: POPDEN
- Choose [Power] smoothing
- Choose the open circle with [Size] .5 for [Symb'l]
- Click OK

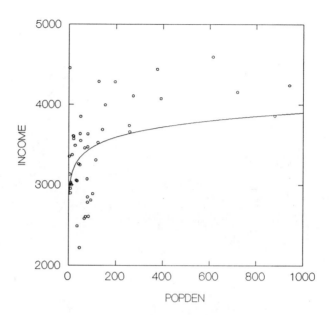

**11.33
Kernel density
estimators**

Bivariate nonparametric kernel density estimators are like continuous histograms (rather than divided into partitions) and show areas where the data are most concentrated in the sample. For [Kernel] smoothing, you select two variables (Y and X) as usual, but SYGRAPH draws a 3-D graph. The densities are shown on the vertical (Z) axis of the plot.

If you use [Kernel] with [Contour], you get a 2-D graph, where the density values are shown with contour lines on the X-Y plane.

The [Kernel] smoothing method uses the Epanechnikov kernel; see Silverman (1986) for more information.

Here is a plot of SUMMER (summer temperatures) against WINTER (winter temperatures) using the US file.

- Select **Plot/Contour** from the **Graph** menu
- Select the variables: SUMMER*WINTER
- Choose [Kernel] smoothing
- Click OK

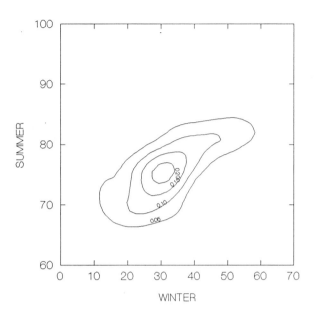

**11.34
Shortening the
domain of
smoothing**

Sometimes you can get into trouble by extrapolating beyond the range of your data when making a prediction. Many of the smoothing methods in SYGRAPH yield curves that extend from the left to the right edges of the plotting frame. If you wish to limit the domain of the smooth to the extreme values of the data on the horizontal axis, click [Short].

Here is a plot with a linear function and confidence interval limited to the range of the X data with [Short]. Compare this to the extrapolated version in Example 11.23.

- Select **Plot/Plot** from the **Graph** menu
- Select the Y variable: WINTER
- Select the X variable: LABLAT
- Choose [Linear] smoothing and click [Confidence bands] and [Short]
- Click OK

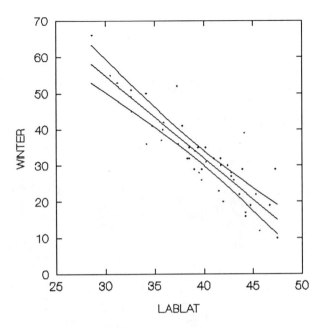

**11.35
Tension
parameter**

The [Tension] option controls a stiffness parameter for [LOWESS], [Spline], [DWLS], or [Kernel] smoothing.

The default value for [LOWESS] is .5 and it can range between 0 and 1. For [Spline], the default is 2, and it can range between 0 and 10. For [DWLS], tension is set at the inverse of the number of cases ($1/n$) and can range between 0 and 10. For [Kernel], it is set to $2n^{-1/6}$, where n is the number of cases.

Increasing tension values makes the smooths stiffer, and decreasing them gives them more local detail, makes them looser, more curvy, more susceptible to individual data points, or however you wish to think about it.

Here is the same plot used to illustrate [LOWESS] in Example 11.24, but with the tension set higher (.9). In this case, 90 percent of the data points are used to smooth each value on the curve.

- Select **Plot/Plot** from the **Graph** menu
- Select the Y variable: PROPERTY
- Select the X variable: LABLON
- Choose [LOWESS] smoothing with [Tension] .9
- Choose the open circle for [Symb'l]
- Click OK

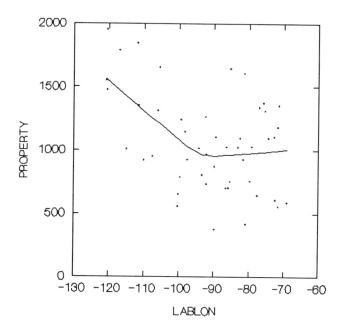

Minimum spanning tree

A minimal spanning tree connects a set of points in a space such that the sum of the lengths of the connecting line segments is as small as possible (Hartigan, 1975). Imagine, for example, that you have a map of the U.S. and you must connect one city in each state with a computer network. The network may have any shape, provided there is only one path along the network from one city to any other. You wish to spend as little as possible on optical cable for the network. The solution to your problem is a minimum spanning tree.

As with **Plot/Voronoi,** which draws Voronoi polygons, the [Span] option presumes you have equivalent distances on the X and Y axis. If your scales differ, adjust the size of the graph to make the physical dimensions of your plot reflect the true scale values. For example, if your vertical scale runs from 0 to 50 and the horizontal from 0 to 100, make the width twice the height.

You can use [Span] on a **Voronoi** tesselation. Each span will be per-pendicular to the edge of a polygon delimiting the closest points.

11.36
Spanning tree

Here is a minimum spanning tree connecting the centroids of each state.

- Select **Plot/Plot** from the **Graph** menu
- Select the Y variable: LABLAT
- Select the X variable: LABLON
- Use the ruler option to make a graph frame twice as wide as tall
- Click [Span]

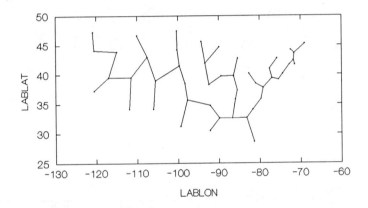

Spikes to data points

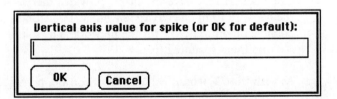

To represent deviations from a constant value, you can plot data with the [Spike] option. This is handy, for example, in plotting residuals from a regression.

- Click [Spike]
- Specify a value to which spikes are drawn
- Click OK

Vertical axis value for spike (or OK for default):

OK   Cancel

If you specify no value, then lines are drawn from each plotting symbol down to the horizontal axis.

If you specify a value, lines are drawn from each symbol to the level on the vertical axis corresponding to the value you have picked.

11.37
Spike plot

Here is an example plotting residuals from the linear regression of SUMMER (average summer temperatures) on WINTER (average winter temperatures for the 48 continental states). These residuals were computed by SYSTAT, but you could get them from any statistical package.

Notice that there is no need to draw a horizontal line at the 0 level of RESIDUAL because we impose our own "subjective contour" at this point anyway. This perception of a horizontal line along spikes like these is well known in the psychological literature (e.g. Levine & Shefner, 1981). The plot shows a distinct heteroscedasticity in the residuals (increasing variance with ESTIMATE). Weighted least squares or a transformation would be appropriate.

- Select **MGLH/Regression...** from the **Stats** menu
- Select the dependent variable: SUMMER
- Select the independent variable: WINTER
- Click [Save residuals]
- Click OK

Open the residuals file and draw the plot.

- Select **Plot/Plot** from the **Graph** menu
- Select the Y variable: RESIDUAL
- Select the X variable: ESTIMATE
- Specify 0 for [Spike]
- Specify [Y min] −20 and [Y max] 20 in the [Axes] dialog box
- Click OK

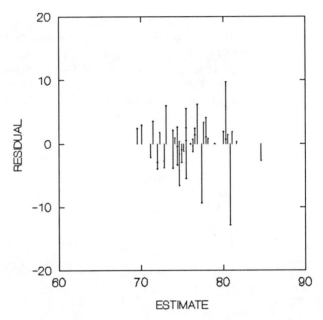

Sunflower plots

Sometimes we have data that overlap at exactly the same values. For example, we may have a questionnaire with a 7 point scale and we wish to plot two items against each other. There are only 49 possible points where we may plot the data. Or, we may have aggregate data and wish to plot them in a scatterplot.

To represent the overlap in these data, you can plot them with special symbols that are light for small values and darker for larger values of a COUNT variable. Most of them look like flowers, so this is often called a sunflower plot. Only 9 symbols are possible, so larger counts are plotted with the darkest, largest symbol (a filled circle).

If you have a count variable, such as in our example below, you need to use weight the cases with **Data/Weight** before using [S'flr].

Otherwise, if your data are not aggregated but nevertheless have duplicate pairs of values, SYGRAPH computes the duplicates. You need only click [S'flr].

See the final section of the chapter, "Jittered plots," (Example 11.40) for another way to deal with overlaps.

11.38
Sunflower plot

Here are the means of PERSON (personal crimes) and PROPERTY (property crimes) within regions of the variables in the US file. COUNT shows the number of states over which the means were computed.

REGION$	COUNT	PERSON	PROPERTY
New England	6	33.2	899.0
Mid Atlantic	3	97.3	1038.3
Great Lakes	5	81.8	1148.8
Plains	7	41.3	891.3
Southeast	8	87.3	1052.3
South	8	67.9	801.5
Mountain	8	59.5	1356.0
Pacific	3	79.3	1661.3

Here we plot these data with [S'flr]. To make the symbols more visible (because there are only a few) we set [Size] to 2.

- Select **Weight** from the **Data** menu
- Select the weight variable: COUNT
- Click OK

- Select **Plot/Plot** from the **Graph** menu
- Select the Y variable: PERSON
- Select the X variable: PROPERTY
- Click [S'flr]
- Specify [Size] 2 in the [Symb'l] dialog box
- Click OK

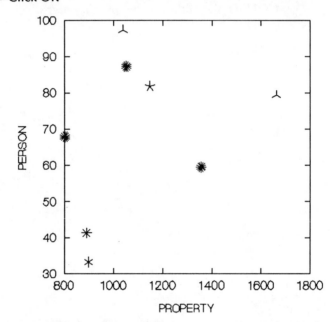

Vector plots

The [Vector] option works like [Spike], except that each point is connected to one point rather than to an axis or plane. This type of plot is especially useful for representing factor loadings and other vector models.

- Click [Vector]
- ○ Specify the origin for vectors
- Click OK

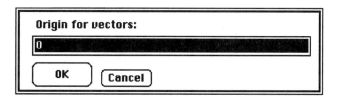

Specify the origin in X,Y coordinates, e.g. 2,3 for X=2, Y=3. The default is 0, which is short for 0,0.

11.39
Vector plot of
factor loadings

Let's get some factor loadings to plot. Let's use the US data and compute principal components with **Factor/Principal components...** from the **Stats** menu (SYSTAT) and save the loadings:

- Select **Factor/Principal components...** from the **Stats** menu
- Choose [Varimax] rotation
- Specify 3 for [Number of factors]
- Click [Save file] to save factor loadings
- Click OK

Here are the resulting data, in the file LOAD:

LABEL$	COL(1)	COL(2)	COL(3)
POPDEN	0.248	-0.180	0.858
PERSON	0.758	0.462	0.170
PROPERTY	0.950	0.033	-0.114
INCOME	0.726	-0.478	0.392
SUMMER	-0.060	0.859	-0.121
WINTER	0.208	0.891	0.126
RAIN	-0.313	0.494	0.731

Use **Data/Transpose...** to transpose the file of loadings. Finally, draw the plot. Notice how we used the [Label] option to label the factor loadings. Here is a plot of the first two components, labeled with the variable name. With these data, because the vectors must emanate from 0 on each axis, we needn't specify a new value in the [Vector] dialog box.

- Select **Plot/Plot** from the **Graph** menu
- Select the Y variable: COL(2)
- Select the X variable: COL(3)
- Click [Vector]
- Specify the variable LABEL$ to label symbols in the [Symb'l] dialog box
- Click OK

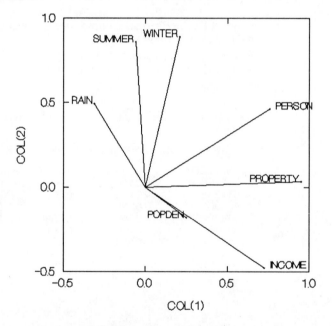

Notice that the plot shows the weather variables grouping together, the crime variables together, and POPDEN and INCOME straggling off somewhere else.

Jittered plots

Sometimes we have data that overlap at exactly the same values. For example, we may have a questionnaire with a 7 point scale and we wish to plot two items against each other. There are only 49 possible points where we may plot the data. Or, we may have aggregate data and wish to plot them in a scatterplot. One way to handle these is by jittering points. Or, you could draw a sunflower plot (discussed earlier in this chapter).

To prevent symbols from overlapping, the [Jitter symbols] option (in the [Symb'l] dialog box) adds a small amount of uniform random error to the location of each point. If you have a count variable, such as in our example, you need to weight the cases with **Data/Weight...** before using [Jitter symbols].

Otherwise, if your data are not aggregated but nevertheless have duplicate pairs of values, SYGRAPH jitters all the duplicates.

**11.40
Jittered
scatterplot**

Here are the means of PERSON (personal crimes) and PROPERTY (property crimes) within regions of the variables in the US file. COUNT shows the number of states over which the means were computed.

REGION$	COUNT	PERSON	PROPERTY
New England	6	33.2	899.0
Mid Atlantic	3	97.3	1038.3
Great Lakes	5	81.8	1148.8
Plains	7	41.3	891.3
Southeast	8	87.3	1052.3
South	8	67.9	801.5
Mountain	8	59.5	1356.0
Pacific	3	79.3	1661.3

We must first weight the data set.

- Select **Weight...** from the **Data** menu
- Select the weight variable: COUNT
- Click OK

Now, we draw the plot. We use hollow circles because they plot well when there are many near overlaps. Notice that if you plot these data without [Jitter symbols], the correlation between the items is not as evident.

- Select **Plot/Plot** from the **Graph** menu
- Select the Y variable: PERSON
- Select the X variable: PROPERTY
- Choose the open circle and click [Jitter symbols] in the [Symb'l] dialog box
- Click OK

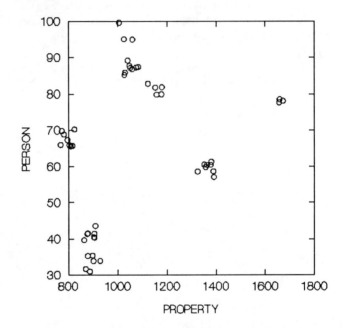

Notice how some of the values randomly extend beyond the frame. If this happens, it is easy to extend the axes with the [Axes] box. In this case, set the limits to [X min] 600, [X max] 1800, [Y min] 20, [Y max] 110.

12   3-D data plots

3-D data plots 12

3-D Plot produces three-way scatterplots of continuous variables. **Spin** lets you spin three-dimensional scatterplots around the X, Y, Z axes. **Spin** is discussed in the *Getting Started* volume.

Plotting

3-D Plot produces three-way scatterplots of continuous variables. **3-D Plot/Spin** spins three-dimensional plots around the X, Y, and Z axes in real time (see the *Getting Started* volume)

To use **3-D Plot**, press and hold the mouse button on **3-D Plot**. A submenu pops up offering **3-D Plot** and **Spin**. Select **3-D Plot** and release the mouse button.

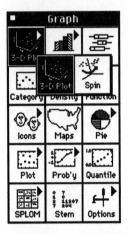

- Select **3-D Plot** from the **Graph** menu
- Select the Z, Y, and X variables, in that order
- Click OK

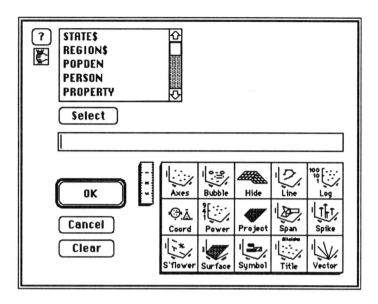

Common options

See the **Common options** chapter for information on how to use [Axes], [Line], [Log], [Power], [Symbol], and [Title]. The [Bubble], [Hide], [Line], [Polar], [Span], [Spike], [S'flower], [Surface], and [Vector] options are discussed and illustrated in this chapter,.

Three-dimensional scatterplots

3-D Plot

3-D Plot plots three variables against each other in a three-dimensional graph.

- Select **3-D Plot/3-D Plot** from the **Graph** menu
- Select a Z variable
- Select a Y variable
- Select an X variable
- Click OK

As we discussed in the graphical perception chapter, three-dimensional plots can be confusing unless they are constructed carefully. Although the SYGRAPH plots are in true perspective, a long focal length has been chosen to avoid distortions.

12.1
3-D scatterplot

Here is a three-dimensional plot of INCOME (per-capita income) against LABLAT (latitude) and LABLON (longitude) from the US file. We have used solid circle symbols to make the points more visible.

- Select **3-D Plot/3-D Plot** from the **Graph** menu
- Select a Z variable: INCOME
- Select a Y variable: LABLAT
- Select an X variable: LABLON
- Choose the circle with black fill for [Symbol}
- Click OK

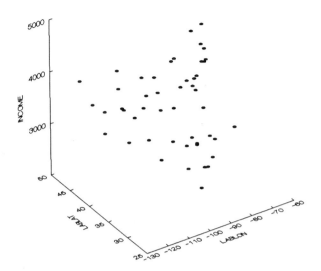

Bubble plots

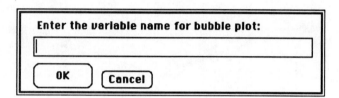

You can use the value of a variable in your file to control the size of a plotting symbol. This way, you can represent a fourth variable against three others in a three-way plot.

- Click [Bubble]
- Specify the variable to be used: DEN
- Click OK

> **Enter the variable name for bubble plot:**
>
> [   ]
>
> (OK) (Cancel)

Caution: the size of the plotting symbols is taken directly from the values in your value. There is no upper or lower limit. If the variable you specify has a tiny or negative value, the point will be invisible; if it has a huge value, it will fill the entire plot. Try a range between 0 and 10. If your sizing variable does not lie in this range, you should rescale it. Finally, you should usually use empty symbols with this type of plot, since filled ones can occlude each other and make the plot difficult to interpret.

12.2
3-D bubble plot

We want to plot PERSON (personal crimes) against LABLAT and LABLON from the US dataset, using bubbles to show population density. This graph might help us determine whether personal crimes have a higher rate of incidence in areas with greater population density. By plotting against LABLAT and LABLON, we produce a quasi-map.

First, let's make a new variable using POPDEN.

- Select **Math...** from the **Data** menu
- Fill in the let statement: Let DEN = 4*SQR(POPDEN/1000)
- Click OK

By this transformation, we have made a variable DEN in the range of 0 to 4 because the maximum population density is 1000. We used square root, because we want the area of the symbols (not their diameter) to be proportional to the value of POPDEN. Now we can use this variable to determine the size of a plotting symbol.

- Select **3-D Plot/3-D Plot** from the **Graph** menu
- Select the variables: PERSON * LABLAT * LABLON
- Specify DEN for [Bubble]
- Choose the open circle for [Symbol]
- Click OK

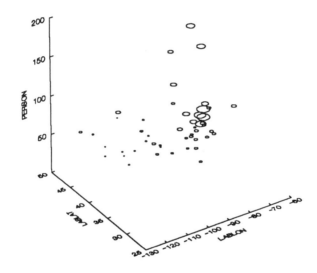

Notice that the large bubbles (high population density) are not all at floating higher than the small bubbles. Higher crime rates do not necessarily correspond to higher population densities.

Line plots

You can plot line graphs in three dimensions.

- Click [Line]
- Choose a type of line, or specify one for each Y variable by typing numbers in the box
- Click [Slope] to adjust the slopes of the lines
- Click OK

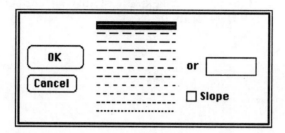

The lines are numbered 1–11 from top to bottom. Specify lines by number in the same order as you selected the dependent variables.

If you do not want to see the symbols that the lines connect, then make them invisible by setting [Size] to 0 in the [Symbol] dialog box.

12.3
3-D line plot

The following data (in the file SPIRAL) comprise a spiral in three dimensions.

X	Y	Z
0.068	0.036	0.923
0.087	0.127	0.846
0.028	0.229	0.769
-0.109	0.288	0.692
-0.288	0.255	0.615
-0.448	0.110	0.538
-0.523	-0.129	0.461
-0.460	-0.408	0.385
-0.245	-0.648	0.308
0.093	-0.764	0.231
0.481	-0.696	0.154
0.818	-0.428	0.077
1.000	0.001	0.000
0.953	0.502	-0.077
0.654	0.951	-0.154
0.147	1.222	-0.231
-0.466	1.222	-0.308
-1.038	0.917	-0.385
-1.420	0.347	-0.462
-1.493	-0.371	-0.539
-1.207	-1.074	-0.616
-0.597	-1.584	-0.693
0.217	-1.756	-0.770
1.052	-1.517	-0.846
1.705	-0.890	-0.923
2.000	0.005	-1.000
1.837	0.970	-1.077
1.219	1.776	-1.154
0.263	2.216	-1.231
-0.824	2.156	-1.308

Here is a plot of these data connected with the [Line] option. We generated these values using SYSTAT. If you want a smoother curve, you can generate more points.

- Select **3-D Plot/3-D Plot** from the **Graph** menu
- Select the variables: Z * Y * X
- Click [Line]
- Click OK

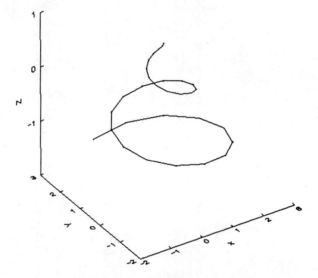

Spirals and other geometric figures appear frequently in the sciences. Krumhansl and Shepard (1979) demonstrated that perception of musical pitch is organized in a three dimensional spiral like the one here.

**Polar
coordinates**

Coord

Ordinarily, you draw plots in Cartesian coordinates—the X-Y(-Z) axis system. You can also plot in polar coordinates by clicking [Coord] and choosing [Polar].

Polar coordinates translate Cartesian coordinates into a circular arrangement. Each point is given by its distance (r) from the origin and the angle (θ) between the X-axis and the vector from the origin to the point. Polar coordinates may seem confusing in some contexts but they are handy for representing many mathematical equations and data profiles. The vertical axis is the usual Z-axis—the height along the Z axis represents distance from the r-θ plane. Thus, polar coordinates in the 3-D option of SYGRAPH are really *cylindrical coordinates*.

SYGRAPH automatically scales polar graphs as well as rectangular graphs. The units printed on the scales are those of the data. You may alter these scales with [Axes]. Use [Y min] and [Y max] for the r axis (distance) and [X min] and [X max] for the θ axis (angle). [Y min] is always at the center of the circle and [Y max] at its periphery. [X min] and [X max] always coincide at the right edge (0 radians). [Z min] and [Z max] behave as usual.

If the data collide with the axes, you can eliminate the axes by clicking off the [Axes] choice in the [Axes] dialog box. If you choose one axis, you get only the circle, omitting the radial axis. If you choose two or more axes, you get both the r and θ axes.

All the other **3-D Plot** options work in polar coordinates. Use them intelligently, however, or you will get bizarre graphs.

12.4
3-D polar plot

Here is a polar plot of RAIN (average annual inches rainfall) on LABLAT (latitude) and LABLON (longitude) expressed in polar coordinates. The minimum and maximum latitude and longitude values have been selected so that the northern hemisphere is displayed as a circle. The Western hemisphere appears in the foreground, with the United States plotted with the first letters of the state names as plotting symbols.

- Select **3-D Plot/3-D Plot** from the **Graph** menu
- Select the variables: RAIN * LABLAT * LABLON
- Click [Spike] (the default value is fine)
- Specify the variable STATE$ for labeling symbols in the [Symbol] dialog box
- Click [Axes]
  - Specify [X min] –180, [X max] 180, [Y min] 0, [Y max] 90
  - Click [X reverse] and [Y reverse]
- Choose [Polar] in the [Coords] dialog box
- Click OK

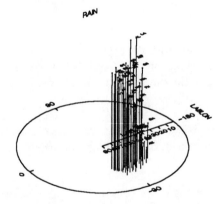

Spherical coodinates

Coord

You can plot data in spherical coodinates by clicking [Coord] and then choosing [Spherical]. If you specify two variables, the points are plotted on the surface of a unit sphere ($\phi=1$). If you specify three variables, the first variable is plotted as ϕ, the second as ρ, and the third as θ.

Minimum spanning tree

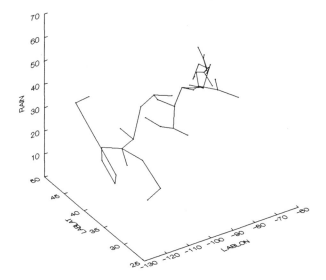
Span

A minimal spanning tree connects a set of points in a space such that the sum of the lengths of the connecting line segments is as small as possible (Hartigan, 1975).

The [Span] option presumes you have equivalent distances on the X and Y axis. If your scales differ, adjust the size of the graph to make the physical dimensions of your plot reflect the true scale values. For example, if your Z scale runs from 0 to 50 and the X and Y from 0 to 100, make the width twice the height.

12.5
3-D minimal spanning tree

Here is a minimum spanning tree connecting the centroids of each state for the rainfall plot.

- Select **3-D Plot/3-D Plot** from the **Graph** menu
- Select the variables: RAIN * LABLAT * LABLON
- Click [Span]
- Click OK

Spikes to data points

To represent deviations from a constant value, you can plot data with the [Spike] option in three dimensions. This is handy, for example, in plotting residuals from a regression. If you use [Spike] without specifying a value, lines are drawn from each plotting symbol down to the horizontal plane. If you specify a value, lines are drawn from each symbol to the horizontal plane at level on the vertical axis corresponding to the value you have picked.

- Click [Spike]
- Specify a value
- Click OK

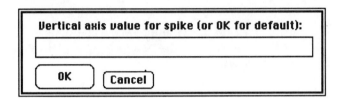

Because three dimensional data plots often seem to float nebulously, it is sometimes helpful to use the [Spike] option to show their location more clearly.

12.6
3-D spike plot

Here is a plot of RAIN (average annual rainfall) against LABLON (longitude of the center of each state) and LABLAT (latitude of the state centers). The [Spike] option makes the heights of the points more comparable. We have used stars to show the points better.

- Select **3-D Plot/3-D Plot** from the **Graph** menu
- Select the variables: RAIN*LABLAT*LABLON
- Click [Spike]
- Choose the star for [Symbol] (18th in the LaserWriter set)
- Click OK

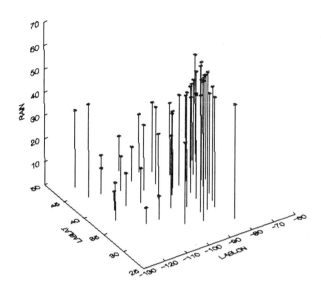

Sunflower plots

Sometimes we have data that overlap at exactly the same values. For example, we may have a questionnaire with a 7 point scale and we wish to plot two items against each other. There are only 49 possible points where we may plot the data. Or, we may have aggregate data and wish to plot them in a scatterplot.

To represent the overlap in these data, you can plot them with special symbols that are light for small values and darker for larger values of a COUNT variable. Most of them look like flowers, so this is often called a sunflower plot. Only 9 symbols are possible, so larger counts are plotted with the darkest, largest symbol (a filled circle).

If you have a count variable, such as in our example below, you need to weight the cases with **Data/Weight...** before using [S'flower]. Otherwise, if your data are not aggregated but nevertheless have duplicate pairs of values, SYGRAPH computes the duplicates. You need only click [S'flower].

See the **Plot** chapter for an example of a sunflower plot in two dimensions.

Surfaces

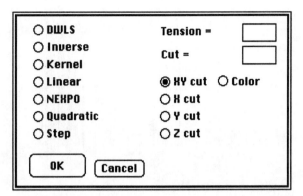

To plot a smooth surface through your data, click [Surface] and go through the [Surface] dialog box.

Choose the method you wish for smoothing and, if you wish, the [Tension] value, number of cuts (wires) in the grid surface, and whether you wish the cuts to run both ways like a mesh [XY cut], along X [X cut], along Y [Y cut], or along Z [Z cut].

Color

Click [Color] to produce a color-contoured surface. Instead of lines, this method uses fill patterns from blue to red in even perceptual gradations that are determined by the height of the surface at a given grid square.

Picking number of cuts in a grid

For contouring and surface plotting in three dimensions, SYGRAPH computes a 30 by 30 square grid. This is usually sufficient to give good resolution while conserving computer time. You can change this value with the [Cut] option, e.g. [Cut=40] or [Cut=10]. You may choose up to 100 cuts and as few as 2 on most machines, but you should rarely need fewer than 10 or more than 40.

You can use [X cut], [Y cut], and [Z cut] to control the grid. [X cut] and [Y cut] control the usual grid marks; [Z cut] produces contours parallel to the X-Y plane, like lifting the contours on an X-Y plot (from **Plot/Contour**) into space.

Setting [Cut=10] and not clicking [Hide] is the best way to save computer time when you are trying to get a rough sketch of a surface. If you want a more detailed view, use the [Hide] option and, perhaps, set [Cut=35]. You may need an even larger value for some complex mathematical functions with steep cliffs.

Hidden surface 3-D plotting

When you plot surfaces in three dimensions, you can occasionally encounter "see through" portions, where parts of the surface overlap. To prevent this overlap, click [Hide], which is an option in the **3-D Plot** dialog box.

[Hide] takes longer to compute, so you may not want to use it until you have a final production graph. On faster machines, you may be able to use it all the time.

12.7
Linear smoothing

For 3-D plots, the [Linear] smoothing option produces a surface based on an equation of the following form:

$$Z = a + bX + cY$$

The data are plotted with the default symbol (a tiny point). If you wish to see them better, use one of the larger symbols. If you want them not to show, set [Size] to 0 in the [Symbol] dialog box. Another option you may wish to consider is [Cut], which sets the number of cuts in the grid surface.

Here is a linear smooth of RAIN (average annual inches rainfall) on
LABLAT (latitude) and LABLON (longitude). The surface shows
higher rainfall in the northeast.

- Select **3-D Plot/3-D Plot** from the **Graph** menu
- Select the variables: RAIN * LABLAT * LABLON
- Click [Surface]
  - Choose [Linear] smoothing
  - Click OK
- Set [Size] to 0 in the [Symbol] dialog box
- Click OK

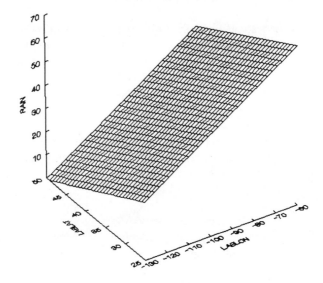

12.8
Negative
exponential
interpolation

You can interpolate a smooth surface through points in 3-D plots. The
method is derived from McLain (1974), in which negative exponential
weights are computed from distances between points in a regular grid
and the irregularly spaced data points in the X-Y plane. These weights
are used in a quadratic function to compute the height of the surface at
each grid point.

Akima, 1978, derived a similar method for 3-D interpolation, which is implemented in SAS (1986). Negative exponential smoothing outperforms Akima's method on Akima's own data, however. Akima sampled the following values from a more detailed surface to see how well his spline interpolation method would do in recovering the original surface.

X	Y	Z
11.160	1.240	22.150
24.200	16.230	2.830
19.850	10.720	7.970
10.350	4.110	22.330
19.720	1.390	16.830
0.000	20.000	34.600
20.870	20.000	5.740
19.990	4.620	14.720
10.280	15.160	21.590
4.510	20.000	15.610
0.000	4.480	61.770
16.700	19.650	6.310
6.080	4.580	35.740
25.000	11.870	4.400
14.900	3.120	21.700
0.000	0.000	58.200
9.660	20.000	4.730
5.220	14.660	40.360
11.770	10.470	13.620
15.100	17.190	12.570
25.000	3.870	8.740
25.000	0.000	12.000
14.590	8.710	14.810
15.200	0.000	21.600
5.230	10.720	26.500
2.140	15.030	53.100
0.510	8.370	49.430
25.000	20.000	0.600
21.670	14.360	5.520
3.310	0.130	44.080

We used [X reverse] and [Y reverse] in [Symbol] to display the surface more clearly. You can try [Contour] (see above in this chapter) to compare the results with Akima's original figures.

- Select **3-D Plot/3-D Plot** from the **Graph** menu
- Select the variables: Z * Y * X
- Click [Surface]
  - Choose [NEXPO] smoothing
  - Click OK
- Click [Axes]
  - Specify [X min] 0, [X max] 25, [Y min] 0, [Y max] 20
  - Click [X reverse] and [Y reverse]
- Set [Size] to 0 in [Symbol]
- Click OK

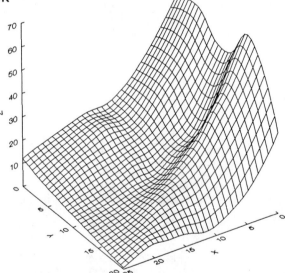

12.9
Inverse squared distance smoothing

[Inverse] squared distance smoothing is a new feature in SYGRAPH. It is similar to [NEXPO] except that no regression estimation is used. The Z height of the curve at a smoothing point is the weighted average of the Y values at X values of the data points, where the weights are the squared Euclidean distances across X and Y.

This method may occasionally produce surfaces that overlap. In these cases, you should click [Hide], which hides parts of surfaces that should not be visible. [Hide] takes longer to compute, because each patch of the surface must be checked for visibility, but it produces clearer plots. Also, you may wish consider altering the number of [Cuts].

Here is the RAIN plot with [Inverse] smoothing.

- Select **3-D Plot/3-D Plot** from the **Graph** menu
- Select the variables: RAIN * LABLAT * LABLON
- Click [Surface]
  - Choose [Inverse] smoothing
  - Click OK
- Click OK

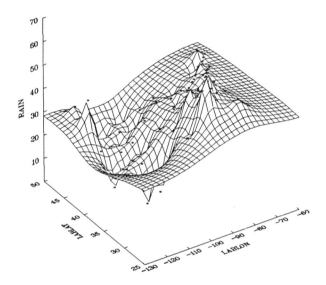

**12.10
Quadratic
smoothing**

For 3-D plots, [Quadratic] smoothing produces a surface based on an equation of the following form:

$$Z = a + bX + cY + dX^2 + eY^2 + fXY$$

This way, the fitted surface can have curvature and tilt.

This method may occasionally produce surfaces that overlap. In these cases, you should click [Hide], which hides parts of surfaces that should not be visible. [Hide] takes longer to compute, because each patch of the surface must be checked for visibility, but it produces clearer plots. Also, you may wish consider altering the number of [Cuts].

Here is a quadratic smooth of RAIN (average annual inches rainfall) on
LABLAT (latitude) and LABLON (longitude). The surface shows
higher rainfall in the northeast.

- Select **3-D Plot/3-D Plot** from the **Graph** menu
- Select the variables: RAIN * LABLAT * LABLON
- Click [Surface]
  - Choose [Quadratic] smoothing
  - Click OK
- Set [Size] to 0 in the [Symbol] dialog box
- Click OK

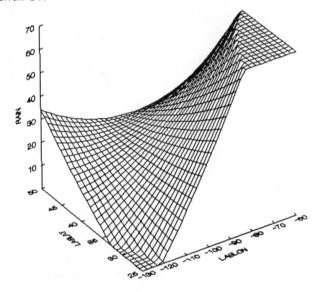

12.11	Distance weighted least squares ([DWLS]) fits a surface through a set of

12.11
Distance
weighted least
squares
smoothing

Distance weighted least squares ([DWLS]) fits a surface through a set of
points by least squares. Unlike linear or low order polynomial smoothing, however, the surface is allowed to flex locally to fit the data better.
The amount of flex is controlled by a tension parameter (see Example
12.14).

If you use DWLS smoothing, be prepared to wait a while, particularly
on slow machines. Every patch on the surface requires four weighted
multiple regressions on all the points. This method produces a locally
weighted three-dimensional surface using an algorithm due to McLain
(1974).

This method may occasionally produce surfaces that overlap. In these cases, you should click [Hide], which hides parts of surfaces that should not be visible. [Hide] takes longer to compute, because each patch of the surface must be checked for visibility, but it produces clearer plots. Also, you may wish consider altering the number of [Cuts].

Here is a distance weighted least squares smooth of RAIN (average annual inches rainfall) on LABLAT (latitude) and LABLON (longitude). We suppress the data values by setting [Size] to 0. The surface adds some detail to the quadratic smooth in Example 12.10.

- Select **3-D Plot/3-D Plot** from the **Graph** menu
- Select the variables: RAIN * LABLAT * LABLON
- Click [Surface]
  - Choose [DWLS] smoothing
  - Click OK
- Set [Size] to 0 in the [Symbol] dialog box
- Click OK

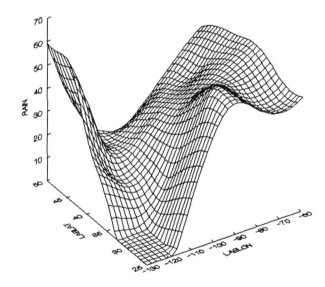

12.12
Step smoothing

You can fit a step function to your data with the [Step] option. [Step] selects the height of the nearest data point as the smoothed surface height. For scattered data, the smoothed surface contains Voronoi polygons at different heights (see the **Plot** chapter). If you input an evenly spaced grid of points, these polygons are squares and you produce a 3-D histogram. To do 3-D histograms in general, it is a good idea to set [Cut] to 80 or so. You may also want to use [X cut] or [Y cut].

If you wish to drop (or rise) immediately from the first point to the second, you need to shift the Y data values one lag down the list for each X in your data.

Here is the rainfall plot with step smoothing.

- Select **3-D Plot/3-D Plot** from the **Graph** menu
- Select the variables: RAIN * LABLAT * LABLON
- Click [Surface]
  - Choose [Step] smoothing
  - Click OK
- Set [Size] to 0
- Click OK

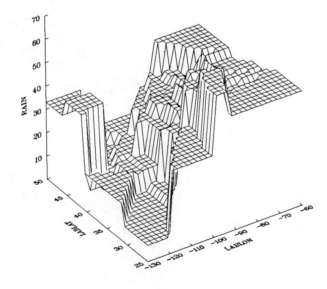

© 1989, SYSTAT, Inc.

12.13
Kernel density
estimators

Bivariate nonparametric kernel density estimators are like continuous histograms (rather than divided into partitions) and show areas where the data are most concentrated in the sample. For [Kernel] smoothing, you select only two variables (Y and X), but SYGRAPH draws a 3-D graph. The densities are shown on the vertical (Z) axis of the plot.

The [Kernel] smoothing method uses the Epanechnikov kernel; see Silverman (1986) for more information.

Here is a kernel density estimate for the bivariate distribution of SUMMER (average summer temperatures) on WINTER (average winter temperatures). You can see a bivariate contouring of this surface in the **Plot** chapter.

- Select **3-D Plot/3-D Plot** from the **Graph** menu
- Select the variables: SUMMER * WINTER
- Click [Surface]
  - Choose [Kernel] smoothing
  - Click OK
- Click OK

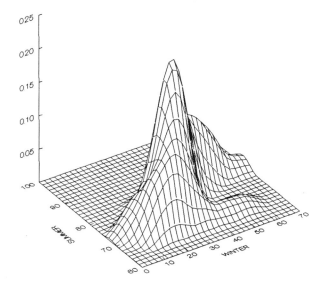

12.14
Tension
parameter

The [Tension] option controls a stiffness parameter for [DWLS] and [Kernel] smoothing. The default tension for [DWLS] is the inverse of the number of cases ($1/n$). The default for [Kernel] is $2n^{-1/6}$, where n is the number of cases. You can set [Tension] to a value between 0 and 10. Increasing these values makes the smooths stiffer and decreasing them makes them looser, more curvy, more susceptible to individual data points, or however you wish to think about it. Here is the same smooth we did in Example 12.11 with a higher tension parameter.

- Select **3-D Plot/3-D Plot** from the **Graph** menu
- Select the variables: RAIN * LABLAT * LABLON
- Click [Surface]
  - Choose [DWLS] smoothing
  - Set [Tension] to .1
  - Click OK
- Set [Size] to 0 in the [Symbol] dialog box
- Click OK

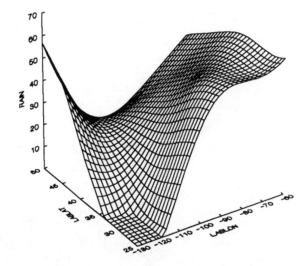

Vector plots

The [Vector] option works like [Spike], except that each point is connected to one point rather than to an axis or plane. This type of plot is especially useful for representing factor loadings and other vector models.

- Click [Vector]
- Specify the origin for vectors
- Click OK

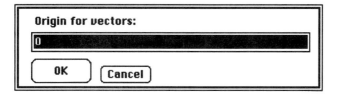

Specify origin coordinates as an ordered triple, e.g. 2,3,4 for X=2, Y=3, Z=4. The default, 0, is short for 0,0,0.

As with other 3-D plots, the vector plot can be difficult to visualize accurately. You can use additional methods to enhance the depth of the plot, however. For example, you can use the [Size] option to make symbols in the foreground larger than those in the background (see the **Using SYGRAPH commands** chapter for an example). Also, you can add the [Spike] option to drop lines to the X-Y plane from the tips of the vectors. This would make a set of right triangles, which would anchor the heights and locations on the X-Y plane.

12.15
3-D vector plots

Let's do the same factor loadings as in the **Plot** chapter. The data are in the file LOAD.

LABEL$	COL(1)	COL(2)	COL(3)
POPDEN	0.248	-0.180	0.858
PERSON	0.758	0.462	0.170
PROPERTY	0.950	0.033	-0.114
INCOME	0.726	-0.478	0.392
SUMMER	-0.060	0.859	-0.121
WINTER	0.208	0.891	0.126
RAIN	-0.313	0.494	0.731

Here we plot the three components in perspective with the labels attached to the end of the vectors. With these data, because the vectors must emanate from 0 on each axis, we use the default "0" for vector origin.

- Select **3-D Plot/3-D Plot** from the **Graph** menu
- Select the variables: COL(3) * COL(2) * COL(1)
- Click [Vector] and specify 0 for origin
- Specify the variable LABEL$ for labeling symbols in the [Symbol] dialog box
- Click OK

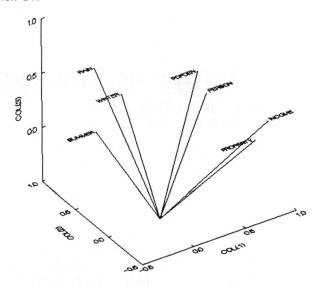

Jittered plots

Sometimes we have data that overlap at exactly the same values. For example, we may have a questionnaire with a 7 point scale and we wish to plot two items against each other. There are only 49 possible points where we may plot the data. Or, we may have aggregate data and wish to plot them in a scatterplot. One way to handle these is by jittering points. Or, you could draw a sunflower plot (discussed earlier in this chapter).

To prevent symbols from overlapping, the [Jitter symbols] option (in the [Symbol] dialog box) adds a small amount of uniform random error to the location of each point. If you have a count variable, such as in our example, you need to weight the cases with **Data/Weight...** before using [Jitter symbols].

Otherwise, if your data are not aggregated but nevertheless have duplicate pairs of values, SYGRAPH jitters all the duplicates.

See the **Plot** chapter for an example of a 2-D jittered plot.

13
SPLOM

SPLOM

Overview

SPLOM stands for "ScatterPLOt Matrix." It is also called a "casement plot" (Cleveland, 1985; Chambers, Cleveland, Kleiner, and Tukey, 1983). Although this graph has been rediscovered several times, the first published reference is in Hartigan (1975a), where it is described as a pairwise plot.

The point of the plot is simple. When you have many variables to plot against each other in scatterplots, why not arrange them in row and column order? **SPLOM** offers several types of symmetrical and asymmetrical SPLOMs.

SPLOM/SPLOM produces a scatterplot matrix or casement plot of the variables you select. If you don't select any variables, **SPLOM** uses all numeric variables in the file by default.

SPLOM/Density produces SPLOMs with density diagrams in the diagonal (label) cells.

To use **SPLOM,** press and hold the mouse button on **SPLOM.** A submenu pops up offering **SPLOM** and **Density.** Slide the pointer to the item you want and release the mouse button.

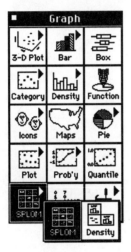

Both items work the same.

- Select **SPLOM/SPLOM** from the **Graph** menu
- Select variables from the left selection list for a symmetric SPLOM
- For an asymmetric SPLOM, select row variables from the left list and column variables from the right list
- Choose [Histogram], [Jitter], or [Stripe] for filling diagonal frames
- Click OK

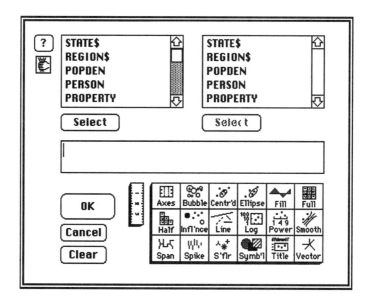

Because SPLOMs are scatterplots, you have almost every option available with **Plot**.

Common options

See the **Common options** chapter for information on [Axes], [Fill], [Line], [Log], [Power], [Symb'l], and [Title]. See below for [Bubble], [Centroid], [Ellipse], [Full], [Half], [Influence], [Smooth], [Span], [Spike], [Sunflower], and [Vector].

SPLOM

SPLOM

13.1
Full symmetric
SPLOM

Here is a scatterplot matrix of the US data.

- Select **SPLOM/SPLOM** from the **Graph** menu
- Click OK

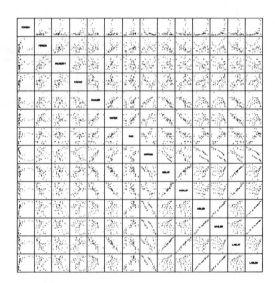

To read the SPLOM, locate the row variable (e.g., POPDEN on the first row) and the column variable (e.g., PERSON in the second column). The intersection is the scatterplot of the row variable on the vertical axis against the column variable on the horizontal. Each column and row is scaled exactly as it is in **Plot** so that the points fill each frame. Tick marks and other labels are omitted because they would distract from the clarity of the plot. If you need scale information on any variable, use **Plot** to produce a separate plot.

Notice that the scatterplots above the diagonal are reflections of those below because the row and column variables are complementary. The overall plot is skew symmetric (the upper half is the mirror image of the lower).

Notice, also, that we didn't need to select the variables. If you don't select any variables, **SPLOM** uses every numeric variable in the file. Watch out if you have a large file of, say, more than a 100 variables. You'll get a scatterplot matrix that looks like a patchwork quilt!

**13.2
Asymmetric
SPLOM**

You can plot one set of variables against another set by selecting some variables from the selection list on the right.

The next example shows SUMMER, WINTER, and RAIN against PERSON and PROPERTY. These particular pairs show up in the earlier SPLOMs, but this orientation allows you to look at cross-relations more easily.

- Select **SPLOM/SPLOM** from the **Graph** menu
- Select row variables from left list: SUMMER, WINTER, RAIN
- Select column variables from the right list: PERSON, PROPERTY
- Click OK

**13.3
Half SPLOM**

You can plot only the lower half of a symmetric SPLOM by using the [Half] option. The full symmetric SPLOM has the same plots above the diagonal but they are transposed. If you can flip things around in your mind's eye, you may want to use the [Half] option all the time. It makes a cleaner graph.

The next example shows all the variables in a half SPLOM.

- Select **Options/Formats…** from the **Graph** menu
- Choose [Swiss] from the [High-res fonts] list
- Click OK

- Select **Options/Global settings…** from the **Graph** menu
- Choose [High resolution] fonts
- Click OK

- Select **SPLOM/SPLOM** from the **Graph** menu
- Click [Half]
- Click OK

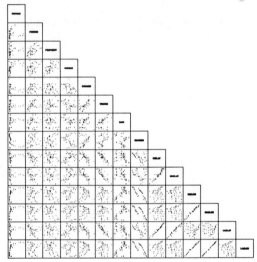

Density

Following Hartigan (1975a), you can insert cute little histograms into the empty cells in the diagonal or the margins of the scatterplot matrix with the [Histogram] option. If you want to add density stripes, click [Stripe]. To add jittered densities, click [Jitter].

13.4
SPLOM with
histograms

The next figure shows histograms in the diagonal elements. These histograms are drawn for each observation on the variable.

- Select **SPLOM/Density** from the **Graph** menu
- Select variables: SUMMER, WINTER, RAIN
- Click [Histogram]
- Click OK

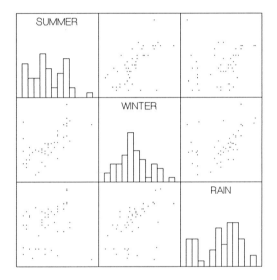

13.5
SPLOM with
density stripes

The next figure shows density stripes instead of histograms in the diagonal elements. These stripes are drawn for each observation on the variable.

- Select **SPLOM/Density** from the **Graph** menu
- Select variables: SUMMER, WINTER, RAIN
- Click [Stripe]
- Click OK

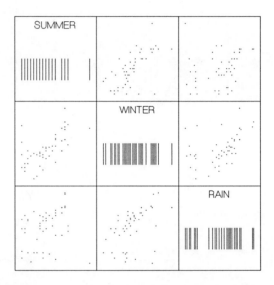

13.6
SPLOM with
jitter plots

The next figure shows jitter plots in the diagonal elements. These plots are drawn for each observation on the variable.

- Select **SPLOM/Density** from the **Graph** menu
- Select variables: SUMMER, WINTER, RAIN
- Click [Jitter]
- Click OK

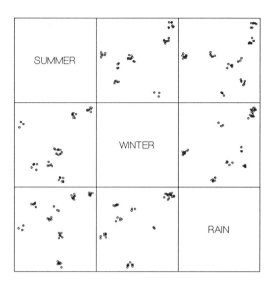

Bubble SPLOMs

Bubble

You can use the value of a variable in your file to control the size of a plotting symbol. This is especially useful to display the value of an additional variable against each pair of variables in a SPLOM.

- Click [Bubble]
- Specify a variable
- Click OK

You can also draw bubble plots by specifying a variable for [Size] in the [Symb'l] dialog box.

One caution. The size of the plotting symbols is taken directly from the values in your file. There is no upper or lower limit., If you size variable has a value as small as .001 or a negative value, the point will be invisible and if it has a value as large as 100, it will fill your entire plot. Try a range of 0 to 10. If your sizing variable does not lie in this range, you should rescale it. Finally, you should usually use empty symbols with this type of plot, since filled ones can occlude each other and make the plot difficult to interpret.

13.7 SPLOM with bubbles

Here is an example. First, we make a new variable using POPDEN from the US dataset.

- Select **Math...** from the **Data** menu
- Fill in the statement: Let DEN = POPDEN/300
- Click OK

By dividing POPDEN by 300, we have placed the new variable DEN in the range of 0 to 4. Now we can use DEN to control the size of each plotting symbol. Notice, by the way, that in the **Plot** chapter we rescaled POPDEN with the formula:

Let DEN = 4*SQR(POPDEN/1000)

This put DEN in approximately the same range as we have now (0 to 4), but the gradations of circle areas were more linear. In the SPLOM below, we are accentuating the larger circles by not using the square root transformation.

Now we draw a scatterplot of climate conditions enhanced by population density.

- Select **SPLOM/SPLOM** from the **Graph** menu
- Select the variables: SUMMER, WINTER, RAIN
- Specify DEN for [Bubble]
- Choose the open circle for [Symbol]
- Click OK

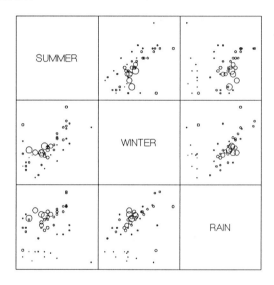

Bivariate confidence intervals

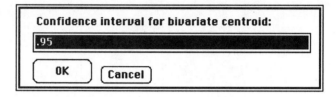

You can draw Gaussian bivariate confidence intervals on centroids in SPLOMs with the [Centr'd] option. As with [Ellipse] (see next), the ellipse produced is centered on the sample means of the X and Y variables. Its major axes are determined by the unbiased sample standard deviations of X and Y and its orientation is determined by the sample Pearson correlation between X and Y. You choose the size of the ellipse by specifying a probability value between 0 and 1, e.g. .95. This size is adjusted by the sample size so that the ellipse will always be smaller than that produced by the [Ellipse] option. The default is .95.

- Click [Centr'd]
- Specify a probability value
- Click OK

Confidence interval for bivariate centroid:

`.95`

[**OK**]　[Cancel]

13.8 Confidence ellipses

Ellipses are superimposed on the SPLOM of SUMMER, WINTER, and RAIN. We have used a 99 percent confidence region on the centroids (ELM=.99). We also place histograms in the diagonal cells.

- Select **Options/Formats...** from the **Graph** menu
- Choose [Swiss] from the [High-res fonts] list
- Click OK

- Select **Options/Global settings...** from the **Graph** menu
- Choose [High resolution] fonts
- Click OK

- Select **SPLOM/Density** from the **Graph** menu
- Select the variables: SUMMER, WINTER, RAIN
- Specify .99 for [Centr'd]
- Click [Histogram]
- Click OK

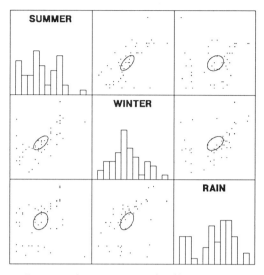

Bivariate ellipses

You can draw Gaussian bivariate sample ellipses on scatterplot matrices assuming a Gaussian (normal) bivariate distribution for your data. The resulting ellipse is centered on the sample means of the X and Y variables. Its major axes are determined by the unbiased sample standard deviations of X and Y and its orientation is determined by the sample covariance between X and Y.

- Click [Ellipse]
- Specify a probability value
- Click OK

You choose the size of the ellipse by specifying a probability value between 0 and 1, e.g..95. If you make an extremely large ellipse (e.g. .999), it may extend beyond the axes of your plot. The default is .5.

Remember, these ellipses are always larger than the confidence ellipses (see the preceding example), because they are for the total sample and the confidence ellipses are for the centroid of the sample. The difference is analogous to the standard deviation versus the standard error of the mean.

**13.9
SPLOM with
ellipses**

Here are ellipses superimposed on the SPLOM of SUMMER, WINTER, and RAIN. We have used the default 50 percent confidence region on the data values.

- Select **SPLOM/SPLOM** from the **Graph** menu
- Select the variables: SUMMER, WINTER, RAIN
- Click [Ellipse]
- Click OK

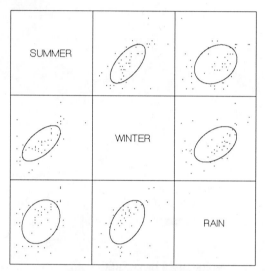

Influence

The influence of a point in a scatterplot on the correlation coefficient is the amount the correlation would change if that point were deleted. Plotting influences can help us determine whether a linear fit to the scatterplot is relatively robust or is dependent on just a few points. **SPLOM** has the same [Influence] option found in **Plot**, which makes the size of the plotting symbol represent the extent of influence from each point. If any large points appear in the plot, we should scrutinize them further with **Plot** before we draw any conclusions concerning the correlation.

You can use any symbol for influence plots, although circles are standard. Positive influences are represented by hollow symbols and negative influences by filled symbols.

Other types of influences on statistical estimators can be represented in SYGRAPH by using the [Size] option on statistics computed in SYSTAT or another statistical package. For example, **MGLH** saves Mahalanobis distances (distances weighted by a covariance matrix) in a file when you do a discriminant analysis or save scores when testing hypotheses. See Gnanadesikan (1977) for further information.

13.10 Influence SPLOM

Here is an influence plot of SUMMER (average summer temperature), WINTER (average winter temperature) and RAIN (annual average inches of rainfall). Notice that some points have large negative influences on the correlation.

- Select **SPLOM/SPLOM** from the **Graph** menu
- Select the variables: SUMMER, WINTER, RAIN
- Click [Influence]
- Click OK

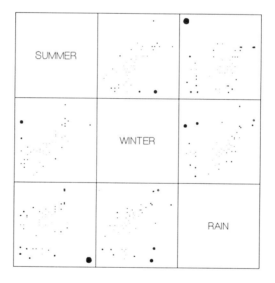

Line SPLOMs

Time series and other data plot best when the points are connected with a line. This is easy to do in SYGRAPH. Just use the [Line] option. You may choose from 11 different types of lines.

- Click [Line]
- Choose a line or specify one by number (1 to 11, top to bottom)
- Click OK

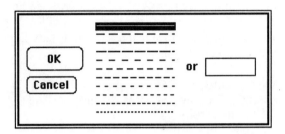

If you do not want to see the symbols that the line connects, make them invisible by setting [Size] to 0 in the [Symbol] dialog box.

**13.11
SPLOM with
lines**

The data in the LABOR file are output productivity per labor hour in 1977 U.S. dollars for a 25 year period from the U.S. Bureau of Labor Statistics.

YEAR	US	CANADA	JAPAN	GERMANY	ENGLAND
1960	62.2	50.3	23.2	40.3	53.8
1965	76.6	62.7	35.0	54.0	63.9
1970	80.0	76.8	64.8	71.2	77.6
1975	92.9	91.8	87.7	90.1	94.3
1980	101.4	101.9	122.7	108.6	101.2
1985	121.8	115.1	159.9	131.9	129.7

The data are in time order in the file. If the data were in some other order, the [Line] option would connect successive points and produce a messy spider web in each cell of the SPLOM.

Here is a SPLOM of each country's productivity against the YEAR variable.

We use [Y min] and [Y max] to keep the vertical scale of each cell the same.

- Select **SPLOM/SPLOM** from the **Graph** menu
- Select row variables from the left list: US, CANADA, JAPAN, GERMANY, ENGLAND
- Select the column variable from the right list: YEAR
- Click the ruler and make the marquee 3 inches tall and 4 inches wide
- Click [Line]
- Set [Size] to 0 in the [Symbol] dialog box
- Set [Y min] to 0 and [Y max] to 200 in the [Axes] dialog box
- Click OK

	YEAR
US	
CANADA	
JAPAN	
GERMANY	
ENGLAND	

Smoothing

The [Smooth] option provides ten types of smoothing. For [Linear] regression smoothing, it further offers confidence bands.

- Click [Smooth]
- Choose the type of smoothing
- For [Linear] regression, click [Confidence bands] and specify the confidence level
- Click [Short] to limit the domain of smoothing to extreme values of the X data
- Specify your own [Tension] level for [LOWESS], [Spline], or [DWLS] smoothing
- Click OK

13.12
Linear regression

The most popular way to smooth data is [Linear] regression. Regression fits a function to data such that the value predicted by the function at each observed value of X is as close as possible to the observed value of Y at the same value of X. Ordinary linear regression uses a straight line for the function and makes the squared discrepancies between predicted and observed Y values as small as possible. The equation for this function looks like this:

$$Y = a + bX$$

where a is a constant term and b is a slope coefficient.

Here is the linear regression smoothing of the climate variables
SPLOM. Notice that the regressions above the diagonal are not the
same as those below. One regresses Y on X and the other X on Y.

- Select **SPLOM/SPLOM** from the **Graph** menu
- Select the variables: SUMMER, WINTER, RAIN
- Choose [Linear] smoothing
- Click OK

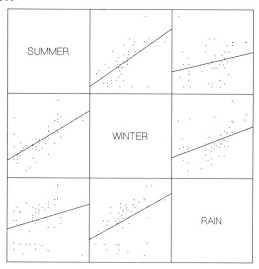

**13.13
Regression with
confidence bands**

Often, we want a confidence interval on a regression line we have fitted
in each cell of a SPLOM. Just click [Confidence bands] and specify a
level.

Say we specify .90. SYGRAPH draws upper and lower hyperbolic bands
around the actual fitted line. These bands mean the following: if the discrepancies (residuals) between the fitted and observed values for Y at
each X are normally distributed and independent of each other and have
the same spread (variance), then 90 times out of a hundred, confidence
intervals constructed by SYGRAPH from data sampled in the same way
you found these data will cover the true regression line relating Y to X.

The next figure shows the 95 percent confidence intervals on the regression lines of SUMMER, WINTER, and RAIN on each other. You must click [Linear] to get the confidence line.

- Select **SPLOM/SPLOM** from the **Graph** menu
- Select the variables: SUMMER, WINTER, RAIN
- Choose [Linear] smoothing and specify .95 confidence
- Click OK

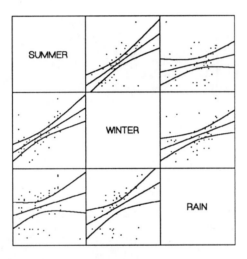

13.14 LOWESS smoothing

Quadratic smoothing, like linear smoothing, presupposes the shape of the function. SYGRAPH offers a smoothing method that requires only that the smooth be a function (i.e., unique Y value for every X). This method is called LOWESS (Cleveland, 1979,1981). It produces a smooth by running along the X values and finding predicted values from a weighted robust average of nearby Y values. Because a lot of computations are involved, the [LOWESS] option can be time consuming for large scatterplots.

This example shows the result for the climate data. Notice that the fit is distinctly curvilinear in most of the cells. It is always a good idea to use LOWESS before fitting a straight line or any other function to data. This way, you can let the data speak for themselves and warn you about whether your model is inappropriate.

The tightness of the LOWESS curve is controlled by a parameter called [Tension], which determines the width of the smoothing window. Normally, the tension is set to .5, meaning that half the points are included in each running window. If you increase the tension, the curve will be stiffer and if you decrease it, the curve will be looser, following local irregularities. [Tension] accepts values between 0 and 1.

- Select **SPLOM/SPLOM** from the **Graph** menu
- Select the variables: SUMMER, WINTER, RAIN
- Choose [LOWESS] smoothing
- Click OK

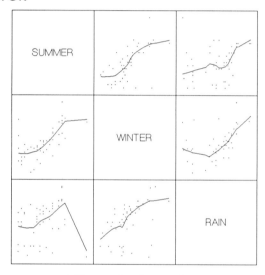

**13.15
Negative
exponentially
weighted
smoothing**

Negative exponentially weighted smoothing ([NEXPO]) fits a curve through a set of points such that the influence of neighboring points decreases exponentially with distance. It is an alternative to [Spline] smoothing for interpolation. The smoothing algorithm is due to McLain (1974). It is closely related to distance weighted least squares regression smoothing.

This example shows a smooth of the LABOR data used to illustrate [Line] in Example 13.11 and [Spline] smoothing in Example 13.19. The primary difference between the two smoothing methods is that negative exponential smoothing is always single valued. For each X value, there is a unique Y value. Spline smoothing, on the other hand, can produce several Y values for a given X value in some contexts.

- Select **SPLOM/SPLOM** from the **Graph** menu
- Select the row variables: US, CANADA, JAPAN, GERMANY, ENGLAND
- Select the column variable: YEAR
- Click the ruler and make the marquee 3 inches tall and 4 inches wide
- Choose [NEXPO] smoothing
- Set [Size] to 0 in the [Symbol] dialog box
- Set [Y min] to 0 and [Y max] to 200 in the [Axes] dialog box
- Click OK

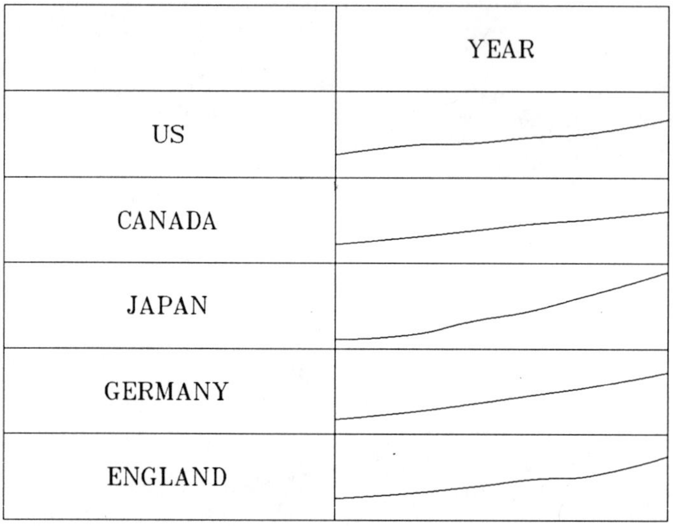

**13.16
Inverse squared
distance
smoothing**

[Inverse] provides inverse squared distance smoothing. This is sometimes called Shepard's method. It is similar to [NEXPO] except that no regression estimation is used. The height of the curve at a smoothing point is the weighted average of the Y values at X values of the data points, where the weights are the squared Euclidean distances from the data points to the smoothing point on the X axis.

This example shows a smooth of the LABOR data used to illustrate [NEXPO] in Example 13.15 and [Spline] smoothing in Example 13.19.

- Select **SPLOM/SPLOM** from the **Graph** menu
- Select the row variables: US, CANADA, JAPAN, GERMANY, ENGLAND
- Select the column variable: YEAR
- Click the ruler and make the marquee 3 inches tall and 4 inches wide
- Choose [Inverse] smoothing
- Set [Size] to 0 in the [Symbol] dialog box
- Set [Y min] to 0 and [Y max] to 200 in the [Axes] dialog box
- Click OK

13.17 Quadratic smoothing

You can fit a quadratic regression curve to your data with the [Quadratic] option. This fits the following type of equation to the data:

$$Y = a + bX + cX^2$$

where a is a constant and b and c are slope coefficients.

Here is the quadratic regression of the climate data. Compare it to the [LOWESS] results in Example 13.14.

- Select **SPLOM/SPLOM** from the **Graph** menu
- Select the variables: SUMMER, WINTER, RAIN
- Choose [Quadratic] smoothing
- Click OK

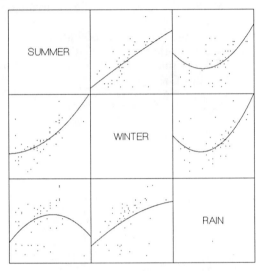

13.18 Distance weighted least squares smoothing

The [DWLS] option—distance weighted least squares—fits a line through a set of points by least squares. Unlike linear or low order polynomial smoothing, however, the surface is allowed to flex locally to fit the data better. The amount of flex is controlled by the [Tension] parameter discussed with Example 13.24.

If you use [DWLS], be prepared to wait a while, particularly on slow machines. Every point on the smoothed line requires a weighted quadratic multiple regression on all the points. This method produces a true, LOWESS curve running through the points using an algorithm due to McLain (1974). If you want to do a regression of one variable on another, but are not positive about the shape of the function, we suggest you use [DWLS] or [LOWESS] first.

Here is a LOWESS least squares smooth of the climate data. Compare it to the smoothing of the same data using [LOWESS]. While not as robust as LOWESS smoothing, DWLS produces smoother curves. We added [Short] (discussed in Example 13.23), because it is extremely misleading to extrapolate from the data using DWLS.

- Select **SPLOM/SPLOM** from the **Graph** menu
- Select the variables: SUMMER, WINTER, RAIN
- Choose [DWLS] smoothing and click [Short]
- Click OK

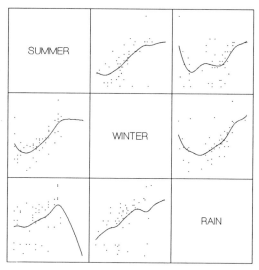

13.19
Spline smoothing

You can fit a spline curve to your data with [Spline] smoothing. Spline smoothing fits a curved line through every point in the plot such that the curve is smooth everywhere. SYGRAPH employs cubic splines (Brodlie, 1980) for smoothing. Cubic splines involve fitting several sections of the curve with cubic equations:

$$Y = a + bX + cX^2 + dX^3$$

where a is a constant, and b, c, and d are coefficients. These curves are joined smoothly at "knots," which usually coincide with the data points themselves.

Cubic splines are especially useful for interpolation, when you need a computer French curve. This means that you should use splines through the data points only when you believe your data contain no error. Otherwise, you should choose one of the regression methods ([Linear], [Quad], [DWLS], or [Locally weighed]).

The tightness of the spline curve is controlled by a tension parameter, which determines how tightly the curves are pulled between the knots. Normally, tension is set to 2, but you can set it down to 0 to make it looser and up to 10 to make it tighter. We hate to say this is a matter of aesthetics, but you really should try several values on the same data to see what we mean.

This SPLOM has a spline smooth of the LABOR data seen earlier in Example 13.11. The smoothing has interpolated flexibly between the 5 year intervals of the original data. Whether this is appropriate depends on how much error you think the data contain. You should use interpolating splines like this only when you want the curve to pass exactly through the points.

Notice the slight upturn at the right end of the curve in the ENGLAND*YEAR plot. Compare this curve to the one with [NEXPO] smoothing in the next example. Splines are not guaranteed to be single valued for every value of the X variable. Because we are fitting a function in this case, the negative exponential smoothing is preferable to the splines.

First, trace a plotting frame 3 inches tall and 4 inches wide.

- Select **SPLOM/SPLOM** from the **Graph** menu
- Select the row variables: US, CANADA, JAPAN, GERMANY, ENGLAND
- Select the column variable: YEAR
- Choose [Spline] smoothing
- Set [Size] to 0 in the [Symbol] dialog box
- Set [Y min] to 0 and [Y max] to 200 in the [Axes] dialog box
- Click OK

13.20
Step smoothing

You can fit a step function to your data with [Step] smoothing. The function begins at the point with the smallest X value and drops (or rises) to the point with the next larger X value. If you wish to drop (or rise) immediately from the first point to the second, you need to shift the Y data values one lag down the list for each X in your data.

Here is the step smooth for the LABOR data. Of all the smoothing
methods for these data, this one is the least appropriate, since it suggests
that productivity changes were discontinuous at five year intervals.

- Select **SPLOM/SPLOM** from the **Graph** menu
- Select the variables: US, CANADA, JAPAN, GERMANY, ENGLAND
- Select a grouping variable: YEAR
- Click the ruler and make the marquee 3 inches tall and 4 inches
  wide
- Choose [Step] smoothing
- Set [Size] to 0 in the [Symbol] dialog box
- Set [Y min] to 0 and [Y max] to 200 in the [Axes] dialog box
- Click OK

	YEAR
US	
CANADA	
JAPAN	
GERMANY	
ENGLAND	

13.21
Log smoothing

[Log] smoothing is a new feature to SYGRAPH. It includes linearizable
functions

$$E[Y] = a + b\ln(X)$$

Here is a log smooth of the climate data. Compare it to the [Quadratic] results in Example 13.17.

- Select **SPLOM/SPLOM** from the **Graph** menu
- Select the variables: SUMMER, WINTER, RAIN
- Choose [Log] smoothing
- Click OK

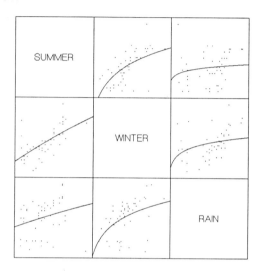

13.22
Power smoothing

[Power] smoothing is a new feature to SYGRAPH. It includes linearizable functions

$$E[Y] = aX^b$$

Here is a power function smooth of the climate data. Compare it to the [Quadratic] results in Example 13.17.

- Select **SPLOM/SPLOM** from the **Graph** menu
- Select the variables: SUMMER, WINTER, RAIN
- Choose [Power] smoothing
- Click OK

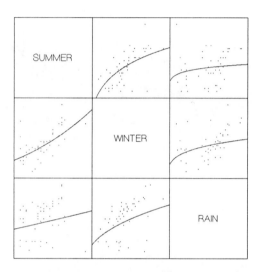

**13.23
Shortening the
domain of
smoothing**

Sometimes you can get into trouble by extrapolating beyond the range of your data when making a prediction. Many of the smoothing methods in SYGRAPH yield curves that extend from the left to the right edges of the plotting frame. If you wish to limit the domain of the smooth to the extreme values of the data on the horizontal axis, click the [Short] option.

This example shows a SPLOM with a linear function and confidence interval limited to the range of the X data. Compare this to the extrapolated version in Example 13.12.

- Select **SPLOM** from the **Graph** menu
- Select the variables: SUMMER, WINTER, RAIN
- Choose [Linear] smoothing with [Confidence bands] and click [Short]
- Click OK

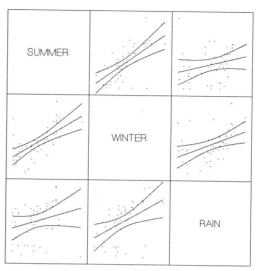

**13.24
Tension
parameter for
LOWESS, spline,
or DWLS
smoothing**

The [Tension] option controls a stiffness parameter for LOWESS, spline, and DWLS smoothing. The default value is .5 for LOWESS and 2 for spline. For DWLS, tension is set at the inverse of the number of cases (1/n).

For LOWESS, [Tension] must be set between 0 and 1. For spline and DWLS, it must be between 0 and 10. Increasing these values makes the smooths stiffer and decreasing them makes them looser, more curvy, more susceptible to individual data points, or however you wish to think about it.

This example shows the same plot used to illustrate LOWESS in Example 13.14, but with the tension set higher at .9. In this case, 90 percent of the data points are used to smooth each value on the curve.

- Select **SPLOM** from the **Graph** menu
- Select the variables: SUMMER, WINTER, RAIN
- Choose [LOWESS] smoothing and set [Tension] to .9
- Click OK

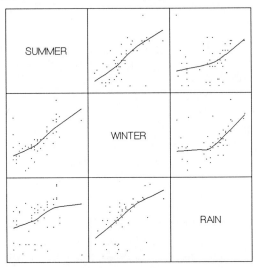

Minimum spanning tree SPLOMs

Okay, folks, what's a minimal spanning tree doing in a SPLOM routine? Well, here's one application. Suppose you've done factor analyses or smallest space analyses or multidimensional scalings in more than two dimensions. Analyzing graphic results from these analyses can be difficult, as many of you who have pored over printouts trying to look at pairs of dimensions on different pages know.

Well, here's the super-duper span SPLOM!

13.25 Super-duper span SPLOM

We did a multidimensional scaling on the US data file. First, we computed a Pearson correlation matrix on the data using SYSTAT:

- Select **Corr/Pearson...** from the **Stats** menu
- Click [Save file]
- Click OK

Then we did a multidimensional scaling on the correlation matrix we saved:

- Select **MDS/Scale...** from the **Stats** menu
- Specify 3 for [Dimension]
- Click [Save file] to save the Final configuration
- Click OK

Here is the output configuration, in the file saved from **MDS**. We added a variable NUM$ and a label (LAB$) to show which variable was which.

LAB$	NUM$	DIM(1)	DIM(2)	DIM(3)
POPDEN	1	0.587	-0.471	-0.643
PERSON	2	0.114	0.104	0.520
PROPERTY	3	0.533	0.680	0.350
INCOME	4	1.243	-0.052	0.066
SUMMER	5	-1.138	0.227	0.221
WINTER	6	-0.759	0.320	-0.022
RAIN	7	-0.579	-0.808	-0.492

Here a minimum spanning tree connects the points in the climate data MDS configuration SPLOM. We've used the numbers in NUM$ to label the points, although you might prefer other symbols. The axis limits have been set with the [Axes] options in order to keep every cell on the same scale.

- Select **SPLOM/SPLOM** from the **Graph** menu
- Select the variables: DIM(1), DIM(2), DIM(3)
- Click [Span]
- Set [X min] to –1.5, [X max] to 1.5, [Y min] to –1.5, and [Y max] to 1.5 in the [Axes] dialog box
- Specify NUM$ for plotting symbols and set [Size] to 3 in the [Symb'l] dialog box
- Click OK

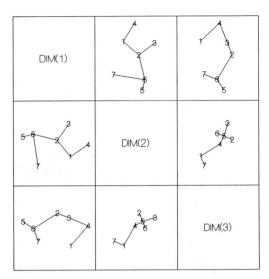

Spikes to data points

Spike

To represent deviations from a constant value, you can plot data with the [Spike] option. This is handy, for example, in plotting residuals from a regression. Lines will be drawn from each plotting symbol down to the horizontal axis in each cell. If you specify a value, e.g., [Spike=10], then lines are drawn from each symbol to the level on the vertical axis corresponding to the value you have picked.

13.26 SPLOM with spikes

We computed residuals from the following regression on the US dataset in SYSTAT:

- Select **MGLH/General linear model...** from the **Stats** menu
- Select the [Dependent] variables: SUMMER, WINTER, RAIN
- Select the [Indep'dent] variables: LABLAT, LABLON
- Click [Save file] (save residuals)
- Click OK

We then plotted residuals against estimates from this multivariate linear regression. We used the file saved from **MGLH**.

- Select **SPLOM/SPLOM** from the **Graph** menu
- Select the row variables: RESIDUAL(1), RESIDUAL(2), RESIDUAL(3)
- Select the column variables: ESTIMATE(1), ESTIMATE(2), ESTIMATE(3)
- Specify Spike=0
- Click OK

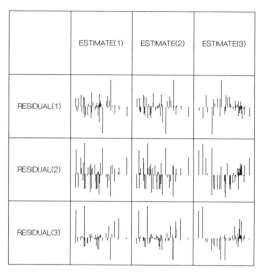

**Sunflower
SPLOMs**

Sometimes we have data that overlap at exactly the same values. For example, we may have a questionnaire with a 7 point scale and we wish to plot two items against each other. There are only 49 possible points where we may plot the data. Or, we may have aggregate data and wish to plot them in a scatterplot.

To represent the overlap in these data, you can plot them with special symbols that are light for small values and darker for larger values of the COUNT variable. Most of them look like flowers, so this is often called a sunflower plot. In the next example, we plot these data with [S'flr]. Only 9 symbols are possible, so larger counts are plotted with the darkest, largest symbol (a filled circle).

See the [Jitter] option for another way to deal with overlaps.

13.27
Sunflower
SPLOM

Here are the means of SUMMER, WINTER, and RAIN within regions of the variables in the US file. COUNT shows the number of states over which the means were computed.

REGION$	COUNT	SUMMER	WINTER	RAIN
New England	6	70.3	25.2	40.7
Mid Atlantic	3	74.8	31.3	39.3
Great Lakes	5	73.6	26.3	34.0
Plains	7	75.7	20.7	25.6
Southeast	8	78.3	43.2	45.0
South	8	81.4	45.1	46.3
Mountain	8	75.3	30.3	11.4
Pacific	3	67.7	39.8	29.7

If you have a count variable, such as in our example, you need to use it to WEIGHT cases before using the [S'flr] option. To make the symbols more visible (because there are only a few) we choose a large symbol size.

- Select **Weight** from the **Data** menu
- Select a weight variable: COUNT
- Click OK

- Select **SPLOM/SPLOM** from the **Graph** menu
- Select the variables: SUMMER, WINTER, RAIN
- Click [S'flr]
- Click OK

If your data are not aggregated but nevertheless have duplicate pairs of values, use **SPLOM** alone. SYGRAPH computes the duplicates before drawing the sunflower plot.

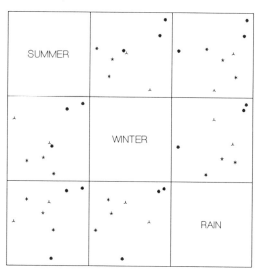

Vector SPLOMs

You can plot factor loadings and other types of vectors in each cell of a SPLOM. The [Vector] option connects points to a single point you specify—usually the origin (0).

- Click [Vector]
- Specify the origin for vectors
- Click OK

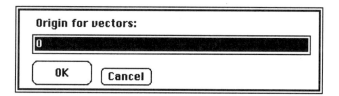

Specify the origin in X,Y coordinates, e.g. 2,3 for X=2, Y=3.

13.28
SPLOM with
vectors

Let's use the same factor loadings we used for illustrating the [Vector] option in the **Plot** chapter, in Example 11.39.

LABEL$	NUM$	COL(1)	COL(2)	COL(3)
POPDEN	1	0.248	-0.180	0.858
PERSON	2	0.758	0.462	0.170
PROPERTY	3	0.950	0.033	-0.114
INCOME	4	0.726	-0.478	0.392
SUMMER	5	-0.060	0.859	-0.121
WINTER	6	0.208	0.891	0.126
RAIN	7	-0.313	0.494	0.731

We've added the variable NUM$ to label each vector in the next figure. Let's plot all three possible pairs of loadings in a single SPLOM with a symbol used at the end of each vector. If you type [Vector] without specifying a point, the vectors are drawn to the near lower left corner of each cell. With these data, because the vectors must emanate from 0 on each axis, we have specified 0 for the origin.

- Select **SPLOM/SPLOM** from the **Graph** menu
- Select the variables: COL(1), COL(2), COL(3)
- Click [Vector] and specify 0 for origin
- Set [X min] to –1, [X max] to 1, [Y min] to –1, [Y max] to 1
- Specify NUM$ for plotting symbols and set [Size] to 2 in the [Symb'l] dialog box
- Click OK

Jittered symbols

Sometimes we have data that overlap at exactly the same values. For example, we may have a questionnaire with a 7 point scale and we wish to plot two items against each other. There are only 49 possible points where we may plot the data. Or, we may have aggregate data and wish to plot them in a scatterplot.

To prevent symbols from overlapping, the [Jitter symbols] option in the [Symbol] dialog box adds a small amount of uniform random error to the location of each point.

Do not confuse the [Jitter symbols] option in the [Symbol] dialog box, which jitters the points in the cells, with the [Jitter] option for **SPLOM/Density**, which puts jittered densities into the diagonals or margins. Both use the same random jittering, but one is for the joint distributions (the off-diagonal cells) and the other is for the marginal (the diagonal or marginal cells).

13.29
Jittered SPLOM

Here are the means of SUMMER, WINTER, and RAIN within regions of the variables in the US file. COUNT shows the number of states over which the means were computed.

REGION$	COUNT	SUMMER	WINTER	RAIN
New England	6	70.3	25.2	40.7
Mid Atlantic	3	74.8	31.3	39.3
Great Lakes	5	73.6	26.3	34.0
Plains	7	75.7	20.7	25.6
Southeast	8	78.3	43.2	45.0
South	8	81.4	45.1	46.3
Mountain	8	75.3	30.3	11.4
Pacific	3	67.7	39.8	29.7

If you have a count variable, such as in our example, you need to use it to weight cases before using the [Jitter symbols] option. Otherwise, if your data are not aggregated but nevertheless have duplicate pairs of values, SYGRAPH will jitter all the duplicates.

- Select **Weight** from the **Data** menu
- Select a weight variable: COUNT
- Click OK

- Select **SPLOM** from the **Graph** menu
- Select the variables: SUMMER, WINTER, RAIN
- Click [Jitter symbols] and choose the open circle in the [Symbol] dialog box
- Click OK

We use open circles because hollow circles plot well when there are many overlaps.

　　　　　　　　　　　　　　　　　　© 1989, SYSTAT, Inc.

14   Function

Function

14

Overview You can plot 2-D and 3-D mathematical functions with **Function**. Many of the same options of **Plot** apply, and **Function** works similarly to **Plot.**.

You can overlay functions on data plots by plotting twice with the Overlay feature. If you use SYSTAT **Nonlin,** you can estimate parameters of functions and plot smooth curves for nonlinear fits this way.

You can plot mathematical functions in two or three dimensions with **Function**.

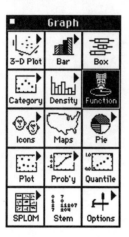

Just type the equation of the function you wish to plot in the **Function** dialog box. You can use the selection list of SYSTAT operators and functions to build your equation. Remember, arguments for functions such as ABS( ) must be placed inside the parentheses, e.g. ABS(X^3).

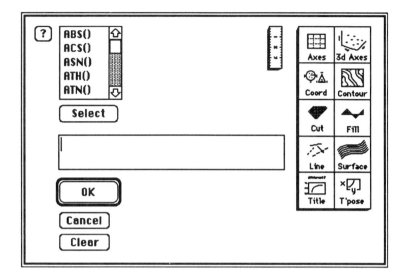

SYGRAPH analyzes your function, determines axis values, and plots it in smooth lines. You need not generate sample values to produce the plot. The notation and syntax for equations follow standard BASIC. For example, the equation "Y=X^2" produces a parabola.

SYGRAPH determines the plotting domain (horizontal axis limits) and range (vertical axis limits) of the function by numerically computing the second derivatives (rate of change in y versus change in x) and indicators of periodicity and monotonicity. If it fails, you can choose limits yourself with [X min], [Y max], etc. in the [Axes] dialog box.

SYGRAPH can generally handle discontinuities in the function as well. It should not blow up with large or small values and it will clip values outside the plotting frame. Sometimes its algorithm will fail, but in these cases, you usually can get a good plot by fiddling with the axis limits.

You do not have to use X, Y, and Z for your variable names. You can use any names that are not names of variables in the current file. These names are used to label the axes unless you use the [X label] and/or [Y label] options in [Axes].

Common options

See the **Common options** chapter for information on [Axes], [3d Axes], [Fill], [Line], [Title], and [T'pose]. Some discussion of [Line] is also given in this chapter. Remaining options [Contour], [Cut], [Surface], and [Coord] are discussed below.

Axes

If you are plotting a three-dimensional function, use the [3d axes] option. If you are plotting a two-dimensional function, use the usual [Axes] option.

Types of plots

Two-dimensional function plots

14.1
2-D function plot

Here is a function from the family used by Rudnic and Gaspari (1987) to model the distribution of the radius of gyration of multidimensional random walks and related fractals.

- Select **Options/Formats...** from the **Graph** menu
- Choose [Hershey] from the [High-res fonts] list
- Click OK

- Select **Options/Global settings...** from the **Graph** menu
- Choose [High resolution]
- Click OK

- Select **Function** from the **Graph** menu
- Specify the function:
  P = SQR(R)*EXP(–R)
- Set [Axes] limits:
  [X min] 0, [X max] 10
  [Y min] 0, [Y max] .5
- Click OK

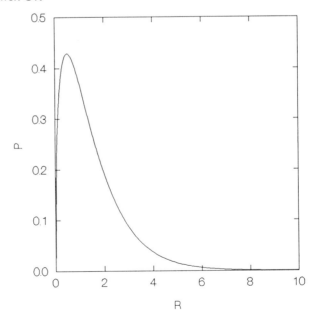

Try some other functions yourself. We love plotting arbitrarily messy and unusual functions to see how they work out. Here are some fun ones. Some require a lot of time to compute.

Y = SIN(COS(TAN(X)))
Y = 1/SIN(X)
Y = SIN(EXP(X))
Y = SIN(1/X)
Y = ATH(COS(X))
Y = 1/X^2 – SIN(X)
Y = 1/LOG(ABS(TAN(X)))

Three-dimensional function plots

SYGRAPH produces three-dimensional function plots when you have two predictors in the equation. For example, if you specify Z=X^2–Y^2, the program recognizes the two predictors X and Y automatically and places the plot in three-dimensional perspective.

Almost always, you should use the [Hide] option (see below), because most mathematical functions produce overlapping surfaces when viewed in perspective. You can try some preliminary plots without [Hide] to save time, however. Another way to save time is to use the [Cut] option (also see below), which modifies the number of cuts in the grid surface. You can make rougher, faster plots by setting [Cut] near 10 and smoother ones by setting it up to 40 or 50.

SYGRAPH tries to adjust scales automatically just as it does in two dimensions. Often, however, you may have to fine tune the scales to get a pleasing figure. The defaults work with a surprising number of graphs.

14.2
3-D function plot

The next figure shows the last example, a damped three-dimensional polar sine wave.

- Select **Function** from the **Graph** menu
- Specify the function:
  Z = 2*SIN(2*SQR(X^2 + Y^2))/SQR(X^2 + Y^2)
- Set the [Axes] limits:
  [X min] –5, [X max] 5
  [Y min] –5, [Y max] 5
  [Z min] –5, [Z max] 5
- Click [Hide]
- Click OK

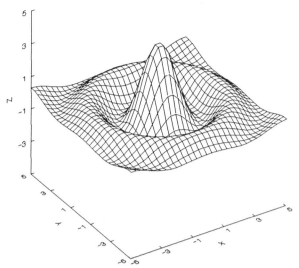

Here are some more fun 3-D functions to try, along with recommended
axes limits. You'll probably want to click [Hide].

Z = X*Y*(X^2 – Y^2)/(X^2 + Y^2)
　　[X min] –10, [X max] 10,
　　[Y min] –10, [Y max] 10,
　　[Z min] –100, [Z max] 100

Z = SIN(SQR(X*X + Y*Y))
　　[X min] –5, [X max] 5
　　[Y min] –5, [Y max] 5
　　[Z min] –1, [Z max] 1

Z = X*X/8 – Y*Y/12
　　[X min] –10, [X max] 10
　　[Y min] –10, [Y max] 10
　　[Z min] –10, [Z max] 10

Picking number of cuts in a grid

Cut

For contouring and surface plotting in three dimensions, SYGRAPH computes a 30 by 30 square grid. This is usually sufficient to give good resolution while conserving computer time. You can change this value with the [Cuts] option. (See also the [Surface] option, which allows you to choose the type of grid.)

- Click [Cuts]
- Specify the number of cut marks
- Click OK

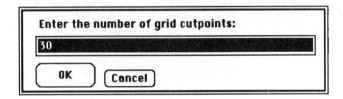

Enter the number of grid cutpoints:

30

OK   Cancel

You may choose up to 60 cuts and as few as 2 on most machines, but you should rarely need fewer than 10 or more than 40.

Setting [Cuts] to 10 and omitting [Hide] (discussed next) is the best way to save computer time when you are trying to get a rough sketch of a surface. If you want a more detailed view, use the [Hide] option and, perhaps, set [Cuts] to 35. You may need an even larger value for some complex mathematical functions with steep cliffs.

Hidden surface plotting

When you plot surfaces in three dimensions, you can occasionally encounter "see through" portions, where parts of the surface overlap. To prevent this overlap, click [Hide] in the [Surface] dialog box.

[Hide] takes longer to compute, so you may not want to use it until you have a final production graph. On faster machines, you may be able to use it all the time.

14.3
Smooth, hidden
surface

Here is an example of an error function plot with 60 cuts. We have used [Z min] and [Z max] in the [Axes] dialog box to scale the vertical axis. The [Hide] option keeps the rear of the surface hidden.

- Select **Options/Formats...** from the **Graph** menu
- Choose [Hershey] from the [High-res fonts] list
- Click OK

- Select **Options/Global settings...** from the **Graph** menu
- Choose [High resolution] fonts
- Click OK

- Select **Function** from the **Graph** menu
- Specify the function:
  Z = EXP(–X^2 – Y^2)
- Set the [Axes] limits:
  [Z min] 0, [Z max] 1
- Click [Hide]
- Specify 60 [Cuts]
- Click OK

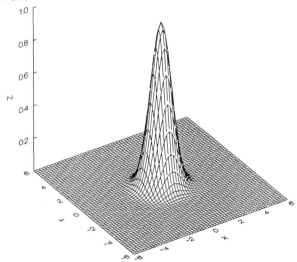

Contouring

You can produce contour plots of functions by clicking the [Contour] option.

SYGRAPH first computes its own square grid of interpolated or directly estimated values. From this grid, contours are followed using the method of Lodwick and Whittle (1970) combined with linear interpolation. This method is guaranteed to find proper contours if the grid is fine enough. The standard grid is 30 by 30. To increase this resolution, use [Cuts] to add up to 60 grid cuts. For rough contours, you can reduce computing time by setting [Cuts] below 30.

SYGRAPH automatically determines the number of contours to draw so that the surface is delineated and the contour labels are round numbers. If you wish to modify this number, use the [Z tick] option in the [Axes] dialog box, which determines the number of tick marks on the third (vertical) axis, and thus the number of contours to be drawn.

Lines or shading
If you just click [Contour], you will get a plot with contour lines. If you click [Contour] and [Fill] both, you get a plot contoured with shading: fill patterns from white to black in even gradations determined by the Z height of the function at a given pixel.

**14.4
Contour plotting
with lines**

Here is a contour plot of a function.

- Select **Function** from the **Graph** menu
- Specify the function:
  Z = SIN(X)*COS(Y)
- Click [Contour]
- Click OK

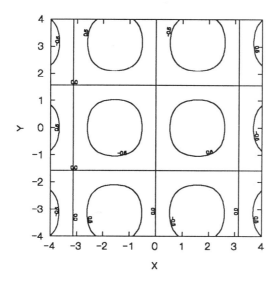

**14.5
Contour plotting
with shading**

You can produce shaded contour plots of functions and smoothed surfaces with the [Contour] and [Fill] options used together. Instead of lines, this method uses fill patterns from empty (white) to full (black) in even gradations that are determined by the height of the function at a given pixel (grid square).

Here is a filled contour plot of the function seen above in Example 14.4. We have added 10 tick marks and 60 cuts to provide finer definition.

- Select **Function** from the **Graph** menu
- Specify the function:
  Z = SIN(X)*COS(Y)
- Click [Contour]
- Click [Fill]
- Specify 60 [Cuts]
- Click [Hide]
- Click OK

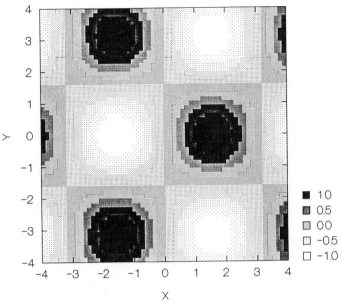

14.6
Contour plotting
with color

You can produce color contour plots of functions by using the [Color]
option in [Surface]. Instead of lines, this method uses fill patterns from
blue to red in even perceptual gradations that are determined by the
height of the function at a given grid square.

Here is how you would produce a color contour plot of the function.
Since this is a two-color manual, it wouldn't make much sense to try to
show the plot here.

- Select **Function** from the **Graph** menu
- Specify the function:
  Z = X^2 – Y^2
- Click [Contour]
- Click [Surface] and click [Color]
- Set [Z tick] to 10, [Z min] to 2, and [Z max] to 2 in the [Axes] dialog
  box
- Specify 60 [Cuts]
- Click [Hide]
- Click OK

Some graphics devices, including color displays that represent fewer
than 256 colors at the same time, cannot produce this plot. Pen plotters
give a fair approximation because SYGRAPH selects the pen with the
closest color appearance, provided the pens are ordered properly in the
carousel.

14.7
Contouring with
triangular
coordinates

You can contour with triangular coordinates. This feature allows you to analyze mixture experiments and examine four dimensional data in two dimensions. See Example 11.17 for an explanation of triangular coordinates. Diamond (1981) summarizes their use and references more advanced material.

Here is a triangular plot of a cubic response surface. This is the only place in SYGRAPH where you can enter three predictors in an equation. Notice that we set the parameters of the contouring axis with [Z min], [Z max], and [Z tick].

You can add grid lines to your triangular plot with [Axes]. All three grid choices produce the same result: a triangular grid. You can estimate trend surfaces with SYSTAT and use the coefficients with SYGRAPH to produce a publication quality plot.

- Select **Function** from the **Graph** menu
- Specify the function: U=V+W^2+X^3-2.5*V*W*X
- Click [Contour]
- Click [Triangle]
- Click [Axes] and set [Z tick] to 10, [Z min] to 0, and [Z max] to 1
- Click OK

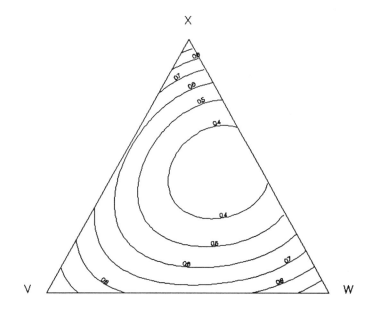

Filled function plots

Fill

You can fill a curve with one of the available fill patterns to highlight its shape. For example, you may want to plot a theoretical probability density with the area under the curve shaded. Or you may wish to reveal the trend across observed data by shading under a line graph. To do this, just click [Fill]. [Fill] fills the area bounded by the curve and a straight line connecting the two endpoints of the curve.

The exact area filled is easier to show in a graph than to explain further. Try the following functions (with recommended [Axes] limits) to see what we mean. You will see that if you want to fill areas under a curve and down to the bottom of the Y axis, you will have to have points at the end of the curve that touch the X axis.

Y = COS(X)
 [X min] 0, [X max] 6.28
 [Y min] –1,[Y max] 1

Y = X^2

Y = –X^2

**14.8
Filled function plot**

Here is a filled sinusoid plot. By limiting the X scale to the interval $(0, 2\pi)$, we get one phase of the function.

- Select **Function** from the **Graph** menu
- Specify the function:
  Y = SIN(X)
- Set [Axes] limits:
  [X min] 0, [X max] 6.28
  [Y min] –1, [Y max] 1
- Click [Fill]
- Click OK

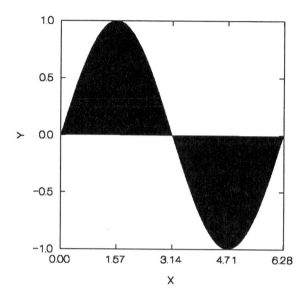

Polar function plots

Coord

Polar coordinates translate Cartesian coordinates into a circular arrangement. Each point is given by its distance (r) from the origin and the angle (θ) of the X-axis and the vector from the origin to the point. Polar coordinates may seem confusing in some contexts but they are handy for representing many mathematical equations and data profiles.

SYGRAPH automatically scales polar graphs as well as rectangular graphs. You may alter the scales with [Axes]. Use [Y min] and [Y max] for the r axis (distance) and [X min] and [X max] for the θ axis (angle). [Y min] is at the center of the circle by default, and [Y max] is at its periphery. [X min] and [X max] always coincide at the right edge (0 radians). [Z min] and [Z max] control Z height as with Cartesian coordinates.

If the data collide with the axes, you can eliminate the axes by clicking off the [Axes] choice in the [Axes] dialog box. If you choose one axis, you get only the circle, omitting the radial axis. If you choose two or more axes, you get both the r and θ axes.

Functions plot in polar coordinates the way you would expect. Just type the function, click [Coord], and choose [Polar].

14.9
Polar function
plot

The next figure plots a flower with 8 petals. You can alter the number of petals by changing 8 to some other number. One revolution of the circle is approximately 6.28 (2π) radians. We have eliminated all labels to keep the flower in its pure, natural state.

- Select **Function** from the **Graph** menu
- Specify the function: Y = SIN(8*X)
- Click [Axes]
  - Click off the [Axes] and [Scales] choices
  - Set the scale limits: [X min] 0, [X max] 6.28, [Y max] 1
  - Specify ' ' for [X label] and [Y label]
- Click [Coord] and choose [Polar]
- Click OK

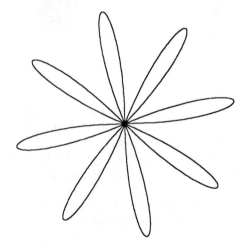

**Spherical
function plots**

Spherical coordinates work like polar coordinates, with an additional parameter for angle of elevation.

14.10
Spherical
function plot

This example illustrates a spherical function. We used [Fill] because [Hide] does not always work well with spherical functions. [Color] works nicely too. If you plot only one variable in the domain, then the equation will be drawn on the surface of a unit sphere.

- Select **Function** from the **Graph** menu
- Specify the function: Z=SIN(X) + COS(Y)
- Click [Coord] and choose [Spherical]
- Click [Fill]
- Click OK

Surface

[Surface] lets you control the type of surface drawn for 3-D function plots.

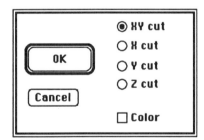

Choose whether you wish the cuts to run both ways like a mesh [XY cut], along X [X cut], along Y [Y cut], or along Z [Z cut].

Use the [Cuts] option in the **Function** dialog box (discussed above) to control the number of cuts in the surface.

Color

Click [Color] to produce a color-contoured surface. Instead of lines, this method uses fill patterns from blue to red in even perceptual gradations that are determined by the height of the surface at a given grid square.

15 Probability

Probability   15

Overview

A histogram is a rather poor method for determining the distribution of your data. A much more powerful visual display is to plot the values of a variable against the corresponding percentage points of a theoretical distribution (Gnanadesikan, 1977). Graphs like this are called probability plots or P-plots.

Specifically, let r be the rank order of an observation in a batch of n observations sorted from smallest to largest. Assume for the moment that we are looking at the normal Gaussian distribution. We estimate an expected normal value corresponding to that observation as the standard normal value corresponding to the probability $(r-.5)/n$. We plot this value on the vertical axis against the value of the observation on the horizontal axis. If the data are from a normal distribution, the plotted values will lie on a straight line. For further information, consult Chambers, Cleveland, Kleiner, and Tukey (1983).

Prob'y offers seven distributions against which you may plot your variable.

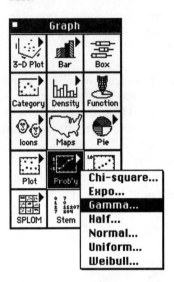

To select a distribution, press and hold the mouse button on **Prob'y**. A submenu pops up offering **Chi-square...**, **Expo...**, **Gamma...**, **Half...**, **Normal...**, **Uniform...**, and **Weibull...** Select the item you want and release the button.

All the items have the same dialog boxes and work the same way, except **Chi-square...** has an option for degrees of freedom ([DF]) and **Gamma...** has an option for specifying a [Shape] parameter.

- Select **Prob'y** from the **Graph** menu
- Select a variable to be analyzed
- Click OK

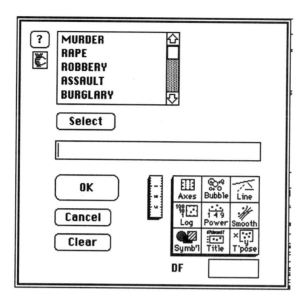

**Common
options**

See the **Common options** chapter for information about [Axes], [Line], [Log], [Power], [Symb'l], [Title], [T'pose]. The [Bubble] and [Smooth] options are discussed below.

Normal...

Normal... produces a normal probability plot.

15.1
Normal
probability plot

Here is a plot of PERSON (person crimes per 100,000) against a standard normal variable.

- Select **Prob'y/Normal...** from the **Graph** menu
- Select a variable: PERSON
- Click OK

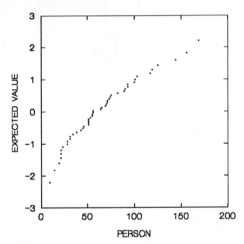

15.2
Normal random
data

Here is another example. We used the SYSTAT normal random number generator ZRN to produce 500 normal random numbers. You can try some other random number seeds.

- Type Z in the first cell of the worksheet
- Select **Fill worksheet...** from the **Data** menu
- Specify number of cases to be filled: 500
- Click OK

- Select **Math...** from the **Data** menu
- Fill in the statement: Let Z = ZRN
- Click OK

- Select **Prob'y/Normal...** from the **Graph** menu
- Select a variable: Z
- Click OK

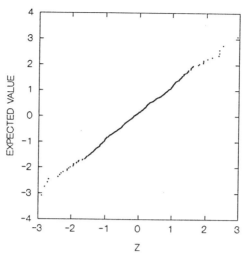

Chi-square... A chi-square variable is the sum of the squares of one or more normal variables. You can plot your data against the quantiles of a chi-square distribution with **Chi-square...** You must specify the degrees of freedom.

Where can we get chi-square data to fool around with? Typically, sums of squares in analysis of variance and Mahalanobis squared distances in multivariate analysis are chi-square distributed when the normality assumptions are appropriate (see, for example, Gnanadesikan, 1977 or Winer, 1971). If you have a 2 by 2 by 2 by 2... analysis of variance, for example, the sums of squares for all effects are single degree of freedom chi-square variables. Probability plots show you which effects stand out.

**15.3
Chi-square
probability plot**

The following example plots Mahalanobis distances of the states from the centroid of all states on PERSON (person crimes) and PROPERTY (property crimes). We computed these distances in SYSTAT:

- Select **MGLH/General linear model...** from the **Stats** menu
- Select the [Dependent] variables: PERSON, PROPERTY
- Click [Indep'dent] to get a CONSTANT term
- Click OK

- Select **MGLH/Test...** from the **Stats** menu
- Click [Save scores and results]
- Click OK

The Mahalanobis distances are saved under the name DISTANCE in the file you save. To plot the distances as 2 degrees-of-freedom chi-square variables, we need to square them. The simplest way to do this is to use the [Power] option with exponent 2 when we graph them. ([Power] is discussed in the **Common options** chapter.) The distances have two degrees of freedom because they are distances squared and summed over two variables (PERSON and PROPERTY).

The x axis scale values are ugly because we used a square transformation and the program could not find evenly spaced round numbers for square roots on the transformed scale. If you really need round numbers, square DISTANCE in DATA before running this plot. The spread of the points will look a bit different, but the overall shape of the data curve will be the same.

- Select **Prob'y/Chi-square...** from the **Graph** menu
- Select a variable: DISTANCE
- Specify 2 degrees of freedom
- Click [Power] and specify 2 for the exponent
- Choose [Linear] smoothing to overlay a linear regression
- Click OK

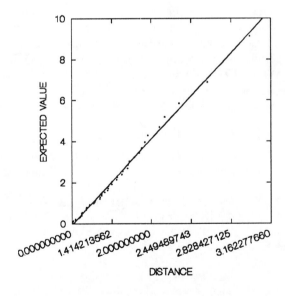

Exponential...   You can plot your data against an exponential distribution with **Expo...** The exponential distribution function is:

$$f(y) = 1 - e^{\left(-\frac{y}{s}\right)}$$

where *s* is a spread parameter. In the transposed probability plot, the slope of the line through the plotted points is an estimate of *s*.

**15.4
Exponential
probability plot**

Here are some data from an unpublished memo by Taylor cited in Maltz (1984) and elsewhere. The data (in the file PAROLE) record the number of Illinois parolees observed to have failed conditions of their parole each month after release. An additional 149 parolees were observed to have failed after 22 months, but we will not graph the data beyond this point.

MONTH	COUNT
.5	29
1	15
2	9
3	8
4	9
5	6
6	5
7	5
8	3
9	2
10	2
11	3
12	3
13	0
14	0
15	2
16	2
17	2
18	0
19	0
20	0
21	0
22	3

Here is an exponential probability plot of these data. Notice that we have weighted the data to cover duplicate values. We have also used the [T'pose] and linear smoothing options. The model appears to fit poorly in the tails, especially the lower tail.

- Select **Weight...** from the **Data** menu
- Select a variable: COUNT
- Click OK

- Select **Prob'y/Expo...** from the **Graph** menu
- Select a variable: MONTH
- Choose [Linear] smoothing
- Click [T'pose]
- Click OK

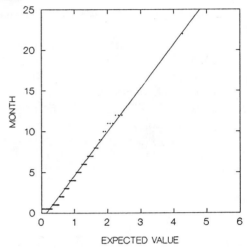

Gamma...

A gamma distribution is a transformed chi-square with real degrees of freedom. You can plot your data against the quantiles of a gamma distribution with **Gamma...** You must specify a shape parameter. Chambers, Cleveland, Kleiner, and Tukey (1983) discuss applications of gamma probability plots in univariate models and Gnanadesikan (1977) shows how to use them for analyzing multivariate data.

**15.5
Gamma
probability plot**

Here is an example. We have plotted the recidivism data used in Example 15.4 ("Exponential probability plot") against a gamma distribution with shape parameter equal to .5. The fit to these data is better than those for the other distributions in this chapter.

- Select **Weight...** from the **Data** menu
- Select a variable: COUNT
- Click OK

- Select **Prob'y/Gamma...** from the **Graph** menu
- Select a variable: MONTH
- Specify the shape parameter: .8
- Choose [Linear] smoothing
- Click [T'pose]
- Click OK

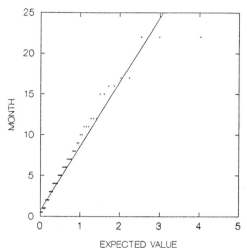

Half-normal... A half-normal distribution is the absolute value of a normal distribution (or the square root of a chi-square with one degree of freedom). You can plot your data against the quantiles of a half-normal distribution with **Half...**

15.6
Half-normal
probability plot

Here is an example. POPDEN looks like half a normal distribution if you do a stem-and-leaf diagram (see the **Stem** chapter). The half-normal probability plot shows it to be otherwise, however, since the points do not plot in a straight line.

- Select **Prob'y/Half...** from the **Graph** menu
- Select a variable: POPDEN
- Click OK

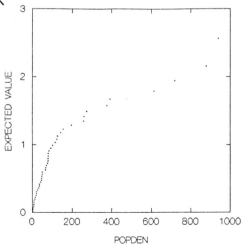

Uniform...

Uniform... produces a uniform probability plot. The uniform distribution has two parameters:

$$f(y) = \frac{y - m}{s}$$

where *m* is a location and *s* is a spread parameter. If you use [T'pose], the slope of the line fitting the points estimates spread, and the intercept estimates location.

15.7
Uniform
probability plot

Here is an example. We used the uniform random number generator in SYSTAT to produce 500 uniform random numbers:

- Select **Fill worksheet...** from the **Data** menu
- Specify number of cases to be filled: 500
- Click OK

- Select **Math...** from the **Data** menu
- Fill in the statement: Let X = URN
- Click OK

- Select **Prob'y/Uniform...** from the **Graph** menu
- Select a variable: X
- Click OK

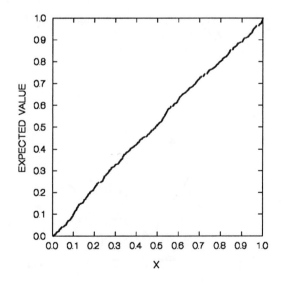

© 1989, SYSTAT, Inc.

Weibull...

You can plot your data against a Weibull distribution with **Weibull...**
The Weibull is a powered exponential distribution:

$$f(y) = 1 - e^{\left(-\frac{y}{s}\right)^t}$$

where s is a spread and t is a power (or shape) parameter. In the probability plot, the slope of the line through the plotted points is an estimate of the inverse of t, and the intercept is an estimate of the log of s. Both axes in the plot are on a natural log scale.

15.8
Weibull
probability plot

Here is a Weibull distribution probability plot of the recidivism data used in the [Exponential] option above in this chapter. Notice that we have weighted the data to cover duplicate values. We have also used the [T'pose] and linear smoothing options (see above in this chapter).

When you read the values, keep in mind that the probability plot for the Weibull distribution transforms both axes with a natural logarithm to achieve linearity. Notice, for example, that the probability plot for the Weibull distribution transforms both axes with a natural logarithm to achieve linearity. If you publish this plot, you should relabel the axes using the [X label] and [Y label] options in the [Axes] dialog box.

- Select **Weight...** from the **Data** menu
- Select a weight variable: COUNT
- Click OK

- Select **Prob'y/Weibull...** from the **Graph** menu
- Select a variable: MONTH
- Choose [Linear] smoothing
- Click [T'pose]
- Specify 'Log of Recidivism Month' for [X label] and
  'Log Weibull Quantiles' for [Y label] in the [Axes] dialog box
- Click OK

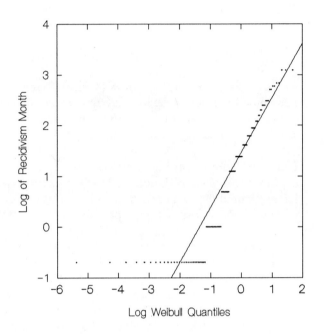

Bubble symbols

You can use the values of a variable in your file to control the size of plotting symbols. Suppose you have two variables and you want to see whether the marginal distribution of one of them is related in some way to the marginal distribution of the other.

- Click [Bubble]
- Specify a variable
- Click OK

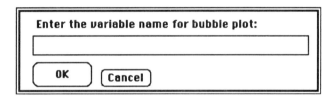

One caution. The size of the plotting symbols is taken directly from the values in your file. There is no upper or lower limit. If the variable you specify for [Bubble] has a value as .001 or a negative value, the point will be invisible. If the variable has a value as large as 100, the symbol will fill your entire plot. Try a range between 0 and 10. If your sizing variable does not lie in this range, you should rescale it. Finally, you should usually use empty symbols with this type of plot, since filled symbols can occlude each other and make the plot difficult to interpret.

**15.9
Probability plot
with bubbles**

Here is an example. First, we make a new variable WIN for the US file.

- Select **Math...** from the **Data** menu
- Fill in the statement: Let WIN = WINTER/25
- Click OK

This brings the values into the range 0 to 3. Now, WIN can serve as a bubble-sizing variable. Normally, we would take the square root of WINTER, because we pay more attention to area than diameter. In this case, however, we want to accentuate the effect.

Here is a normal probability plot of SUMMER. The upside-down U shape of the plot (with a central dip) indicates short tails. Notice that the larger symbols are near both tails, indicating that the states with unusually warm winters have summers that do not follow the same distribution as the remaining states.

- Select **Prob'y/Normal...** from the **Graph** menu
- Select a variable: SUMMER
- Specify WIN for [Bubble]
- Choose the open circle for [Symb'l]
- Click OK

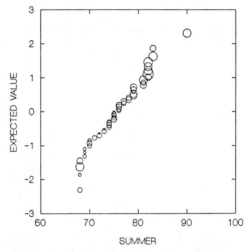

Smoothing

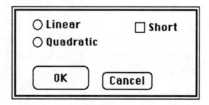

The [Smooth] option lets you overlay a linear regression or a quadratic curve on your probability plot.

- Click [Smooth]
- Choose [Linear] or [Quadratic] smoothing
- Click OK

Click [Short] to limit the smoothing to the domain of the data. (This is illustrated in Example 15.12.)

15.10
Linear regression

You can fit a linear regression to your probability plot with [Linear]. Regression fits a function to data such that the value predicted by the function at each observed value of X comes as close as possible to the observed value of Y at the same value of X. Ordinary linear regression uses a straight line for the function and makes the squared discrepancies between predicted and observed Y values as small as possible. The equation for this function looks like this:

$$Y = a + bX$$

where a is a constant term and b is a slope coefficient.

The slope and intercept provide rough estimates of the spread and location parameters in most of the distributions in **Prob'y**, provided you transpose your plot by clicking the [T'pose] option. Keep in mind, however, that this information is useful only if the regression line passes evenly through the points, with little bending of the points on one or the other side of the line. We have used linear smoothing in most of the plots in this chapter because it reveals how ill-fitting many of the plots are.

Here is the linear regression smoothing of the probability plot of WINTER (average winter temperatures). The line is a reasonable fit for a sample this size.

- Select **Prob'y/Normal...** from the **Graph** menu
- Select a variable: WINTER
- Choose [Linear] smoothing
- Click [T'pose]
- Click OK

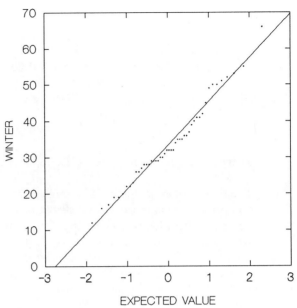

15.11
Quadratic
smoothing

You can fit a quadratic regression curve to your data with [Quadratic].
This fits the following type of equation to the data:

$$Y = a + bX + cX^2$$

where a is a constant and b and c are slope coefficients.

You might want to use this option to enhance visually any bendings in
your probability plot. The more curved the fit, the more poorly fit is the
distribution.

Here is the quadratic regression of the same data (WINTER) used in
Example 15.10 for linear smoothing.

- Select **Prob'y/Normal...** from the **Graph** menu
- Select a variable: WINTER
- Choose [Quadratic] smoothing
- Click [T'pose]
- Click OK

       © 1989, SYSTAT, Inc.

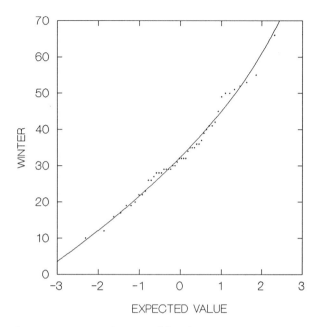

15.12 Shortening the domain of smoothing

Sometimes you can get into trouble when smoothing by extrapolating beyond the range of your data. Linear and quadratic smoothing for probability plots yield curves that extend from the left to the right edges of the plotting frame. If you wish to limit the domain of the smooth to the extreme values of the data, click [Short].

Here are the instructions for a plot with a quadratic smooth limited to the range of the data by the [Short] option.

- Select **Prob'y/Normal...** from the **Graph** menu
- Select a variable: WINTER
- Choose [Quadratic] smoothing and click [Short]
- Click [T'pose]
- Click OK

16   Quantile

Quantile

16

Overview **Quantile** produces quantile plots, or Q plots (Gnanadesikan, 1977). We have seen how probability plots compare a sample to a theoretical probability distribution. Sometimes we want to compare a sample to its own quantiles (a one-sample plot) or two samples to each other. The quantile of a sample is the data point corresponding to a given fraction of the data.

Quantile produces quantile plots.

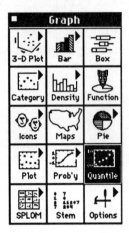

- Select **Quantile** from the **Graph** menu
- Select one variable from the left selection list for a one-sample plot; or, for a two-sample plot, select a Y variable from the left list and an X variable from the right list
- Click OK

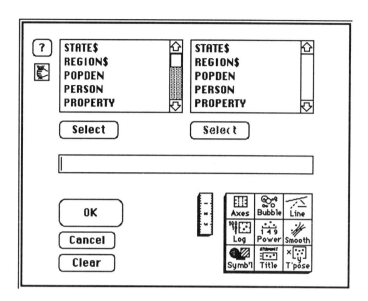

Common options

See the **Common options** chapter for information on [Axes], [Line], [Log], [Power], [Symb'l], [Title], and [T'pose]. Other options, [Bubble] and [Smooth] are discussed below.

Types of plots

One-sample plots

One sample plots compare one sample (one variable) to its own quantiles. The quantile of a sample is the data point that corresponds to a given fraction of the data.

A single sample quantile plot looks like a cumulative sample distribution function. A sample from a normal distribution, for example, should plot in an S or "ogive" shape. A sample from a uniform distribution should plot roughly as a straight line. Samples from skewed distributions should plot as asymmetric functions.

**16.1
Quantile plot**

The next figure shows a Q plot for INCOME (per-capita income) from the US dataset. The plot is slightly S-shaped, indicating lumpiness in the middle and two tails.

- Select **Quantile** from the **Graph** menu
- Select one variable from the selection list at the left: INCOME
- Click OK

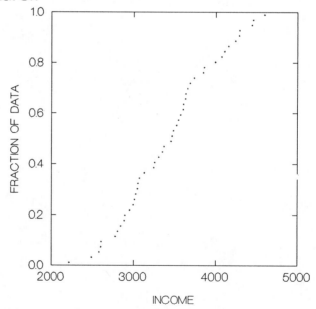

Two-sample plots

A two-sample quantile plot relates two sample distributions. It should look approximately like a straight line if the two samples are from the same distribution. Otherwise, the quantile plot can reveal the area of the distribution where the samples differ most. These are sometimes called Q-Q plots.

16.2
Q-Q plot

Here is a Q-Q plot of PERSON (person crimes) against PROPERTY (property crimes) from the US dataset.

- Select **Quantile** from the **Graph** menu
- Select the Y variable from the list on the left: PERSON
- Select the X variable from the list on the right: PROPERTY
- Click OK

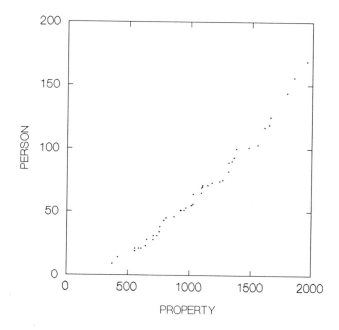

Bubble symbols

You can use the values of a variable in your file to control the size of plotting symbols. See Example 15.9 in the **Probability** chapter for an example of bubbles in probability plots.

- Click [Bubble]
- Specify a variable
- Click OK

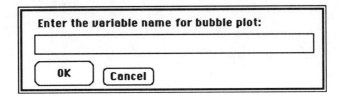

One caution. The size of the plotting symbols is taken directly from the values in your file. There is no upper or lower limit. If the variable you specify for [Bubble] has a value as .001 or a negative value, the point will be invisible. If the variable has a value as large as 100, the symbol will fill your entire plot. Try a range between 0 and 10. If your sizing variable does not lie in this range, you should rescale it. Finally, you should usually use empty symbols with this type of plot, since filled symbols can occlude each other and make the plot difficult to interpret.

16.3
Bubble quantile
plot

Here is an example for quantile plots. First, make a new variable DEN for the US file:

- Select **Math...** from the **Data** menu
- Fill in the statement: Let DEN = 4*SQR(POPDEN/1000)
- Click OK

This brings the values of DEN to between 0 and 4 because 1000 is the maximum value of POPDEN in the file. Now, DEN can serve as a bubble variable.

Here is a quantile plot of SUMMER (average summer temperatures). The states with the highest population densities are concentrated at middle values of the temperature distribution.

- Select **Quantile** from the **Graph** menu
- Select a variable: SUMMER
- Specify DEN for [Bubble]
- Choose open circles for [Symb'l]
- Click OK

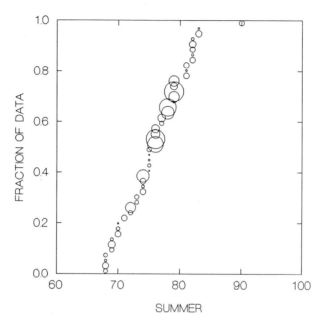

Smoothing

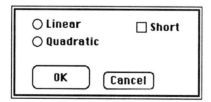

The [Smooth] option lets you overlay a linear regression or a quadratic curve on your probability plot.

- Click [Smooth]
- Choose [Linear] or [Quadratic] smoothing
- Click OK

○ **Linear**   □ **Short**
○ **Quadratic**

OK   (Cancel)

Click [Short] to limit the smoothing to the domain of the data. (This is illustrated in Example 15.12.)

Options

16.4
Linear regression

You can fit a linear regression to your quantile plot with the [Linear] option. Regression fits a function to data such that the value predicted by the function at each observed value of X is as close as possible to the observed value of Y at the same value of X. Ordinary linear regression uses a straight line for the function and makes the squared discrepancies between predicted and observed Y values as small as possible. The equation for this function looks like this:

$$Y = a + bX$$

where a is a constant term and b is a slope coefficient.

Here is the linear regression smoothing of the quantile plot of PERSON (person crimes). Notice how the line accentuates the S-shape of the curve, telling us the distribution is not uniform. In a quantile-quantile plot, deviations of the curve from a straight line tells us that the distributions have a different shape.

- Select **Quantile** from the **Graph** menu
- Select a variable: PERSON
- Choose [Linear] smoothing
- Click OK

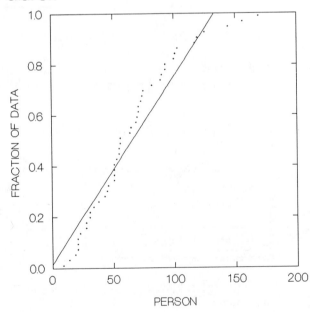

16.5
Quadratic
smoothing

You can fit a quadratic regression curve to your data with the
[Quadratic] option. This fits the following type of equation to the data:

$$Y = a + bX + cX^2$$

where *a* is a constant and *b* and *c* are slope coefficients.

You might want to use this option to enhance visually any bendings in
your quantile plot.

Here is the quadratic regression of the same data (PERSON) used in
Example 16.4 for linear smoothing.

- Select **Quantile** from the **Graph** menu
- Select a variable: PERSON
- Choose [Quadratic] smoothing
- Click OK

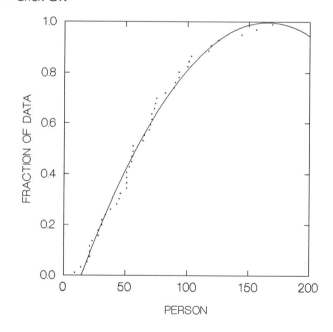

17 Icon

Icon   17

Overview

Icons are pictures for displaying multivariate data (Everitt, 1978
Cleveland, 1985). Given a dataset containing measurements of n cases
on p variables, you plot n icons (one for each case) with p different features in each icon.

SYGRAPH offers a variety of icons for representing multivariate data:
cartoon faces, Fourier blobs, stars, histograms, rectangles, and others.
You should try several of these on the same data to see how they work.
You should also compare them to automated techniques such as discriminant analysis and clustering. For some data you will be able to locate clusters that elude automated methods because your eye can perceive nonlinear, disjunctive relationships. Icons cannot replace formal
statistical models, but they are indispensable exploratory tools.

Unlike most graphs in SYGRAPH, icons are not designed to communicate absolute numerical information. They are intended, instead, for recognizing clusters of similar objects. Icons are useful for sorting or organizing objects that differ in many respects.

Some theorists find the use of icons subjective and ad hoc. They have ridiculed, for example, Chernoff's faces as being facetious and cartoon-like. In such conclusions they have ignored cognitive science research on multi-attribute visual processing, which shows that people can accurately categorize multivariate data based on appropriate visual cues (Garner, 1974 Spohr and Lehmkuhle, 1982).

Variable scales

For all icon methods, it is important to have all variables on common or comparable scales. Otherwise, individual features in each icon will dominate the whole picture, distorting comparisons. The US file variables SUMMER and WINTER, for example, are both measured in degrees Fahrenheit, so they do not need rescaling when used together. For other variables, however, you probably want to click the [Standardize] option to standardize values on each variable to z scores before drawing icons.

Ordering the variables

The shape of icons depends on the mapping of variables to icon features. For all SYGRAPH icons, this mapping is done in the order you select variables. With Chernoff's faces, for example, the first variable is assigned to mouth curvature, the second to angle of brow, and so on.

Some have criticized icons for the arbitrariness of this assignment. There are ways to circumvent this problem, however. Research in cognitive processing (e.g. Garner and Felfoldy, 1970) has shown that integrated displays are more effective for communicating multidimensional information. Correlated information is best presented within integrated features, rather than across disparate features. One way to accomplish this is to order the variables by some seriation method before selecting them for **Icon**.

For example, use a cluster analysis program which orders tree branches (e.g. **Cluster** in the **Stats** menu of SYSTAT) and then use the ordering for **Icon**. Alternatively, order the variables according to the loadings on the first principal component of the correlation matrix of variables (**Factor** from the **Stats** menu). Even better, use the one dimensional multidimensional scaling (**MDS** from the **Stats** menu) of this matrix. This way, similar features of faces, blobs, stars, etc. will be assigned to correlated variables. Freni-Titulaer and Louv (1984) have demonstrated that cluster-ordered icons result in fewer judgment errors than randomly ordered icons.

In the examples in this chapter, we have determined order from the multidimensional scaling seriation of the correlation matrix of the variables.

Icon offers eight types of icons: Fourier blobs, Chernoff faces, histograms, profiles, rectangles, stars, arrows (vectors), and vanes (weathervanes).

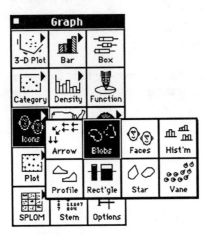

To use **Icon**, press and hold the mouse button on **Icon**. A submenu pops up offering **Arrow**, **Blobs**, **Faces**, **Hist'm**, **Profile**, **Rect'gle**, **Star**, and **Vane**. Select the item you want and release the mouse button.

All the items work the same and offer similar dialog boxes.

- Select **Icon** from the **Graph** menu
- Select variables, in order
- Click OK

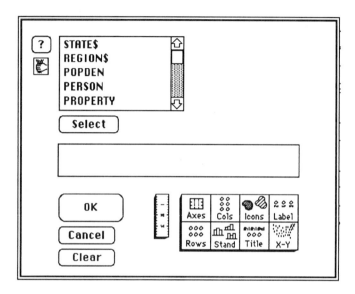

Common options

See the **Common options** chapter for information on [Axes], and [Title]. The [Icons] option collects the relevant features of [Fill], [Color], and [Size] into a single dialog box. You should read those sections in the **Common options** chapter to learn how to use the [Icons] option. [Label] works just like the [Label symbols with variable] option of the [Symbol] dialog box. [Symbol] is also discussed in the **Common options** chapter. [Cols], [Rows], [Stand], and [X-Y] are described in the "Options" section below.

Ordering the icons

Sometimes you may wish to publish a matrix of icons clustered according to similarity. One way to do this is to cluster analyze a dataset and reorder the cases according to a seriation based on cluster membership. Then, when you use **Icon,** the icons will be arranged in clustered order. Another way to do this is to order the icons yourself and rearrange the cases in a file according to your visual ordering:

- Print a plot and label each icon with a number
- Clip out each icon with scissors
- Sort them into piles of similar icons
- Enter the sequence of numbers in a new variable of the data file
- Sort the file by that variable
- Plot the icons again (in sorted order) with their actual labels

This procedure avoids the bias of knowing the categories in advance.

Fourier blobs

Blobs

Blobs produces Fourier blobs. Fourier blobs are polar coordinate Fourier waveforms. Fourier functions have the following form:

$$f(t) = \frac{y_1}{\sqrt{2}} + y_2\sin(t) + y_3\cos(t) + y_4\sin(2t) + y_5\cos(2t) + \ldots$$

where y is a p–dimensional variate and t varies from -3.14 to 3.14 (π radians on either side of zero). The result of this transformation is a set of waveforms made up of sine and cosine components. Each waveform corresponds to one case in the dataset. Cases that have similar values across all variables have comparable waveforms. Cases with different patterns of variation have contrasting waveforms. When these waveforms are transformed into polar coordinates, they look like blobs or amoebae. The information contained in Fourier blobs is therefore identical to that of the Andrews' Fourier plot (see **Fourier** in the **Plot** chapter). The advantage of blobs is that they do not overlap and they can be used as plotting symbols in a dimensional plot.

How do you interpret these blobs? What are the variable values? Keep in mind what we mentioned at the beginning of this chapter. The point of the icon is not to translate back to numerical values. The Fourier transformation is too complex for us to compute those values mentally. Instead, look for similar blobs and then go back to the raw data to examine actual values with other types of graphs.

The shape of the blobs depends on the order you select the variables. Variables selected earlier are weighted with lower frequency components in the above equation and later ones with higher frequency.

17.1
Blob plot

This example shows blobs of the variables in the US file. Compare this result to the other icon representations in this chapter. We label the blobs with state names and click [Stand] to standardize the variables. (You almost always want to standardize variables for every icon type.) To keep things clear on this small page, let's plot only the New England states.

- Select **Select Cases...** from the **Data** menu
- Fill in the statement: Select REGION$='New England'
- Click OK

- Select **Icons/Blob** from the **Graph** menu
- Select variables, in order: INCOME, POPDEN, PROPERTY, PERSON, RAIN, WINTER, SUMMER
- Click [Stand]
- Specify STATE$ for [Label]
- Click OK

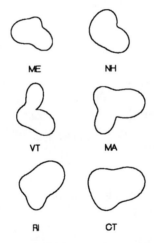

Chernoff's faces

Don't laugh. Faces are one of the most effective graphical icons for visually clustering multivariate data, particularly for long term memory processing. Chernoff (1973) introduced the idea of using a cartoon face to represent many variables. Wang (1978) contains a number of articles on applications of faces to multivariate data. Wilkinson (1982) showed that faces can be more effective than many other icons for similarity comparisons.

Reviewers have criticized the faces for their arbitrary assignment of variables to features on the face. Chernoff and Rizvi (1975) and Jacob (1983) address this problem. See the [Theory] section in this chapter for ways to make a rational assignment to features. Here is the order of features assigned to the variables by **Icon/Faces**:

1 Curvature of mouth
2 Angle of brow
3 Width of nose
4 Length of nose
5 Length of mouth
6 Height of center of mouth
7 Separation of eyes
8 Height of center of eyes
9 Slant of eyes
10 Eccentricity of eyes
11 Half-length of eyes
12 Position of pupils
13 Height of eyebrow
14 Length of brow
15 Height of face
16 Eccentricity of upper ellipse of face
17 Eccentricity of lower ellipse of face
18 Ear level
19 Radius of ear
20 Hair length

If you select variables A, B, C, and D in that order, for example, A, B, C, and D are assigned to the first four features in the list. You may select variables more than once to make multiple assignments (e.g. A, A, B, C), but we would do this only for correlated features such as mouth curvature and brow tilt.

You can exclude features by typing a period in the variable selection box. For example, this selection

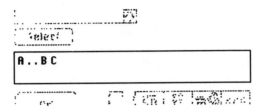

assigns A to curvature of mouth, skips brow angle and nose width, assigns B to length of nose, and assigns C to length of mouth.

If you select more than 20 variables, SYGRAPH reports an error instead of plotting.

**17.2
Chernoff plot**

This example shows faces of the 7 variables in our US file. Notice the features not assigned to variables (such as shape of face) are constant.

- Select **Select Cases...** from the **Data** menu
- Fill in the statement: Select REGION$='New England'
- Click OK

- Select **Icons/Faces** from the **Graph** menu
- Select variables: INCOME, POPDEN, PROPERTY, PERSON, RAIN, WINTER, SUMMER
- Click [Stand]
- Specify STATE$ for [Label]
- Click OK

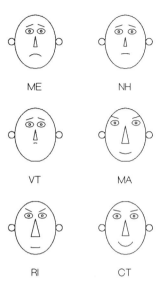

Histogram icons

Hist'm

The histogram icon assigns one histogram bar from left to right to each variable you choose in order in the **Icon** dialog box. The bars are scaled so that the largest value in the data is the tallest bar and the smallest value is the shortest (i.e. zero height). Freni-Titulaer and Louv (1984) show examples of this icon.

It helps to order the variables according to a clustering or some other seriation. We have used the multidimensional scaling seriation of the variables to determine their order for **Icon**.

As with the other icons, you should make sure that the variables are on similar scales. Otherwise, one bar will be tall in all the icons and the rest will be barely visible. In the next figure, we click [Stand] to standardize the variables on a common scale within the New England region before plotting. You can compare the results to blobs, faces, and the other icons in this chapter.

17.3
Histogram icon
plot

Again, the New England data.

- Select **Select** from the **Data** menu
- Fill in the statement: Select REGION$='New England'
- Click OK

- Select **Icon/Hist'm** from the **Graph** menu
- Select variables: INCOME, POPDEN, PROPERTY, PERSON, RAIN, WINTER, SUMMER
- Click [Stand]
- Specify STATE$ for [Label]
- Click OK

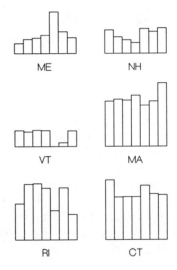

Profile icons

Chambers, Cleveland, Kleiner, and Tukey (1983) discuss profile icons. They are identical to histogram icons except the tops of the bars are connected by lines and the bars are not drawn. Here are Rhode Island's histogram and profile icons:

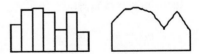

Stars (discussed next) are profile icons drawn in polar coordinates. To our knowledge, there is no research showing which of the three is better.

Profile assigns one profile point to each variable in the order that you select them. Profiles can be improved by drawing them in a rational order. As with the other icons in this chapter, we have used the seriation from a multidimensional scaling of the variables to determine the order of entering the variables.

As with the other icons, you should make sure that the variables are on similar scales. Otherwise, one point will be high in all the icons and the rest will be barely visible.

17.4
Profile icon plot

In this example, we click [Stand] to standardize the variables on a common scale. You can compare the results to blobs, faces, and the other icons in this chapter.

- Select **Select Cases...** from the **Data** menu
- Fill in the statement: Select REGION$='New England'
- Click OK

- Select **Icons/Profile** from the **Graph** menu
- Select variables: INCOME, POPDEN, PROPERTY, PERSON, RAIN, WINTER, SUMMER
- Click [Stand]
- Specify STATE$ for [Label]
- Click OK

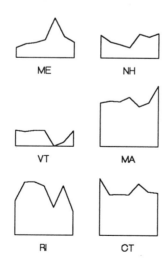

Star plots

Star

Star icons are profile icons in polar coordinates. Imagine that you have 12 variables, for example. For each case, draw a clock with 12 hands, one pointing to each hour, where the length of each hand is determined by the value of the variable. Next, draw a line connecting the tips of each hand. Finally, erase the clock.

Here are Rhode Island's profile and star icons:

[Star] can represent up to 200 variables (hands), but you usually don't want to do more than a few.

17.5
Star icon plot

As with the other icons, it is helpful to order the variables around the circle (clock) so that correlated variables are near each other. We did this by using the multidimensional scaling seriation of our US variables, which we described in the introduction to this chapter.

- Select **Select Cases...** from the **Data** menu
- Fill in the statement: Select REGION$='New England'
- Click OK

- Select **Icons/Star** from the **Graph** menu
- Select variables: INCOME, POPDEN, PROPERTY, PERSON, RAIN, WINTER, SUMMER
- Click [Stand]
- Specify STATE$ for [Label]
- Click OK

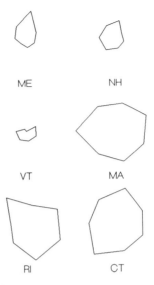

Framed rectangle icons

Cleveland and McGill (1984) discussed an icon to represent a single variable. Framed rectangles are like little thermometers that show the "temperature" of a single variable for each case.

Since [Rect] can be used to represent only one variable, it is the most useful icon for representing an extra variable on a map or scatterplot in combination with X and Y (see below in this chapter).

You can also represent two variables with [Rect]. Following Dunn (1987), we have made it possible to vary the width of each rectangle (thickness of each thermometer) with a second variable.

As Dunn points out, counts or sample sizes (or their square roots) are particularly appropriate as width variables. SYGRAPH requires that the width variable be between 0 and 1; values 1 or larger produce maximum width rectangles.

**17.6
Rectangle icon
plot**

This example uses the data we used in the **Category** chapter.

REGION$	COUNT	INCOME
New England	6	3730.2
Mid Atlantic	3	4114.0
Great Lakes	5	3867.2
Plains	7	3396.9
Southeast	8	3272.6
South	8	2753.8
Mountain	8	3345.5
Pacific	3	3903.7

To represent COUNT with areas instead of widths, make a WIDTH variable:

- Select **Math...** from the **Data** menu
- Fill in the statement: Let WIDTH = SQR(COUNT/8)
- Click OK

We select the "temperature" variable first and the width second.

- Select **Icons/Rect'gle** from the **Graph** menu
- Select the variables, in order: INCOME, WIDTH
- Specify REGION$ for [Label]
- Click OK

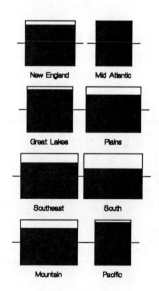

　　　　　　　　　　　　　　　　　© 1989, SYSTAT, Inc.

Arrow plots

Arrow

Arrow icons are for representing two variables only. The first variable is assigned to the length of the arrow and the second to its direction (from 0 to 360 degrees). Zero and 360 degrees are vertical orientations for arrows. For length, the minimum value of the data is set to zero length and the maximum value to a scaled length. The arrowhead is not rescaled. For direction, minimum and maximum values in the data are scaled between 0 and 360 degrees.

You can regulate the scale of the icon variables with the [Z min] and [Z max] settings. If you specify them, these limits are used to set the minimum and maximum values for both length and direction. First, the data are rescaled to new values:

$$Z = \frac{X - ZMIN}{ZMAX - ZMIN}$$

(ZMIN and ZMAX represent the values you specify for [Z min] and [Z max].) For length, values less than or equal to zero produce zero length arrows. Unit length corresponds approximately to 10 percent of the display width. For direction, zero and unit direction correspond to a vertical orientation, as do any integers beyond one, since a unit is a complete rotation of 360 degrees. Be careful when you use the absolute scaling option with [Z min] and [Z max]. Length has no upper limit, so you can produce icons that overflow your plotting window.

Arrow plots are often used to show fluid flow over a surface. You can overlay them on a scatterplot or function plot, for example, with the [X–Y] option.

17.7
Arrow plot

The following example shows an arrow plot for the ROTATE data used to illustrate bivariate regression in the SYSTAT manual. The data are reaction times to recognize an object when rotated by various degrees. We have standardized both variables to similar scales.

- Select **Icon/Arrow** from the **Graph** menu
- Select variables: RT, ANGLE
- Click [Stand]
- Click OK

Vane plots

Vane icons look like weathervanes (Bruntz *et al.*, 1974; see also Gnanadesikan, 1977). They are used to represent three variables. The first determines the radius of the central circle. The second variable determines the length of the vane, and the third, its direction. See the **Arrow** icon directly above for information concerning scaling of the length and direction of the vector.

17.8
Weathervane
plot

Here is an example, which shows rainfall as the size of the circles, and summer and winter temperatures as the length and direction of the vectors, respectively. The data have not been standardized.

- Select **Icon/Vane** from the **Graph** menu
- Select variables: RAIN, SUMMER, WINTER
- Click OK
- Specify LABLON for [X] and LABLAT for [Y] with [X-Y]

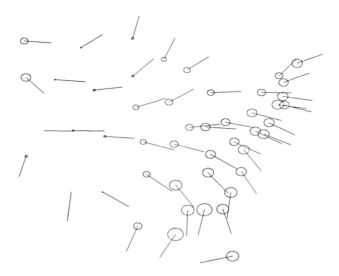

Notice that rainfall is concentrated on the coasts. Summer temperatures do not vary substantially (the lengths of the lines are similar). Average winter temperatures, on the other hand, show substantial variation.

Options

Standardizing scales

All the icons work best when the variables are on common scales. For example, all variables should be measured in inches, centimeters, minutes, degrees, etc.. If they are not, then some features of the icons will dominate others because some numbers are large relative to the others.

If variables are on different scales, then you can standardize them first to z scores by subtracting out the sample means and then dividing by the sample standard deviations. You do this by clicking [Stand].

17.9 Unstandardized icons

Since we have clicked [Stand] for every other example, let's try one without. Notice how INCOME dominates the histograms so that other variation is undetectable. Compare this result to the same plot standardized in Example 17.3.

- Select **Select Cases...** from the **Data** menu
- Fill in the statement: Select REGION$='New England'
- Click OK

- Select **Icons/Hist'm** from the **Graph** menu
- Select variables: INCOME, POPDEN, PROPERTY, PERSON, RAIN, WINTER, SUMMER
- Specify STATE$ for [Label]
- Click OK

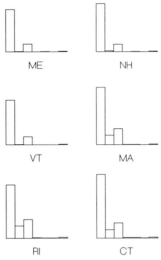

Controlling the number of columns and rows

As you have seen in the previous figures, SYGRAPH determines the number of rows and columns for displaying your icons. If you want a different shaped matrix or rectangle of icons, use the [Cols] and [Rows] options. If you set [Cols], SYGRAPH draws as many rows as necessary to cover all your cases, or vice versa. If you set [Rows=*r*] and [Cols=*c*,] SYGRAPH draws only the first *rc* icons.

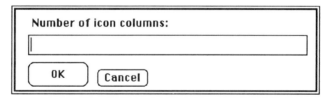

- Click [Cols] or [Rows]
- Specify the number of columns or rows
- Click OK

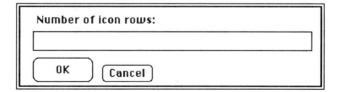

17.10
Four column star plot

Here is a star plot of the US variables with 4 columns. Notice that the symbols are reduced in size to fit in the window.

- Select **Icon/Star** from the **Graph** menu
- Select the variables, in order: INCOME, POPDEN, PROPERTY, PERSON, RAIN, WINTER, SUMMER
- Specify 4 for [Cols]
- Specify STATE$ for [Label]
- Click OK

                                              © 1989, SYSTAT, Inc.

Icon-enhanced scatterplots

Wainer and Thissen (1981), Chambers, Cleveland, Kleiner and Tukey (1983), and others discuss using icons to enhance scatterplots by placing them at the location of X and Y variables. Icons can be placed on maps, for example, or on scatterplots of two related variables.

After you click [X–Y], you get two dialog boxes, one at a time.

- Click [X–Y]
- Specify the X variable
- Specify the Y variable
- Click OK

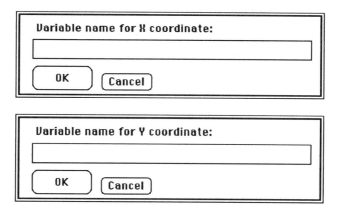

Use [X–Y] to specify the variables that determine the horizontal and vertical locations of the icons, respectively. You may have to fiddle with [Size] in the [Icons] option and perhaps move the locations slightly to keep icons from colliding.

The [X min], [X max], [Y min], and [Y max] options of [Axes] control the axis limits if you are using the [X–Y]. They work exactly the way they do for **Plot**. Since axes are not drawn when you use icons this way, you may wonder why these limits are necessary, especially when SYGRAPH automatically determines them from the data values. The reason they are here, however, is to allow you to combine maps, plots, and other graphs with icons in a single display and insure that the icons are correctly located.

17.11
Icons overlayed
on a map

This example shows a plot of the Mountain states on the US variables. The two additional variables we have used, LABLAT and LABLON, are the latitudes and longitudes of the centers of the states respectively. Before making the plot we select **Window/Graph Placement...** and choose **Overlay graphs.**

- Select **Select Cases...** from the **Data** menu
- Fill in the statement: Select REGION$='Mountain'
- Click OK

- Select **Icons/Face** from the **Graph** menu
- Select the variables: INCOME, POPDEN, PROPERTY, PERSON, RAIN, WINTER, SUMMER
- Click [Stand]
- Specify LABLON for [X] and LABLAT for [Y] with [X–Y]
- Set [Size] to 2 with [Icons]
- Set [Axes] limits:
  [X min] –120, [X max] –105,
  [Y min] 30, [Y max] 50
- Click OK

- Select **Map** from the **Graph** menu
- Set [Axes] limits:
  [X min] –120, [X max] –105,
  [Y min] 30, [Y max] 50
- Click OK

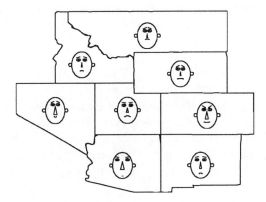

18   Map

Map

18

Map   18

Overview

SYGRAPH produces maps with the **Map** item. The standard package includes a boundary map of the continental United States with borders having a resolution of several miles; when enlarged, this map even shows Wellfleet Harbor of Cape Cod. Because of this high resolution, the U.S. map takes a long time to draw. The [Sketch] option produces rougher maps much more quickly.

If you plan to do much work with maps, you really should read some of the research on map coloring, shading, and contouring. Much literature on these topics exists, of course, in geography. Gale (1982) discusses continuously shaded maps, which you can do in SYGRAPH with the [Fill] option. Shaded maps, however, suffer from the perceptual biases we discussed in the **Cognitive science and graphic design** chapter. Trumbo (1981) and Wainer and Francolini (1980) discuss problems in coloring statistical maps.

Standard latitude and longitude text files of city, county, state, and international maps that SYGRAPH can process are available from a variety of sources. See Appendix V for further information on boundary files.

You must have two files in your SYSTAT folder. **Both must have the same name:** one with the extension .MAP and the other with no extension. The boundaries of regions are taken from the .MAP file. Other labeling information is taken from the regular data file.

The first three examples in this chapter use the US and US.MAP files. The last example demonstrates global mapping and uses the WORLD and WORLD.MAP files. To draw a map, you must open the US or WORLD file. SYGRAPH knows to find the US.MAP or WORLD.MAP file. More information about map files appears in Appendix V of this volume, **Map boundary files.**

The maps take a while to draw because there are tens of thousands of boundary points in the map files. Maps with lower resolution are drawn much faster. On some computers, you may not have enough memory to draw these maps. Try the [Sketch] option if this happens or choose a map file with fewer coordinates.

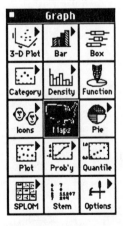

- Select **Maps** from the **Graph** menu
- Click OK

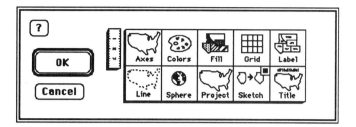

**Common
options**

See the **Common options** chapter for information on [Axes], [Colors], [Fill], [Line], and [Title]. [Axes] is also discussed in this chapter.

The [Label] option is similar to the [Label symbols with variable] option of the [Symbol] option that appears in many of the **Graph** items. Consult the **Common options** chapter for information on [Symbol]. The [Grid], [Project], [Sphere], and [Sketch] options are discussed below.

Selecting subsets

You can use **Data/Select Cases...** to map only part of your file, just as you can do graphs on subsets of your data. For instance, you can use **Data/Select Cases...** to select only the Mountain States:

- Select **Select Cases...** from the **Data** menu
- Fill in the statement: Select REGION$='Mountain'
- Click OK

Now, **Maps** would produce a map of only the Mountain states. Recall that **Select Cases...** remains in effect until you make another selection, open a new data file, or select **Data/Select Cases...** and click OK. Note that REGION$ is a variable in the US file—not the US.MAP file.

Drawing a map
18.1
Map of United
States

Here is an example of an unlabeled map of the contiguous United States. Since no projection is used, the actual latitudes and longitudes are plotted as rectangular coordinates.

- Select **Maps** from the **Graph** menu
- Click off the [Sketch] option
- Click OK

Grid lines

Grid

The [Grid] option produces a grid over the map. The default number of grid lines is 18 (vertical and horizontal). You may choose a different number if you wish.

Geographic projections

Project

Projections are transformations of spherical to rectangular coordinates. You can think of them as mathematical methods for taking an orange peel and stretching it to lie flat on a table. **Maps** offers oblique gnomonic, oblique stereographic, Mercator conformal, and oblique orthographic projections.

- Click [Project]
- Choose a projection
- Click OK

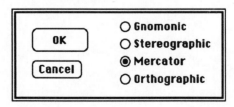

These projections are documented in Appendix B of Richardus and Adler (1972).

　　　　　　　　　　　　　　　　　　　　　　　© 1989, SYSTAT, Inc.

18.2
Map with
stereographic
projection and
grid lines

Here is a map of the U.S. using an oblique stereographic projection. We have chosen the longitude and latitude limits so that the grid marks indicate five degrees of latitude and ten degrees of longitude.

- Select **Maps** from the **Graph** menu
- Choose [Stereographic] projection
- Click off [Sketch]
- Specify [Xmin]=–130, [Xmax]= –60, [Ymin]=20, [Ymax]=55 in the [Axes] dialog box
- Specify 7 [Grid] lines
- Click the ruler icon and set [Height] to 3in and [Width] to 4in
- Click OK

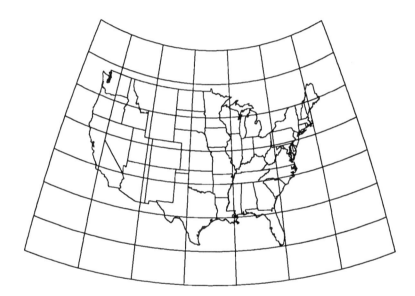

Sketching maps

Sometimes you want a quicker look at a complex map before drawing it in high resolution. The [Sketch] option produces maps with lower resolution, saving time and storage. You can expect to save a half to a tenth of the normal computing time depending on the size of the map. The lower resolution slightly compromises boundaries between states or regions, however.

SYGRAPH's default is for [Sketch] to be on—that is, unless you click [Sketch] off, you will get sketched maps. Click [Sketch] off when you are ready to make final copy.

Limits of maps

The [X min], [X max], [Y min], and [Y max] options of [Axes] control the axis limits of latitude and longitude in case you need to superimpose plots on a map. They work exactly the way they do for **Plot** and other graphs. Since axes are not drawn when you do maps, you may wonder why these limits are necessary, especially when SYGRAPH can determine them automatically from the data values. The reason they are included, however, is to allow you to combine maps, plots, and other graphs in a single display and insure that the points are correctly located. You can see some examples of this in the **Using SYGRAPH commands** chapter.

18.3
Squished map

Here is how to squish the U.S. sideways. We've set the axis limits to two different ranges. Keep in mind that the scales you use affect horizontal and vertical orientation. If you wish to proportion the map more familiarly, make the ranges the same. This will make the projections sensible as well. The limits you select are identical to the ones you get if you plot latitude and longitude with **Plot**. This way, any numerical information you have in a data file can be coordinated with the map.

- Select **Maps** from the **Graph** menu
- Set [Axes] limits:
  [X min]=–140, [X max]=–60,
  [Y min]=20, [Y max]=50
- Click OK

© 1989, SYSTAT, Inc.

Global maps

Sphere

You can map on a globe. The default latitude and longitude are [Ymin]=–90, [Ymax]=90, [Xmin]=–180, [Xmax]=180. Do not change these unless you want a bizarre map. (The British could again achieve world dominance, for example, by wrapping England around the globe.) The [Hide] option is automatically used with global mapping to hide the opposite side of the globe. You can change the viewpoint by selecting **Options/Formats...** from the **Graph** menu and changing the [Eye] setting.

18.4
The world

Here is a map of the Western hemisphere. You must have WORLD.SYS and WORLD.MAP in your directory. We have included grid lines on the map.

- Select **Maps** from the **Graph** menu
- Click [Sphere]
- Click [Grid]
- Click OK

19 Using SYGRAPH commands

Using SYGRAPH commands **19**

Overview   Parallel to its iconic interface, SYGRAPH contains a programming language for producing graphs in large batches and for customizing displays. This chapter is divided into two parts: "Commands" and "Examples." The examples will produce identical graphs on any machine running SYGRAPH.

If you open the Command window and continue to do your work using the point-and-click (mouse) interface, the Command window will generate the commands corresponding to your actions. Observing the Command window while you work will teach you how to use commands easily and painlessly.

Here is a table of all the SYGRAPH commands:

Graphics	*General*	*Controls*
BAR	BY	COLOR
BOX	HELP	SEPARATE
CPLOT	NOTE	EYE
DRAW	OUTPUT	DEPTH
DENSITY	QUIT	FACET
ICON	SELECT	FORMAT
MAP	SUBMIT	ORIGIN
PIE	USE	THICK
PLOT	WEIGHT	TYPE
PPLOT		SCALE
QPLOT		WAY
SPLOM		BEGIN
STEM		END
WRITE		

These commands are discussed in Appendix I, **Command reference.** The examples below will illustrate their use.

Commands

The graphics commands are equivalent to the icons in the graphics menu as follows:

Command	Menu equivalent
BAR	Bar
BOX	Box
CPLOT	Category
DRAW	Window/Plot Tools
DENSITY	Density
ICON	Icon
MAP	Map
PIE	Pie
PLOT	Plot, Function, 3-D Plot
PPLOT	Prob'y
SPLOM	SPLOM
STEM	Stem
WRITE	Window/Plot Tools

The Control commands—color, separate, eye, depth, facet, format, origin, thick, type, scale, way, begin, and end—function parallel to the options available in the **Options** items of the **Graph** menu. The following examples illustrate their use.

To do these graphs, you must be able to draw repeatedly on a single page or screen. The BEGIN and END commands function like the [Overlay plot] option with the main (mouse) interface. They allow you to overlay several SYGRAPH plots. The examples in this and the next chapter are surrounded with BEGIN and END markers and are submitted from a command file or from the Clipboard.

Examples

Scatterplots
19.1
Plotting a curve
on points from a
spreadsheet

Spreadsheets can perform sophisticated numerical analyses and can produce simple XY plots and line plots. When you use a spreadsheet for forecasting or creating theoretical mathematical curves, however, there is no way to plot a smooth curve unless you compute many points and connect them with a line. The interpolation methods among SYGRAPH's smoothing routines allow you to do this.

The following data are adapted from Nelson (1987). They constitute the results of a spreadsheet analysis using internal rate of return (IRR) and net present value (NPV) functions on earnings from an undeveloped land holding. Nelson standardized both measures to allow a common vertical scale on his graph.

YEAR	IRR	NPV
1	-24.9	-12.07
2	12.8	-3.54
3	19.6	2.98
4	20.9	7.80
5	20.9	11.19
6	20.6	13.37
7	20.1	14.54
8	19.7	14.87

Although the spreadsheet calculated the values of these functions for only 8 points (years), we can plot them as continuous functions with spline smoothing.

You should compare this graph with the graph in the original article to see the improvement with smoothing. Spline smoothing works well provided you have enough points to define the curve that underlies the points. We increased the standard tension (TENSION=5) in order to make the IRR curve straighter on the left.

```
TYPE=BRITISH
PLOT IRR,NPV*YEAR,
  / SMOOTH=SPLINE, SYMBOL=2,3, FILL=1,1,
  TENSION=5, YLABEL='YIELD'
```

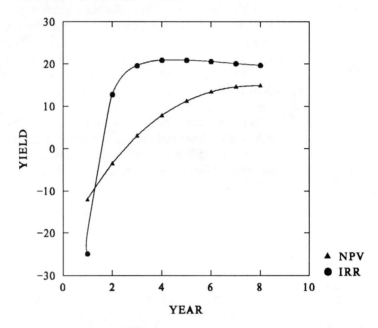

19.2
Plotting a
theoretical curve
on data

You can plot a theoretical curve on top of data in two steps. The following data, saved in the FADE dataset, are adapted from Giloh and Sedat (1982), who showed that the chemical n-propyl gallate reduces the rate of fading of fluorescence of cell structures labeled with tetramethylrhodamine for microscopy. The variable T_HALF represents time in minutes for 50 percent loss of initial fluorescence and CONCENT represents concentration of propyl gallate (percentage, weight to volume).

CONCENT	T_HALF
.2	1.8
.3	5.0
.6	10.0
1.0	15.0
2.0	18.0
4.0	27.0
10.0	34.0

We used SYSTAT to fit a model to these data:

```
NONLIN
MODEL T_HALF=A + B*CONCENT + C*SQR(CONCENT)
```

Although it is nonlinear in the parameters, this model happens to be linear, so we could have used **MGLH** in SYSTAT to fit it. Either way, the parameter estimates are A=−7.147, B=−3.446, C=23.882. Now we can plot the fitted function and the raw data in the same graph. Notice that we had to define the axis limits to make them correspond in the two plot commands. The resulting smooth is remarkably close to the one the authors presented in the article, although they do not give the smoothing method.

You can use the equation plotting feature in SYGRAPH to plot any theoretical curve on raw data. We happened to create a somewhat ad-hoc smoother, but there are many applications where you may want to plot both theoretical and fitted curves in the same graph.

```
BEGIN
PLOT T_HALF*CONCENT,
 /AXES=2, SYMBOL=2, FILL=1,
  XMIN=0, XMAX=10, YMIN=0, YMAX=40,
  XLABEL='Concentration of propyl gallate',
  YLABEL='t1/2 (minutes)'
PLOT Y=-7.147 - 3.446*X + 23.882*SQR(X),
 !AXES=0, SCALE=0,
  XMIN=0, XMAX=10, YMIN=0, YMAX=40,
  XLABEL=' ', YLABEL=' '
END
```

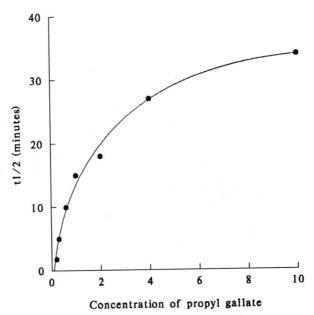

Concentration of propyl gallate

**19.3
Plotting
confidence limits
for polynomial
regression
models**

The following variables X and Y were created in SYSTAT using the equation:

$$X = u + i - 10$$
$$Y = 2 + 3x + 4x^2 + 5x^3 + 500z$$

where u is a uniform random variable, i is an index running from 1 to 20, and z is a standard normal random variable.

The variable ESTIMATE was estimated from a cubic regression model computed with the **MGLH** regression program in SYSTAT. Finally, the variables UPPER and LOWER were computed with DATA from the variable SEPRED (standard error of the predicted values) created by MGLH. UPPER is two standard errors above ESTIMATE and LOWER is two standard errors below.

```
LET UPPER = ESTIMATE + 2*SEPRED
LET LOWER = ESTIMATE - 2*SEPRED
```

X	Y	ESTIMATE	UPPER	LOWER
-8.472	-2598.746	-2680.917	-1915.487	-3446.347
-7.570	-1981.547	-1975.207	-1419.687	-2530.727
-6.058	-916.427	-1113.931	-713.743	-1514.119
-5.666	-1543.242	-947.304	-555.893	-1338.715
-4.005	392.356	-450.719	-50.705	-850.733
-3.353	-501.377	-330.748	71.349	-732.844
-2.898	-516.368	-266.045	134.056	-666.145
-1.425	-406.352	-133.613	242.519	-509.745
-0.081	321.691	-62.792	283.751	-409.335
0.807	-844.989	-11.042	324.172	-346.256
1.006	-211.789	3.306	337.631	-331.018
2.064	311.474	108.577	449.465	-232.310
3.054	1070.435	270.706	631.626	-90.214
4.238	1188.001	580.501	970.489	190.513
5.510	459.061	1099.617	1510.074	689.160
6.150	1594.951	1449.868	1862.904	1036.831
7.398	2438.986	2335.840	2743.716	1927.964
8.108	2535.208	2975.190	3386.096	2564.284
9.902	4708.076	5096.305	5651.865	4540.744
11.000	7250.791	6802.599	7607.337	5997.861

The point of this example is to show you that you can use the standard errors of the predictors output from a statistics package to place confidence intervals on the estimated regression line from a polynomial model. Note that these upper and lower limits do not form a band for the entire curve, but are calculated using only one x value at a time. The example here is two standard errors on either side of the estimate. If you wish, you can use an F distribution to set the width at a given probability value (see, for example, Daniel and Wood, 1971). Here are the values plotted and smoothed. Notice that we have suppressed the axes and labels the second time around.

```
BEGIN
PLOT Y*X / SYMBOL=2
PLOT UPPER,ESTIMATE,LOWER*X,
 / SMOOTH=SPLINE, SIZE=0, AXES=0, SCALE=0,
  XLABEL=' ', YLABEL=' ', SHORT
END
```

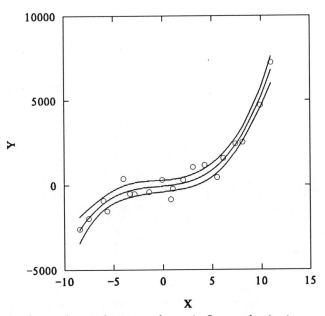

**19.4
Flow graphs for
price/
consumption
and other data**

Line graphs can be used to trace dynamic flow and price/consumption indices in economics. In these graphs, successive points are connected in a trace that is not a function of the horizontal axis variable. A price/consumption chart shows price plotted against consumption with points connected in time order.

The following data are adapted from a graph in Harris (1987) on tobacco prices and consumption. PRICE is in 1986 dollars a pack and CONSUMP is in packs per person per day.

CONSUMP	PRICE	YEAR
0.575	1.00	1964
0.584	1.02	1965
0.588	1.04	1966
0.580	1.07	1967
0.575	1.08	1968
0.545	1.10	1969
0.543	1.13	1970
0.552	1.10	1971
0.553	1.11	1972
0.567	1.05	1973
0.566	1.00	1974
0.565	0.98	1975
0.561	0.96	1976
0.557	0.94	1977
0.543	0.91	1978
0.530	0.88	1979
0.529	0.83	1980
0.526	0.80	1981
0.512	0.85	1982
0.480	0.99	1983
0.475	1.02	1984
0.462	1.05	1985
0.450	1.10	1986

We can make a price/consumption graph by plotting PRICE against CONSUMP and connecting successive points by a line. Because the dataset is in time order, the trace of the line will follow years. In the graph, 1964 begins on the right and 1986 ends on the left.

```
TYPE=SWISS
BEGIN
PLOT PRICE*CONSUMP,
 / LINE, SYMBOL=2, HEIGHT=3IN, WIDTH=4IN, FILL=1,
   YLAB='Price per Pack',
   XLAB='Packs Consumed per Day'
WRITE '1964',
 / X=3.5IN, Y=1.6IN,
   HEIGHT=6PT, WIDTH=6PT, CENTER
WRITE '1986',
 /X=1IN, Y=2.6IN,
   HEIGHT=6PT, WIDTH=6PT, CENTER
END
```

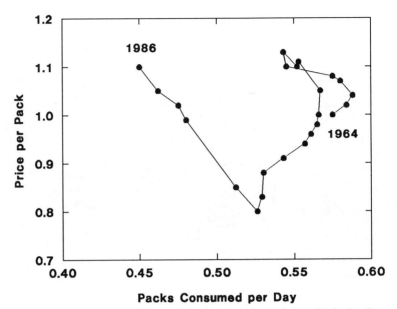

A random walk is a two-dimensional trace of a path in which the direction taken at each step is given by a random variable. Here is a program in SYSTAT for generating a random walk in two dimensions.

```
DATA
SAVE WALK
REPEAT 1000
HOLD
LET R=URN
IF R<.25 THEN LET X=X+1
ELSE IF R<.5 THEN LET Y=Y+1
ELSE IF R<.75 THEN LET X=X-1
ELSE LET Y=Y-1
RUN
```

Here is a plot of the output of this program. We have left out the axes to emphasize the shape itself. This elongated (non-globular) shape is typical of random walks and is somewhat counter-intuitive. Rudnick and Gaspari (1987) discuss the shapes of random walks and show several examples that look like this.

```
PLOT Y*X,
 / LINE, AXES=0, SCALE=0, HEIGHT=4IN, WIDTH=4IN,
  SIZE=0, XLABEL=' ', YLABEL=' '
```

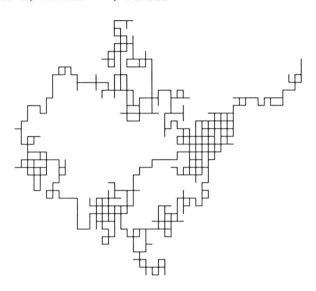

**19.6
Bordering
scatterplots**

You can do several panels of scatterplots on a common scale bordered by box plots or other types of graphs. The **Plot/Borders** item of the **Graph** menu provides this graph automatically; the commands below are equivalent. You can study these commands to see how you might build similar graph variations.

Here is an example using our U.S. data. You might want to substitute density stripes or jitter plots for the box plots.

```
TYPE=HERSHEY
BEGIN
ORIGIN=0,0
PLOT RAIN*SUMMER,
 / HEIGHT=3IN, WIDTH=1.5IN, SYMBOL=2
ORIGIN=2.5IN,0
PLOT RAIN*WINTER,
 / AXES=4, HEIGHT=3IN, WIDTH=1.5IN, SYMBOL=2
ORIGIN=4IN,0
BOX RAIN,
 / TRANS, AXES=0, SCALE=0, HEIGHT=3IN, WIDTH=1.5IN,
  XLABEL=' '
ORIGIN=2.5IN, 3IN
BOX WINTER,
 /AXES=0, SCALE=0, HEIGHT=1.5IN, WIDTH=1.5IN,
  XLABEL=' '
ORIGIN=0,3IN
BOX SUMMER,
 /AXES=0, SCALE=0, HEIGHT=1.5IN, WIDTH=1.5IN,
  XLABEL=' '
END
```

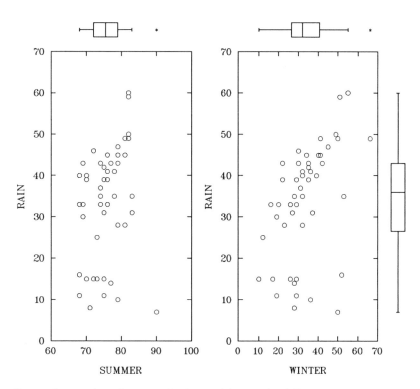

19.7
Plotting long time series

Long time series often require long, thin graphs. This is easy to do with SYGRAPH. Just use the HEIGHT and WIDTH options to rescale the size of the graph. Cleveland, McGill, and McGill (1986) discuss the implications of this scaling for plotting time series and other data. The next figure shows a series of 256 points scaled in this way. We have removed the points themselves by including SIZE=0. In the upper section of the figure, we have used the FILL option to highlight the periodicity in the same data.

```
TYPE=HERSHEY
BEGIN
ORIGIN=-.5IN,0
PLOT RATE*TIME,
 /HEIGHT=.75IN,WIDTH=5IN,LINE,SIZE=0,
  XMIN=0,XMAX=7
ORIGIN=-.5IN,3IN
PLOT RATE*TIME,
 /HEIGHT=.75IN,WIDTH=5IN,LINE,SIZE=0,
  XMIN=0,XMAX=7,FILL=1
END
```

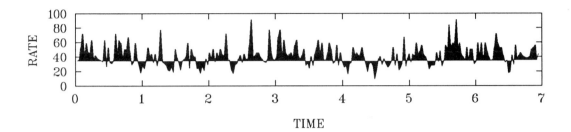

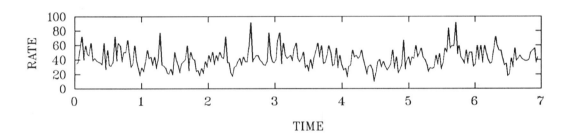

**19.8
Contouring over
filled contours**

You can enhance filled contours by adding contour lines for reference. Here is an example of this. These are contours of INCOME (per-capita income) against LABLAT and LABLON (latitude and longitude of the centers of the states). The contours help to delineate the darker and lighter areas without destroying the continuity of the gray scale.

```
BEGIN
PLOT INCOME*LABLAT*LABLON,
 /CONTOUR, FILL,
  XMIN=-125, XMAX=-65, YMIN=25, YMAX=50
PLOT INCOME*LABLAT*LABLON,
 /CONTOUR, ZTICK=10,
  XMIN=-125, XMAX=-65, YMIN=25, YMAX=50
END
```

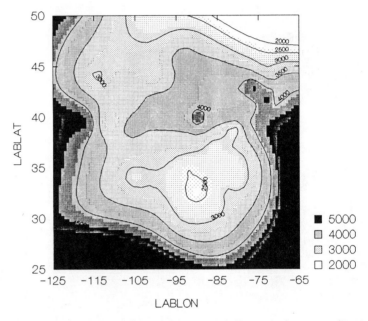

Bar charts

19.9
Dual histograms
and pyramid
graphs

Dual histograms and pyramid graphs reveal differences between distributions in groups because they place them side by side. The most popular form of these graphs is the age-sex pyramid. The following data from the 1980 U.S. Census show the distributions of males and females within age groups. Each age group is the upper age limit of its members. The last group (90) is open ended.

AGE	MALES	FEMALES
5	9230	8806
10	8608	8213
15	8762	8340
20	9445	9107
25	10515	10479
30	10886	10865
35	10096	10171
40	8741	8967
45	6889	7166
50	5679	5969
55	5281	5660
60	5380	5957
65	5120	5877
70	4254	5176
75	3213	4352
80	2135	3360
85	1153	2176
90	773	1938

Here is a graph of these data. The graph explains itself, but there are a
few things to note. The YREV option reverses the left graph segment.
The ORIGIN command moves the origin over so that the second half
can be plotted. The final BAR command is necessary because
SCALE=−4 in the previous BAR command prints only the right-hand
vertical scale. By adding the other options (SIZE=0, etc.), we cause
SYGRAPH to print only the scale values at the bottom right side of the
graph. If you have a color graphics device, it helps to use a different
color for each side of the graph instead of the fill patterns.

```
TYPE=HERSHEY
BEGIN
ORIGIN=0,0
BAR MALES*AGE,
 /TRANS, XMIN=0, YMIN=0, YMAX=12000, BWID=5,
  FILL=5, HEIGHT=4IN, WIDTH=2IN, TICK=4, YREV
ORIGIN=2IN,0
BAR FEMALES*AGE,
 /TRANS, XMIN=0, YMIN=0, YMAX=12000, BWID=5,
  FILL=7, HEIGHT=4IN, WIDTH=2IN, TICK=4,
  XLABEL=' ', SCALE=-4
BAR FEMALES*AGE,
 /TRANS, XMIN=0, YMIN=0, YMAX=12000, AXES=0,
  SCALE=1, HEIGHT=4IN, WIDTH=2IN, TICK=4,
  BWIDTH=5, XLABEL=' ', YLABEL=' '
END
```

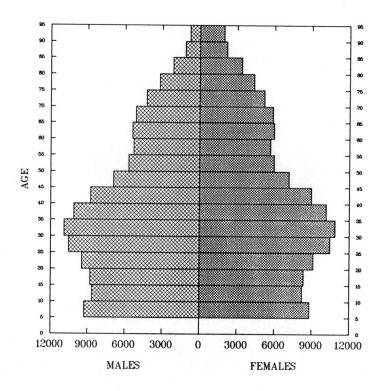

19.10
A pretty bar
graph

The following data are adapted from an editorial in *The New York Times* (December 3, 1987). They represent the duration of various plays, films, and operas.

TITLE$	HOURS
SHOA	9.0
ELECTRA	6.5
NICKLEBY	8.6
MAHABHAR	9.0
EINSTEIN	4.0
PARSIFAL	5.0
STALIN	12.0
HITLER	7.0

We plot this graph in italic Hershey font to suit the nature of the titles. While there are many commands, most of them are devoted to annotating the graph. The positioning of the text is determined by the height and width we chose. By keeping an even number (HEIGHT=4.5IN, WIDTH=6IN), we were able to determine the text positions in advance. The 4.5 inches of height was chosen because there are 8 bars each a half an inch plus two half bar spaces on either end of the bars. You'll have to make your view window very large, so that the plot fits. Also, you must open the data file with the Editor *closed* (i.e., uncheck the [Edit] box in the **Open...** dialog box) in order for the WRITE command to work properly. Otherwise, SYSTAT will try to write to a data file.

```
BEGIN
TYPE=HERSHEY
ORIGIN=-1IN,0
BAR HOURS*TITLE$,
 /FAT, TRANS, SORT, AXES=1, SCALE=1, XLABEL=' ',
  YMIN=0, YMAX=12, STICK, HEIGHT=4.5IN, WIDTH=6IN
WRITE 'OPERA'/X=-.3IN, Y=3.5IN, ANGLE=90
WRITE 'THEATER'/X=-.3IN, Y=2IN, ANGLE=90
WRITE 'FILM'/X=-.3IN, Y=.75IN, ANGLE=90
TYPE HERSHEY/ITALIC
WRITE 'The Life and Times of Joseph Stalin',
 /X=.1IN, Y=3.9IN, HEIGHT=.2IN, WIDTH=.1IN
WRITE 'Parsifal',
 /X=.1IN, Y=3.4IN, HEIGHT=.2IN, WIDTH=.1IN
WRITE 'Einstein on the Beach',
 /X=.1IN, Y=2.9IN, HEIGHT=.2IN, WIDTH=.1IN
WRITE 'The Mahabharata',
 /X=.1IN, Y=2.4IN, HEIGHT=.2IN, WIDTH=.1IN
WRITE 'Nicholas Nickleby',
 /X=.1IN, Y=1.9IN, HEIGHT=.2IN, WIDTH=.1IN
WRITE 'Mourning Becomes Electra',
 /X=.1IN, Y=1.4IN, HEIGHT=.2IN, WIDTH=.1IN
WRITE 'Shoa',
 /X=.1IN, Y=.9IN, HEIGHT=.2IN, WIDTH=.1IN
WRITE 'Our Hitler',
 /X=.1IN, Y=.4IN, HEIGHT=.2IN, WIDTH=.1IN
END
```

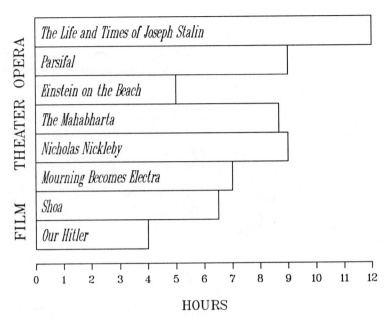

19.11
A really
complicated bar
graph

The following example is adapted from Warner, Mathewes and Clague (1982). The data give the incidence of fossil specimens of various flora found at various elevations of a site in British Columbia. The numbers have been interpolated from the graph, and may not accurately reflect the original data. Nevertheless, we have attempted to reproduce the graph literally, except for selecting four flora out of ten to save room in the dataset below. We have also omitted an illustration of the geological strata next to the vertical scale. This graph takes a lot of work to produce. Notice that two of the bottom scales are logarithmic and the widths have been adjusted to fit on a page. We have included this example to show you how much custom work you can do with SYGRAPH. Despite the lengthy setup, it should take less time than consulting with an illustrator.

HEIGHT	CHARA	NITELLA	JUNCUS	RUMEX
5	1	0	52	0
10	2	0	65	4
15	1	0	18	20
20	0	0	9	10
25	0	0	4	8
30	3	0	4	4
35	180	0	0	9
40	260	18	0	0
45	280	0	0	0
50	500	0	10	0
55	190	18	0	0
60	390	20	0	0
65	690	38	0	4
70	720	95	0	0
75	600	85	0	0
80	425	148	10	0
85	550	85	0	0
90	30	50	6	0
95	40	90	0	0
100	550	12	0	0
105	550	0	0	0
110	550	0	0	0

```
BEGIN
ORIGIN = 0,0
PLOT CHARA*HEIGHT,
 /SIZE=0, AX=-2, SCALE=-2,
  YTICK=12, YMIN=0, YMAX=120, YPIP=2,
  HEIGHT=2IN, WIDTH=3.25IN, STICK,
  YLABEL='Height of sampled exposure (cm)',
  XLABEL='Macrofossils per 100 cubic centimeters'
WRITE '(logarithmic scale) <-1',
 /HEIGHT=6PT, WIDTH=6PT,
  X=1.12IN, Y=-.8 IN
ORIGIN=.125IN,0
BAR CHARA*HEIGHT,
 /LOG=10, XMIN=0, YMIN=0, BWID=5, FILL=1, TRANS,
  AXES=-1, SCALE=-1, XLABEL=' ', YLABEL=' ',
  HEIGHT=2IN, WIDTH=1IN, PIP=9, STICK
WRITE 'Chara oospores',
 /X=.1IN, Y=2.1IN, HEIGHT=6PT, WIDTH=6PT, ANGLE=40
ORIGIN=1.25IN,0
BAR NITELLA*HEIGHT,
 /LOG=10, XMIN=0, YMIN=0, BWID=5, FILL=1, TRANS,
  AXES=-1, SCALE=-1, XLABEL=' ', YLABEL=' ',
  HEIGHT=2IN, WIDTH=1IN, PIP=9, STICK
WRITE 'Nitella oospores',
 /X=.1IN, Y=2.1IN, HEIGHT=6PT, WIDTH=6PT, ANGLE=40
ORIGIN=2.375IN,0
BAR JUNCUS*HEIGHT,
 /XMIN=0, YMIN=0, BWID=5, FILL=1, TRANS, AXES=-1,
  SCALE=-1, XLABEL=' ', YLABEL=' ',
  HEIGHT=2IN, WIDTH=1IN, PIP=5, STICK
WRITE 'Juncus',
 /X=.1IN, Y=2.1IN, HEIGHT=6PT, WIDTH=6PT, ANGLE=40
ORIGIN=3.5IN,0
BAR RUMEX*HEIGHT,
 /XMIN=0, YMIN=0, BWID=5, FILL=1, TRANS, AXES=-1,
  SCALE=-1, XLABEL=' ', YLABEL=' ',
  HEIGHT=2IN, WIDTH=1IN, PIP=5, STICK
WRITE 'Rumex',
 /X=.1IN, Y=2.1IN, HEIGHT=6PT, WIDTH=6PT, ANGLE=40
END
```


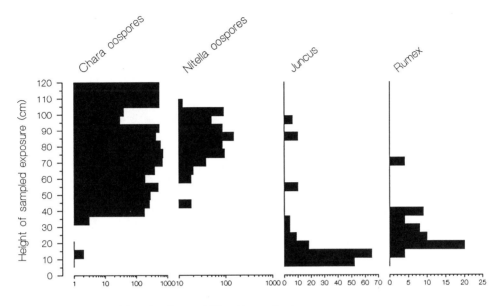

Macrofossils per 100 cubic centimeters

(logarithmic scale) <-1

Category plot
19.12
Multi-valued
category plots
with lines
(ANOVA plots)

In the analysis of variance, we often plot the results of a factorial design using lines connecting levels of a factor. This highlights interaction effects and trends. Here are the cell means from a repeated measures example in Winer (1971, page 525).

A1	A2	B$
2.33	5.33	B1
1.33	3.67	B2
5.33	7.00	B3
3.00	7.67	B4

Notice that you should use the CPLOT command because the factors are categorical. Choose the factor you want on the horizontal axis for your character variable in the file (B$ in this case) and make a separate variable for each level of the other factor (A in this case). You can plot up to 12 levels on the second factor this way in a single CPLOT command. If there are more groups, you can use separate CPLOT commands (with AXES=0 and MIN and MAX options) to superimpose results.

```
TYPE=SWISS
CPLOT A1,A2*B$ / LINE, SYMBOL=2,3, FILL=1,1, SIZE=2
```

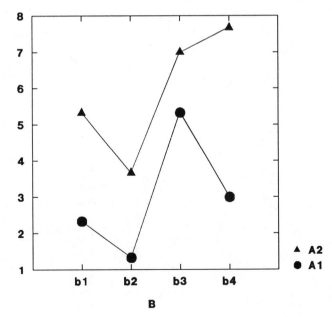

© 1989, SYSTAT, Inc.

3-D plots

Working in three dimensions requires thinking about facets of the graph you are creating. You can apply any two-dimensional plot like wallpaper on the surface of a three-dimensional box in perspective with the FACET command. We discuss using the FACET command in this chapter, and the examples show some applications.

EYE, FACET, and DEPTH

The commands you will need for more complex 3-D graphics are EYE, FACET, and DEPTH. These commands regulate the perspective, orientation, and position of planes in a 3-D space. What you draw on those planes depends on the subsequent graphics commands you choose. Once you have set these three control commands, you may proceed with other graphics commands as if you were working in two dimensions.

You can also use the [Eye], [Facet], and [Depth] options in **Options/Formats...** in the **Graph** menu. Enter values in these boxes in the **Options/Formats...** dialog box just as you would specify them with the commands. Also, you should use that dialog box in the same sequence (relative to other **Graph** items) as with commands.

Perspective

The EYE command regulates perspective. You need to specify three coordinates of the viewing eye to change the standard perspective. These coordinates are multiples of a standard unit cube whose lower near left corner (from the standard viewing perspective) is the (0,0,0) origin.

The default setting is EYE=–8,–12,8. You may put your viewing eye anywhere, including inside the cube, but some viewpoints will produce weird perspectives. Example 19.13 shows some examples. The first example uses the default perspective. By typing EYE with no numbers following (or deleting the numbers in the dialog box), the perspective is reset to the default perspective. If you have not set it to some other value during your session, this is optional. The last example in 19.13 shows a viewpoint underneath the cube.

Facets

The FACET command defines the facet of 3-D space on which you wish to plot 2-D graphs. FACET=XY defines the X-Y plane. FACET=YZ defines the Y-Z. FACET=XZ defines the X-Z.

Depth

The position of a plane along a facet is defined by the DEPTH command. The normal setting is DEPTH=50, which is 50 percent of the viewing area before perspective transformation. For the XY facet, DEPTH=50 defines the top of the default viewing cube. For the YZ facet, it defines the right rear plane. For the XZ facet, it defines the left rear plane. It is usually easier to define a depth in inches or centimeters, however, so you can think of the actual measurements of the physical object you are constructing. The examples in this chapter are done this way. In Example 19.13, we use DEPTH=0 with FACET=XY to mark the floor of the standard cube.

19.13
Some boxes

As with the two-dimensional plots above, you will need to use the BEGIN and END commands to superimpose several graphics commands on the same screen or page.

```
BEGIN
EYE
FACET=XY
DEPTH=0
DRAW BOX/HEIGHT=2IN, WIDTH=2IN, FILL=5
DRAW BOX/HEIGHT=2IN, WIDTH=2IN, ZHEIGHT=2IN

ORIGIN=3IN,0
EYE=.3,-.5,.5
FACET=XY
DEPTH=0
DRAW BOX/HEIGHT=2IN, WIDTH=2IN, FILL=5
DRAW BOX/HEIGHT=2IN, WIDTH=2IN, ZHEIGHT=2IN

ORIGIN=0,2IN
EYE=-.5,-.5,.5
FACET=XY
DEPTH=0
DRAW BOX/HEIGHT=2IN, WIDTH=2IN, FILL=5
DRAW BOX/HEIGHT=2IN, WIDTH=2IN, ZHEIGHT=2IN

ORIGIN=-2IN,0
EYE=.2,-1,-.8
FACET=XY
DEPTH=0
DRAW BOX/HEIGHT=2IN, WIDTH=2IN, FILL=5
DRAW BOX/HEIGHT=2IN, WIDTH=2IN, ZHEIGHT=2IN
END
```

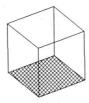

19.14 Writing on the facets of a cube

Let's try writing on the faces of a rectangular box to see how these options work. The example below shows how to use DEPTH and FACET. Notice that you have to keep track of which facet of the box you are laying a graph on. HEIGHT and WIDTH always refer to the height and width of the selected facet. You can adjust DEPTH to any setting you wish, but you have to take care to keep things from colliding or going off the page. When you are working in 3-D, it may take several tries to get things right.

FACET XY puts the plane on the XY axes, perpendicular to Z, and DEPTH 0 puts it at the floor of the cube. FACET XY and DEPTH 3IN lets us plot at the ceiling of the cube. FACET XZ plots on the XZ axes, perpendicular to Y, and DEPTH 3IN moves the plane to the rear left wall of the cube. FACET YZ plots on the YZ axes, perpendicular to X, and DEPTH 3IN moves the plane to the rear right wall of the cube.

```
BEGIN
FACET=XY
DEPTH=0
DRAW BOX/HEIGHT=3IN WIDTH=1IN FILL=5
TYPE=SWISS
DRAW BOX/HEIGHT=3IN WIDTH=3IN ZHEIGHT=3IN
FACET=YZ
DEPTH=3IN
WRITE 'YZ'/HEIGHT=1IN WIDTH=1IN X=1.5IN Y=1IN CENTER
FACET=XZ
DEPTH=3IN
WRITE 'XZ'/HEIGHT=1IN WIDTH=1IN X=1.5IN Y=1IN CENTER
FACET=XY
DETPH=3IN
WRITE 'XZ'/HEIGHT=1IN WIDTH=1IN X=1.5IN Y=1.5IN CENTER
END
```

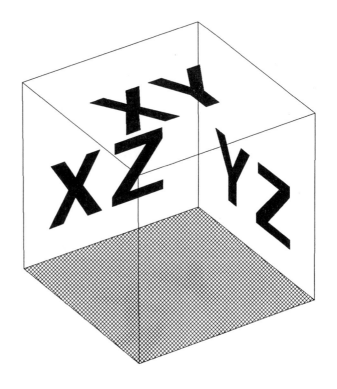

19.15
Drawing on the
facets

The following is an outlandish graph that has no real application. Its purpose is merely to show you how the EYE, FACET, and DEPTH commands interact with the graphics commands to produce a complex 3-D plot.

This example plots all the graphs on the surface of a box. The box is only to make the orientations clear.

Two other commands should be of use. ORIGIN will set the 2-D origin to wherever you wish. If you precede the 3-D plotting commands with an ORIGIN command, then the entire graph will be shifted to the area you wish. Furthermore, if your final graph proves too large or small, you can use the SCALE command to reduce or enlarge the entire image.

Notice that the separator for the equation (function) plot is an exclamation point (!) rather than a slash (/). This is because a slash is a divide sign in the mathematical expression.

```
TYPE=SWISS
BEGIN
DRAW BOX / ZHEIGHT=3IN, HEIGHT=4IN, WIDTH=5IN
FACET=ZX
DEPTH=4IN
WRITE 'A Whatsit Plot' / HEIGHT=.4IN, WIDTH=.25IN,
  X=2.5IN, Y=3.75IN, CENTER
SPLOM SUMMER,WINTER,RAIN / HEIGHT=3IN, WIDTH=5IN, ELL=.5
SELECT REGION$="New England"
FACET=XY
DEPTH=0
MAP / HEIGHT=4IN, WIDTH=5IN
FACET=ZY
DEPTH=5IN
PLOT Y=SIN(COS(TAN(X))), ! HEIGHT=3IN,
  WIDTH=4IN, AXES=0, SCALE=0, XLAB=' ', YLAB=' '
END
```

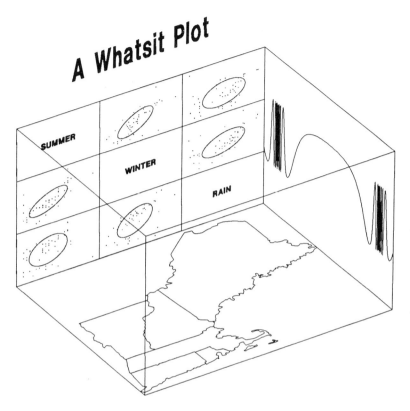

**19.16
Adding
perspective to
3-D plot symbols**

The perspective transformation in SYGRAPH is mild. That is, the graphs have a long focal length so as to avoid perspective distortions. Close points in a 3-D plot are in fact larger than distant points, but the effect is barely noticeable. Sometimes you might want to enhance the perspective effect, however, when you are trying to distinguish among plotting symbols.

One way to do this is to create a variable that you can use with the SIZE option to make close points larger and distant points smaller. This variable (say, DIST) should be a weighted sum of the two variables used on the bottom XY plane for the normal viewing position. This way, if a point has large values on X and Y, the DIST variable will have a large value and if the X and Y values are small, the DIST variable will be small.

463

The DIST variable should range from about .5 to 2.5 when used to size plotting symbols. If you let it range more broadly, the depth effect will be too exaggerated. Let's consider plotting RAIN (annual rainfall) against LABLAT (latitude) and LABLON (longitude) from the US file. Since LABLAT and LABLON will be on the XY plane, we want a combination of these two that will range from about .5 to 2.5. We need to check the data to find the minimum and maximum values on these variables, namely LABLAT (31 ... 47) and LABLON (–120 ... –69) approximately. Thus, our new variable DIST should be:

```
LET DIST=2.5-(LABLAT-31)/16-(LABLON+120)/51
```

The 16 and 51 values are the approximate ranges of the two variables.

If you save this variable DIST into the file along with the data, you can use it to control the size of the plotting symbols. Filled circles (SYMBOL=2,FILL=1) work well with this type of plot, although sometimes you may want to make them hollow (SYMBOL=2) to allow show-through. Five axes clarify it a bit.

```
PLOT RAIN*LABLAT*LABLON / SIZE=DIST, SYMBOL=2, AXES=5
```

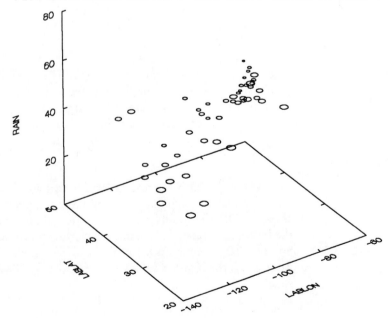

© 1989, SYSTAT, Inc.

19.17
Overlaying facets
in three
dimensions

The next example shows how you can overlay three-dimensional plots.
For this example, we plot RAIN against SUMMER and WINTER
temperatures in a 3-D scatterplot with filled circles twice as large as the
default.

Next, we plot two scatterplots at the margins of SUMMER and
WINTER. The first we place on the XZ facet, perpendicular to the Y
axis on the left rear. This panel reveals the joint distribution of RAIN
and WINTER temperatures. Then we change the facet to YZ, perpendicular to the X axis on the right rear in order to plot RAIN against
SUMMER temperatures. Notice that we have to use XREV to reverse
the bottom axis because of the location of the origin. Finally, we revert
to the bottom of the graph on the XY facet (FACET=XY and
DEPTH=0) to plot contours.

```
BEGIN
DEPTH
PLOT RAIN*SUMMER*WINTER,
 / SYMBOL=2, SIZE=2, FILL=1, AXES=0
FACET=XZ
PLOT RAIN*WINTER,
 / SCALE=0, XLABEL=' ', YLABEL=' ', ZLABEL=' '
FACET=YZ
PLOT RAIN*SUMMER,
 / XREV, SCALE=0, XLABEL=' ', YLABEL=' ', ZLABEL=' '
FACET=XY
DEPTH=0
PLOT RAIN*SUMMER*WINTER,
 / SCALE=0, CONTOUR, SMOOTH=DWLS, ZTICK=10,
   XLABEL=' ', YLABEL=' '
END
```

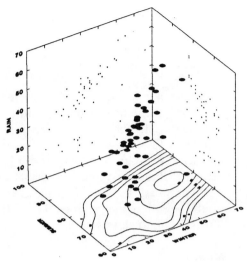

19.18
3-D grid lines

The next example shows how to place grid lines on any facet of a three-dimensional plot. The default grid lines for 3-D plots are on the bottom facet of the axis frame. To put grid lines or other material on the other facets, use the FACET command. The XREV option in the second PLOT command is not necessary because we are not plotting data or scale values. Nevertheless, you should keep in mind that plots on the XZ facet need to be reversed on the X axis if you are blending them with 3-D plots.

```
BEGIN
DEPTH
PLOT RAIN*LABLAT*LABLON,
 / SYMBOL=2, SIZE=2, AXES=9, GRID=3
FACET=YZ
PLOT RAIN*LABLAT,
 / XREV, SCALE=0, GRID=3, SIZE=0,
  XLABEL=' ', YLABEL=' ',
FACET=XZ
PLOT RAIN*LABLON,
 / SCALE=0, GRID=3, SIZE=0,
  XLABEL=' ', YLABEL=' '
END
```

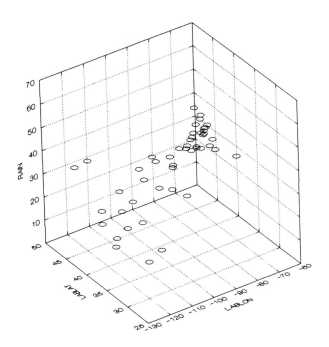

**19.19
Contouring on a
globe**

You can contour on the surface of the globe. Here is an example showing infant mortality. We used United Nations data aggregated by country and consulted an atlas for the latitude and longitude of the center of each country. The sampling points in this example are not well distributed across the globe, so the results should be interpreted with caution. In addition, since contours are drawn across oceans, it is preferable to use physical variables such as temperature or rainfall in plots like this. See example 17.11 in the **Icons** chapter and 11.21 in **2-D data plots** chapter for more information.

```
USE WORLD
BEGIN
THICK=1.5
EYE=8,8,4
MAP / SPHERE,HIDE
USE MYWORLD
THICK
PLOT BABYMORT*LAT*LON / CONTOUR,XMIN=-180,XMAX=180,
    YMIN=-90,YMAX=90,SMOOTH=INVERSE,SPHERE,HIDE,
      ZTICK=25,SCALE=-5,CUT=60
END
```

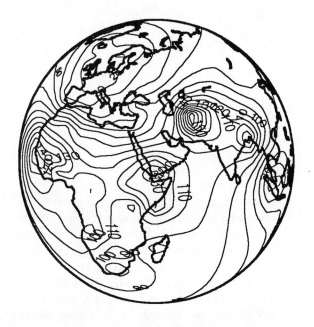

**19.20
Using symbols to identify multivariate outliers**

You can plot Mahalanobis distances to detect multivariate outliers in a distribution. Here is an example of how to do it in three dimensions. Use **MGLH** in SYSTAT to compute the distances and then used them with the SIZE option to represent outliers. Then use DATA to merge the distances with the variables in the US file and save them into a new file called WEATHER.

```
MGLH
USE US
MODEL SUMMER,WINTER,RAIN = CONSTANT
ESTIMATE
HYPOTHESIS
SAVE CANON
TEST

DATA
USE US CANON
SAVE WEATHER
RUN
```

The next figure shows the result of plotting the data in the WEATHER
file. You may have to rescale the Mahalanobis distances with other data
before using them to control the size of the plotting symbols.

```
TYPE=HERSHEY
PLOT RAIN*SUMMER*WINTER / SYMBOL=2, SIZE=DISTANCE
```

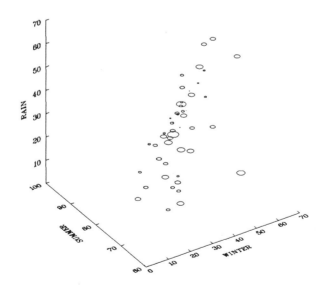

19.21
Perspective maps

Although they can distort, perspective maps have their uses. The trick in producing them in SYGRAPH is to line up the scales for whatever you are plotting over the map and the scales for the map itself. Here we do this with the US map. Setting FACET=XY and DEPTH=0 places the map on the floor of the subsequent plot.

We have chosen a stereographic projection for the map and plots. Notice that we must specify axis limits to use the PROJ option in the PLOT command. How do you know what limits to choose? Check the MINLAT, MINLON, MAXLAT, and MAXLON variables in the SYS file accompanying your map. Round the largest and smallest of these values up and down, respectively, to make the map fit as much of the plotting window as possible. See Appendix V for further details.

```
TYPE=HERSHEY
BEGIN
FACET=XY
DEPTH=0
MAP,
  / XMIN=-125, XMAX=-65, YMIN=25, YMAX=50,
  HEIGHT=3IN, WIDTH=5IN, PROJ=STEREO
ORIGIN=0,1.5IN
PLOT RAIN*LABLAT*LABLON,
  / XMIN=-125, XMAX=-65, YMIN=25, YMAX=50,
  SMOOTH=NEXPO, HIDE, HEIGHT=3IN, WIDTH=5IN,
  AXES=0, SCALE=0, PROJ=STEREO, SIZE=0,
  XLABEL=' ', YLABEL=' ', ZLABEL=' '
FACET
WRITE 'Average Annual U.S. Rainfall',
  / X=2.5IN, Y=4.5IN, CENTER
END
```

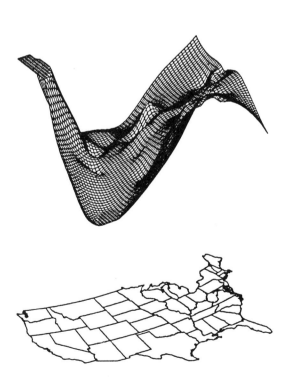

Average Annual U.S. Rainfall

**19.22
3-D functions
and contours**

You can place contours below 3-D function plots in the same graph. Here is an error function with contours below. We chose the default perspective and lengthened the Z axis (ZHEIGHT=75 instead of the default ZHEIGHT=50) to keep the upper plot from hiding the contours. You may wish to try two other methods to keep the plots visible. First, you can adjust the perspective with the EYE command (e.g. EYE=–9,–8,3). Second, you can use the ORIGIN command to move the surface higher (e.g. ORIGIN=0,1IN).

Here, we plot the contours first. Set FORMAT=1 to keep the labels on the contours to one decimal. We set CUT=50 to make the contours smoother and ZTICK=20 to draw more than a few contours. Next, do the upper plot. This time, set CUT=60 to make the mesh finer. Finally, make ZHEIGHT=75 to enlarge the vertical axis. The normal size of 3-D figure axes is 50 percent of the display area.

The final set of commands draws the axes. This is a rather sleazy method just to produce axes, but it works and saves having an extra command. Any old data will do, as long as X is a variable in the file. We just make SIZE=0 so that the plotting symbols don't appear.

```
TYPE=HERSHEY
BEGIN
FORMAT 1
FACET=XY
DEPTH=0
PLOT Z = EXP(-X^2)*EXP(-Y^2)*X,
   ! CONTOUR, ZMIN=-.5, ZMAX=.5, CUT=50, ZTICK=21,
   AXES=0, SCALE=0, XLABEL=' ', YLABEL=' ',
   XMIN=-3, XMAX=3
PLOT Z = EXP(-X^2)*EXP(-Y^2)*X,
   ! ZMIN=-.5, ZMAX=.5, HIDE, AXES=0, SCALE=0,
   CUT=60, XLABEL=' ', YLABEL=' ', ZLABEL=' ',
   ZHEIGHT=75, XMIN=-3, XMAX=3
USE AFIFI
PLOT SYSINCR*SYSINCR*SYSINCR,
   / XMIN=-3, XMAX=3, YMIN=-3, YMAX=3,
   ZMIN=-.5, ZMAX=.5, SIZE=0, XLABEL='X',
   YLABEL='Y', ZLABEL='Z', AXES=5, ZHEIGHT=75
END
```

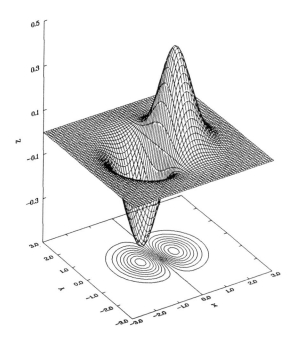

19.23
Time ordered
spectra and 3-D
function plots

Time ordered spectral plots are used frequently in chemistry, acoustics, image processing, medicine, and other fields. Two forms are popular. The first uses darkness to represent magnitude across time. This plot is produced by some laboratory spectral decomposition equipment. Speech samples and bird calls, for example, have been displayed this way. The graph looks like a smear of light and dark patches. The second form is a three-dimensional plot in which magnitude is assigned to the third dimension. This latter graph looks like a range of mountains in perspective.

Here is this second type of spectral plot. The data are from Michalske and Bunker (1987). They are the Fourier transformed infrared spectroscopy data for a chemical reaction involving methanol. This graph shows spectra at only three time points. We have estimated the data by interpolating their graph at several points. The vertical scale was not given in the article, so we standardized it to 1.0 maximum.

FREQ	TIME1	TIME2	TIME3
950.00	0.40	0.30	0.15
940.00	0.50	0.31	0.16
930.00	0.44	0.29	0.14
920.00	0.55	0.32	0.19
910.00	0.79	0.51	0.23
900.00	0.81	0.58	0.26
890.00	0.98	0.76	0.31
880.00	0.50	0.49	0.13
870.00	0.02	0.02	0.01

This type of plot is useful for other purposes. You can display a family of curves (such as chi-square with increasing degrees of freedom) in one plot with each curve plotted behind the last. By choosing your perspective carefully, you can show all the curves in a continuous surface.

If you do not wish to use the mild perspective transformation as here, you can accomplish the same effect by using the ORIGIN command with two-dimensional plots to shift the curves, e.g.

```
BEGIN
ORIGIN=0,0
PLOT Y=SQR(X)*EXP(-X) ! AXES=0, SCALE=0
ORIGIN=1CM,1CM
PLOT Y=SQR(2*X)*EXP(-2*X) ! AXES=0, SCALE=0
ORIGIN=2CM, 2CM
PLOT Y=SQR(3*X)*EXP(-3*X) ! AXES=0, SCALE=0
END
```

and so on.

```
BEGIN
FACET=ZX
DEPTH=0
PLOT TIME1*FREQ,
  / SMOOTH=SPLINE, XMIN=870, XMAX=950,
  XTICK=8, XREV, YMIN=0, YMAX=1,
  HEIGHT=3IN, WIDTH=4IN, AXES=1, SCALE=1,
  XLABEL='WAVENUMBERS', YLABEL=' '
DRAW BOX / HEIGHT=3IN, WIDTH=4IN
DEPTH=1IN
PLOT TIME2*FREQ,
  / SMOOTH=SPLINE, XMIN=870, XMAX=950,
  XTICK=8, XREV, YMIN=0, YMAX=950,
  HEIGHT=3IN, WIDTH=4IN, AXES=1, SCALE=0,
  XLABEL=' ', YLABEL=' '
DRAW BOX / HEIGHT=3IN WIDTH=4IN
DEPTH=3IN
PLOT TIME3*FREQ,
  / SMOOTH=SPLINE, XMIN=870, XMAX=950,
  XTICK=8, XREV, YMIN 0, YMAX=1,
  HEIGHT=3IN, WIDTH=4IN, AXES=1, SCALE=0,
  XLABEL=' ', YLABEL='MAGNITUDE'
DRAW BOX / HEIGHT=3IN, WIDTH=4IN
FACET=XY
DEPTH=0
DRAW BOX / HEIGHT=3IN, WIDTH=4IN
WRITE 'TIME (MINUTES)',
  / X=-.8IN, Y=1.5IN, CENTER, ANGLE=270,
  HEIGHT=.1IN, WIDTH=.1IN
END
```

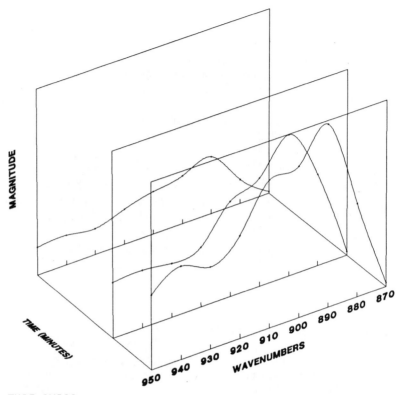

19.24
And now, a word
from our sponsor

```
TYPE=SWISS
BEGIN
FACET=XY
DEPTH=0
SELECT STATE$='IL'
MAP / HEIGHT=6IN, WIDTH=6IN
COLOR GRAPH=GREEN
ORIGIN=-.2IN,1.4IN
WRITE 'SYSTAT' / HEIGHT=.5IN,  WIDTH=.5IN
DRAW BOX / HEIGHT=.11IN, WIDTH=2.9IN, Y=.62IN, FILL=1
DRAW BOX / HEIGHT=.11IN, WIDTH=2.9IN, Y=-.23IN, FILL=1
DRAW BOX / HEIGHT=.11IN, WIDTH=1.93IN, Y=.86IN, FILL=1
DRAW BOX / HEIGHT=.11IN, WIDTH=1.93IN, X=.97IN,
  Y=-.47IN, FILL=1
END
```

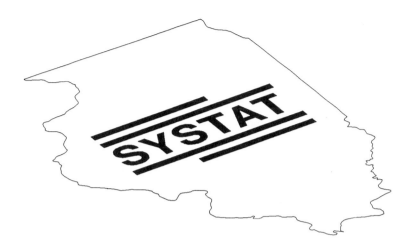

Appendix I: Command reference

Appendix I: Command reference

Overview

You may sidestep SYGRAPH's point-and-click menu interface by using the optional command interface. Just select **Command** from the **Window** menu. The Command window appears, and your first prompt ">" awaits orders.

The quickest way, perhaps, to learn the command line interface is to open the Command window and continue using the menus. The Command window follows along, showing you all the command line equivalents to your pointing and clicking. After a while, you'll get the idea and start using commands naturally.

This appendix explains the command syntax and defines all the options and arguments. First, we list some reasons you might want to use the command interface, and we give instructions for editing and submitting batch files. The remaining sections are references: lists of every command with syntax instructions, organized in parallel with the chapters in the manual.

Introduction

Why commands?

Why would you want to use the command interface? Because if you're doing a lot of repetitive analyses, generating a lot of variables algebraically, or using ranges of variables frequently, command lines are probably faster. If you're going to draw the same type of graph repeatedly, with only minor changes, chances are good that you could get done sooner typing.

What if you forget the syntax? Pull down a menu, do it once with the mouse, and see what shows up in the Command window!

Commands are better for a number of tasks:

Reproducing results

Suppose you're doing work that someone else will want to repeat. Perhaps you're doing consulting work, and your client wants to see a command file so she can verify your results. Perhaps someone wants to elaborate on your work, and he wants to see how you did it.

It would be difficult to give someone a comprehensive list of point-and-click instructions. Instead, you can hand over a list of exact commands. Many government agencies, in fact, *require* that command files be submitted with reports that include computer-generated results.

If all you want is a record of your work, you don't even need to use commands. Just open the Command window before you start working, do your usual point-and-click routine, and save or print the contents of the Command window. If you publish your results and a reader disputes your analyses, you can recreate your work from start to finish with SYGRAPH's commands. Otherwise, you cannot defend your work. In the private sector, auditors often require lists of command statements. See Weber (1982).

Batching

You can write batch files of commands to be executed in succession. In other words, you enter a series of commands into a file and then submit the file, leave for coffee, and come back to get your results. The batch file could include commands to save and print results. You can also edit the command file and resubmit it.

Modifying previous work
You can edit the Command window after an interactive session and re-submit the commands as a batch.

Submitting

The basic strategy for using batches is first to type a batch file or edit a portion of the Command window and then to submit that file or the portion from the window as a batch.

Creating a batch

There are two basic ways to create a batch: either type a bunch of commands from scratch, or edit something already in the Command window. The variations, though, are endless. You can type commands from scratch in any word processor and save them as a text file, or you can cut or copy them to the Clipboard. You can edit in either the SYSTAT Analysis window or the Command window. You can cut and paste between the windows. You can save your editing work in a file, or copy it to the Clipboard, or cut it to the Clipboard.

All windows in SYSTAT and SYGRAPH, except the graphics View window, are little text processors. You can do anything you want in them. If you have SYSTAT results in the Analysis window that you want to use elsewhere, you can cut them, type some comments around them, select a chunk, and print it. Snip out the comments, paste in some results from the correlation from half an hour ago (the one you still have in the window, because you remembered to "Scroll analyses"), select a chunk, save it to a file, and then edit it a little more into a set of commands. Copy it to the Clipboard, submit the Clipboard, sit back, and watch.

The catch: you have to clean out the garbage. Commands must look just as they do if you type them at prompts. No extra words, no extraneous characters (except spaces, commas, and tabs), no old prompts. So, if you're resubmitting some commands in the Command window, you must edit out the prompts and any SYSTAT messages (like "Series is cleared"). Each command should be on a separate line.

Quick and dirty:

- Type or edit something into shape:
  One command per line
  No extra junk—no prompts, comments, or weird characters
  Proper command syntax
- Save it in a file or copy it to the Clipboard:
  Select the text you want
- Use **File/Save selected text as...** to put it in a file
  Use **Edit/Copy Text** or **Edit/Cut Text** to put it in the Clipboard
  Use a word processor to save it in a text file

Submitting a batch

Once you've created a batch and saved it in a file or the Clipboard, you can submit it. SYGRAPH processes the commands as if you were doing everything the usual, interactive way.

To submit a batch file, enter the command SUBMIT *"filename"*, or use the mouse.

- Select **Submit command file...** from the **File** menu
- Specify the file to be used
- Click Submit

To submit a batch from the Clipboard, type Command-F or use the mouse.

- Select **Submit Clipboard** from the **File** menu

General strategy

We discuss command syntax, rules for how to type commands, and guidelines for deciphering our notation in the section "Command syntax," below. Here, we discuss the general strategy for using SYGRAPH's command interface.

The first step when using commands for anything is the same as the first step without commands: open a data file. The command equivalent for **File/Open...** is USE:

USE US

SYGRAPH remembers what file you opened with USE even if you switch to and from **Stats** modules in SYSTAT. The files always follow you around through the various parts of SYSTAT and SYGRAPH, just as they do when you are using the usual mouse interface.

If you need to do anything to "adjust" the way you use data, you can do it at any time. So, if you need **Data/By groups...**, **Select...**, or **Weight...**, you can do that now with commands like the following:

```
WEIGHT COUNT
SELECT REGION$='New England'
BY GROUP1
```

You can start a SELECT, a BY, or a WEIGHT at any time. These three things stay in effect across modules. So, to turn them off, you have to either issue the command again, but without an argument, or you have to USE a new data file (or use the same one again).

```
WEIGHT        or        USE MEDICAL
SELECT
BY
```

You can also "turn off" a BY, SELECT, or WEIGHT command by issuing a new one:

```
WEIGHT X(1)
SELECT GROUP=3
BY REGION$
```

When in doubt, start fresh: USE the file anew. That way, you're sure that you're using the whole dataset in your analyses.

The next thing you must do is "switch to a module." A module could be any of the SYSTAT modules, like CORR or STATS, or else GRAPH for SYGRAPH. (SYSTAT modules are discussed in more detail in the SYSTAT manual's **Command reference** chapter.) So, if you are about to draw a graph, your first command is:

```
GRAPH
```

Next, you type the command or commands needed to do the analysis. Suppose you want to get a bar chart of INCOME by REGION$ from the US dataset. The command you need is the same as the menu item's name (**Bar/Bar**). The first thing you would do in the dialog box is select variables, and that's the first thing you do with the command.

```
BAR INCOME*REGION
```

You may need to use *options* with the command. *Options* are items controlled by the row of buttons in the dialog box, like "Axes," "Title," "Sort," "Polar," etc. Options for SYGRAPH commands come after a slash (/). We'll discuss command syntax in more detail later. For now, let's just consider our BAR example. Suppose we would click "T'pose" in the dialog box. The command equivalent is obvious:

```
BAR INCOME*REGION / TRANSPOSE
```

Organization of the reference

To help ease your transition to the command interface, we have organized the command reference to follow the organization of the menus and dialog boxes.

The first sections discuss the command equivalents of items found in the **File, Edit, Data,** and **Window** menus. Next, we discuss the equivalents for items in **Options** menu: **Color...** and **Formats...** These commands all control global settings for color, typeface, positioning facets, etc. Then we discuss equivalents for common options (equivalents for those items introduced in the **Common options** chapter at the front of the book): "Axes," "Error," "Symbol," and so on.

Finally, we show the commands for each type of graph, in the same order as they were discussed in the manual. In the left margin of each page, where you usually see section headings, we have shown the **Graph** menu equivalent. Commands are grouped according to "module," or menu item. We show the menu item, like **Bar** or **Plot** or **Map**, in boldface.

For each major command, we list the common options that can be used for that type of graph. Consult the "Common options" section for information on using those options.

Remember: you can always get help for any command. Just type "HELP *command*," where *command* is the name of the command that confuses you. For instance, if you need help with PLOT or any of its options:

```
HELP PLOT
```

Finally, if you are in doubt about how to use commands to accomplish a particular type of graph, look in the manual for an example that is similar to what you are trying to do. Make a note of its number—e.g., Example 7.3 or 8.6, etc. The next appendix, **Command equivalents for examples,** shows the command equivalents to the mouse instructions we give for each example in the manual. The examples are grouped by chapter and retain the same numbering as in the chapters.

HOT and COLD commands

Some commands are HOT. Some commands are COLD. When you type a HOT command you see an immediate action—the screen fills with graphics, the printer starts working, etc. COLD commands turn switches on and off, specify conditions, and select options.

Generally, you use COLD commands to set global options—like when you use TYPE=BRITISH so that all subsequent graphs will be done using the British SYGRAPH font. The HOT command sets the procedure in motion. Since the COLD commands all just set up the procedure, you can usually put them in any order. The important thing is that the HOT command comes last.

In the reference, we identify the COLD commands at the end of the description paragraph.

For example, suppose you have just started SYGRAPH up for the day and want to draw a bar chart of INCOME by REGION$, and you want the text to be printed in the Hershey typeface. You also want to save the graph in a file, so you add a PICT command to the list.

```
USE US
GRAPH
PICT 'bar'
TYPE=HERSHEY
BAR INCOME*REGION$
```

First, you USE the data file, then "switch" to GRAPH, and then set up the global options. These are all COLD commands. Note that once you have USE and GRAPH done (in either order), the remaining COLD commands can be in any order. After everything is set up, you do the HOT BAR command.

Again, when in doubt, use HELP and check the **Command equivalents for examples** chapter.

BEGIN and END

Two special commands can only be used with batch files: BEGIN and END, which are used for overlaying plots. When you submit a batch file, each file is drawn separately (as if you were sitting at your Mac clicking "Stack plot" in between each graph). If you surround several plotting commands with BEGIN and END, they are overlayed (as if you were clicking "Overlay plot").

BEGIN begins a graph. It is needed when you are plotting several graphs on the same page or screen. Here is an example:

```
BEGIN
PLOT Y=X
PLOT Y=X^2
END
```

Use END to complete the block of commands. With this construction, both plots will be superimposed. The BEGIN-END block can be used only with batch files. The advanced **Two-dimensional plots** and **Three-dimensional plots** chapters illustrate what you can do with BEGIN-END blocks of graphics commands.

Command syntax

"Syntax" is grammar. Command syntax is all the typing rules: this word has to come first, slashes come later, quotation marks do this, filenames have to look that way, and so on.

Prompts

The "greater than" sign (>) in the Command window is your "prompt." A prompt tells you that SYSTAT is waiting for you to tell it something. After you type a command, press Return. If you typed a HOT command, SYSTAT begins work and you do not see another prompt until SYSTAT is done. If you typed a COLD command, you get another prompt right away.

Upper- and lower-case

You can type commands in upper or lower-case. Commands are not case sensitive except when they include text values, which *are* case sensitive.

Abbreviations

Command words can be abbreviated to the first three letters, but function names and variable names must always be typed fully. Commas, spaces, and tabs are interchangeable.

Order

Commands consist of several parts. The first is the command word: the part that says what the command is supposed to do. "PLOT" is a command word that means "draw a scatterplot."

The next part is the "argument": the object of the command. The argument answers the question, "Plot *what*?!" You answer the question by listing some variables:

```
PLOT Y*X
```

Sometimes, arguments are optional; for instance, if you don't say which variables, BOX draws box plots for all the numeric variables it can find.

The last part of any command is the option list. The option list is (how could you guess?) optional. Put a slash (/) before the option list and then list all the options you want.

One exception: when you use PLOT for function plots, separate the options from the command with an exclamation point (!) instead of a slash. This is because the slash is a division symbol for functions.

You only need one slash (or exclamation point), no matter how many options you use. Each command has a set of options. Some options are exclusive—if you pick A, you can't pick B. These are listed together in our reference, separated with bars: SMOOTH=NORMAL | KERNEL. You can pick NORMAL, or you can pick KERNEL, or you can skip it entirely and SYSTAT uses its *default*: the thing it does if you don't tell it otherwise. More on defaults below.

Placeholders

Placeholders tell you what to type. For instance, we show the place-holder *yvar* where you're supposed to type a dependent variable name. Placeholders are always shown in *italic* typeface.

depvar	dependent variable (vertical axis for graphs)
indvar	independent variable (horizontal axis for graphs)
var$	character variable
gvar	grouping variable
varlist	one or more variables (variations: *xvarlist, yvarlist, gvarlist, var$list*)
"filename"	any valid filename; must be surrounded by double or single quotation marks if it contains path (folder) information, spaces, or symbols
"char"	one or more characters, for instance a value for a character variable; must be surrounded by double or single quotation marks
exprn	any mathematically valid expression

Brackets

Items enclosed in brackets are optional. We don't bother putting brackets around the list of options, since it is understood that options are optional. Usually, things that involve brackets are explained in detail in the description of the command to the right.

Quotation marks

Quotation marks that are included in the syntax demonstrations and in example commands are *required*. Quotation marks are required for all text values and any filenames that contain spaces or symbols.

Long commands

If a command is too long to fit on one line, put a comma at the end of the line, press Return, and continue typing. You can stretch a single command down several lines as long as you keep using commas.

Slashes

As we mentioned above, slashes set off options, such as sizes, symbol sizes, etc. You *must* type the slash as part of the command. Use only one slash per command, regardless of the number of options; in other words, the slash divides the command-argument half of the command from the option half.

Items that follow slashes are understood to be optional. For clarity, we do not enclose the lists of options inside brackets.

For example, the following PLOT commands are all valid. Note that spaces and commas are interchangeable:

```
PLOT Y*X
PLOT A,B*X/SYMBOL='a','b'
PLOT Y W    *X/ERROR=SD
PLOT Y*X/SMOOTH,CONF=.95, SIZE=.5 XMIN=4,XMAX=14
PLOT Y*X/    SYMBOL=1
```

Note: there is one exception. When plotting functions, use an exclamation point (!) to set off options rather than a slash, which indicates division in SYSTAT BASIC.

The following are correct:

```
PLOT Z = X^2 + Y^2 ! HIDE XMIN=0 YMIN=0 ZMIN=0
PLOT Y=X ! LINE=11
```

Vertical bars

A vertical line (|) means "or." For example, you can use NORMAL or KERNEL smoothing for DENSITY:

```
SMOOTH=NORMAL |
      KERNEL
```

Options that are separated by vertical bars are exclusive. You can use only one at a time (or none). For example, SMOOTH=NORMAL | KERNEL means that you can normal *or* kernel smoothing but not both.

Defaults

Defaults are preset option selections that take effect unless you change them. Defaults are underlined. For example, in the option above, the underlining indicates that if you type SMOOTH without an argument, you will get NORMAL smoothing.

Sometimes you see underlining without the vertical "or" bar. This indicates a default that doesn't necessarily exclude other options listed with it.

Command reference

File menu Open...	**EDIT** "*filename*"	Opens data file *filename* and displays it in Data Editor. If you do not specify *filename*, SYGRAPH opens a new (empty) worksheet. HOT.
	GET "*filename*"	Opens text file *filename*. Use in conjunction with INPUT command. COLD.
	USE "*file1* " [(*varlist*)]	Opens a data file without the Data Editor. If you include *varlist*, only those variables are opened. You must enclose *varlist* in parentheses. HOT.
Save as...	**MAC** "*filename*"	Saves current file into tab delimited text file named *filename*. HOT.
	PUT "*filename*"	Creates a text file of the current data file. The text file is comma delimited with quotation marks around character values. HOT.
	WRITE "*filename*"	Saves current worksheet in data file named *filename*. HOT.
	TYPE=CORRELATION | COVARIANCE | DISSIMILARITY | <u>RECT</u> | SIMILARITY | SSCP	Specifies the type of matrix being entered. All but RECT are triangular matrices such as are saved by procedures in CORR.
Save graph as...	**PICT** "*filename*"	Saves graph currently in View window in PICT file named *filename*. HOT.

Submit command file...	**SUBMIT** "*filename*"	Reads and executes commands contained in *filename. Filename* must be a text file. HOT.
	/ECHO	Displays the commands in *filename* as they are processed.
Results to Screen/ Printer/File as...	**OUTPUT=*** I DISPLAY I@ I PRINTER I "*filename*"	Sends subsequent output to the specified device. Asterisk (*) or DISPLAY, the default, sends output to the screen only. At-sign (@) or PRINTER sends output to a printer and the screen. *Filename* sends output to the screen and a text file called *filename*. Not available in the Data Editor. COLD.
Quit	**QUIT**	Exits SYGRAPH to the Finder. HOT.

Edit menu Clear Case…	**DELETE**	Prevents current case from being saved into a new file. Usually used with IF-THEN; e.g., IF X>10 THEN DELETE. COLD.
Preferences… /Analysis section	**PAGE**	Selects screen display and printer output format and characteristics with the options that follow. COLD.
	/FILE=*n*	Specifies the number of lines per page in a text file. The default value is 56. Specify 0 for no page breaks.
	PRINTER=*n*	Specifies the number of lines per printed page. The default value is 56. Specify 0 for no page breaks.
	<u>NARROW</u> | WIDE	Specifies the number of columns used for analysis (text) output. NARROW, the default, specifies 80 columns; WIDE specifies 132.
	TITLE='*line1*', '*line2*', …	Specifies a title for each page of output. You may specify up to 10 title lines; each line may be up to 132 characters long. SYSTAT centers each line on the page.
	FORMAT=*n*	Specifies the number of decimals to display in output ($0 \leq n \leq 9$). The default is 3. COLD.
	/UNDERFLOW	Prints tiny numbers that otherwise would appear as "0" in exponential notation.
Preferences…/ Editor section	**FORMAT=*n***	Specifies the number of decimals to display in the data editor. The default is 3. COLD.

Data menu Math…	**LET** *var=exprn*	Assigns value specified by *exprn* to *var*. HOT.
Recode…	**IF** *exprn* **THEN LET** *var=exprn*	If *exprn* is true, the LET statement is executed. HOT.
Find Case… Find Next	**FIND** *exprnlist*	Finds the first case below the cursor's position that meets the condition specified by *exprnlist*. If you do not include *exprnlist*, SYSTAT uses the previous *exprnlist*. HOT.
Fill Worksheet…	**REPEAT** *n*	Fills *n* cases in the worksheet with missing values. You must label variables before you use REPEAT. HOT.
By Groups…	**BY** *gvarlist*	Specifies grouping variables for subgroup analysis. Analyses are performed separately for each subgroup.
Select Cases…	**SELECT** *exprn1* […]	Selects a subgroup of cases for analysis. You may include up to 10 expressions. Only cases meeting all the expression conditions are used. Using the SELECT command without an argument ends current selection conditions. COLD.
Weight…	**WEIGHT**=*var*	Weights each observation with the value of *var*. The sample size for analyses is the sum of the values of *var*. The values of *var* are truncated to integers before processing. Issuing the WEIGHT command without an argument clears the current weight selection. Not available with the MDS or SERIES items. COLD.

Window menu Help	**HELP** *command*	Displays help for specified *command*. HOT.

Plot Tools...

DRAW ARROW

Draws an arrow.

/ X1, X2, Y1, Y2, Z1,
Z2=*n* | *n* IN | *n* CM

Specifies the starting (X1, Y1, and Z1) and ending (X2, Y2, and Z2) coordinates of the arrow relative to the origin. Z coordinates are used only for 3-D plots. The default value for each coordinate is 0.

DRAW BOX

Draws a box. Specify height and width with the HEIGHT and WIDTH options.

/ X, Y, Z=*n* | *n* IN | *n*
CM

Specifies the coordinates for the lower left (bottom) corner of the box. The Z coordinate is only used for 3-D plots.

CENTER

Redefines X and Y so that they locate the center of the box.

ZHEIGHT=*n* | *n* IN | *n*
CM

Specifies the "altitude" or height of the *z* axis for a 3-D box.

DRAW LINE

Draws a line.

/ X1, X2, Y1, Y2, Z1,
Z2=*n* | *n* IN | *n* CM

Specifies the starting (X1, Y1, and Z1) and ending (X2, Y2, and Z2) coordinates of the line relative to the origin. Z coordinates are used only for 3-D plots. The default value for each coordinate is 0.

DRAW OVAL	Draws an oval. Specify height and width with the HEIGHT and WIDTH options.
/ X, Y, Z=*n* I *n* IN I *n* CM	The oval is centered on the point whose coordinates you give. The Z coordinate is used only for 3-D plots.
DRAW SYMBOL	Draws the specified symbol. Specify height and width with the HEIGHT and WIDTH options.
/SYMBOL="*char*" I *n*	Specifies the symbol to draw. Choosing a number ($1 \le n \le 21$) selects a preset symbol. You can specify any symbol by enclosing it in quotation marks.
/ X, Y, Z=*n* I *n* IN I *n* CM	The symbol is centered on the point whose coordinates you give. The Z coordinate is used only for 3-D plots.
DRAW TRIANGLE	Draws a triangle. Specify height and width with the HEIGHT and WIDTH options.
/ X, Y, Z=*n* I *n* IN I *n* CM	Specifies the coordinates of the lower left corner of the triangle. The Z coordinate is only used for 3-D plots.
CENTER	Redefines X, Y, and Z so that they locate the center of the triangle.

Common options   COLOR   FILL   HEIGHT
WIDTH

Plot Tools…	**WRITE** *"char"*	Writes *char* to the output destination.
	/ANGLE=*n*	Writes text at angle *n* ($0 \leq n \leq 360$).
	X, Y, Z=*n* | *n* IN | *n* CM	Specifies the location of the lower left corner of the text. X specifies the horizontal distance from the origin to the corner and Y specifies the vertical distance. Z is used for 3-D plots only.
	CENTER	Redefines X, Y, and Z so that they locate the center of the text.

Common options	COLOR	HEIGHT	WIDTH

Appendix I: Command reference

<table>
<tr>
<td>Commands
without menu
equivalents</td>
<td>NAMES</td>
<td>Displays variable names in current file. Not available in the Data Editor. HOT.</td>
</tr>
<tr>
<td></td>
<td>REM comment</td>
<td>REM lets you put comments in command files. All text on the same line is ignored.</td>
</tr>
<tr>
<td></td>
<td>RSEED=n</td>
<td>Specifies the random number seed n to be used for any random data generated by the SYSTAT functions (used with IF...THEN and LET). You can specify any integer between 1 and 30,000.</td>
</tr>
<tr>
<td></td>
<td>BEGIN</td>
<td>Opens the graphics output device. Use BEGIN...END to overlay plots. You can only use this command in a batch file</td>
</tr>
<tr>
<td></td>
<td>END</td>
<td>Closes the graphics output device. Use BEGIN...END to overlay plots. You can only use this command in a batch file.</td>
</tr>
</table>

Options

The following SYGRAPH commands, which are equivalents to **Color...**, **Formats...**, and **Global settings...** from the **Options** menu do not produce graphics. They are COLD commands (switches) that affect subsequent commands. They all stay set

Color...

COLOR *item=color*

Plots the graph *item* in the specified *color* in the graphs that follow. You can specify item as BACK (background), FORE (foreground), GRAPH (graph), or LABEL (labels on the graph).

You can specify colors by name (RED, ORANGE, YELLOW, GREEN, BLUE, VIOLET, BLACK, WHITE, GRAY, BROWN) or by wavelength in nanometers. You must include all items in one COLOR command.

Formats...

CS= *n*

Sets the size of characters used in all subsequent graphs (excepts those produced by the WRITE command). The default is CS=1. CS=2 produces characters twice as large as usual in graphs, scales and labels.

DEPTH= *depth unit*

Specifies the depth of the plane along the facet. The default is 50%. The default unit is %. You may specify units of % (for percent), IN (for inches) or CM (for centimeters).

EYE= *xeye, yeye, zeye*

Specifies the point of view for a three dimensional graph. *Xeye, yeye,* and *zeye* specify units from the origin from which to view the plot. The default values are -8, -12, 8.

FACET *axis1 axis2*

Specifies the plane onto which subsequent two dimensional graphs are plotted.

SCALE *x unit, y unit*

Rescales the graph to a specified size. The *x* and *y* values refer to the size of your display window. The default is 100,100. the default *unit* is % (percent). Other units available are IN (for inches) and CM (for centimeters).

SEPAR *color*

Plots only the areas of the subsequent graphs which are the specified *color*. Valid colors are RED, ORANGE, YELLOW, GREEN, BLUE, VIOLET, BLACK, WHITE, GRAY, BROWN or the color in nanometers.

THICK thickness

Specifies the thickness of lines on subsequent graphs. The default *thickness* is 1. Larger *thickness* values will make lines that many times thicker (e.g. THICK=2 will make lines twice as thick as THICK=1). You can specify any positive value for *thickness*.

TYPE *typeface*

Specifies the typeface (or font) for your graph. The default is STROKE. Other available typeface are BRITISH, SWISS, HERSHEY and GREEK.

/ITALIC

Specifies an italic typeface.

TICK=INTERVAL I RATIO

This command is used when logging scales with XLOG etc. TICK=INTERVAL gives equally spaced tick marks; TICK=RATIO gives logarithmic tick marks.

INDENT

Indents the first and last scale values on each axis so they don't overlap.

Common options

The following options are provided for most SYGRAPH commands. Below each command appears a list of the common options that apply. See also TICK, above.

Axes

AXES=*n*	Specifies the number of axes to plot. For 2-D graphs, *n* must be between 0 and 4, inclusive. For 3-D graphs, *n* must be between 0 and 12, inclusive. Specify a negative number to print only that axis.
GRID=1	2	3	Overlays a grid on the plot. 1 specifies vertical grid marks, 2 specifies horizontal, and 3 both vertical and horizontal. The default is no grid.
XLIMIT, YLIMIT=*n, p*	Adds dashed horizontal lines to mark control limits. You must specify both *n* and *p*. Limits are not plotted for numbers outside the axis extremes; therefore, to plot only one line, specify a value outside this range.
SCALE=*n*	Specifies which axes to print scales on. For 2-D graphs, *n* must range from 0 to 4. For 3-D graphs, *n* must range from 0 to 12. Specify a negative number to print a scale for only that axis.
STICK	Forces tick marks to face outside the graph frame.
XTICK, YTICK, ZTICK=*n*	Specifies the number of tick marks along each axis.
XLABEL, YLABEL, ZLABEL="*char*"	Labels the corresponding axis with the text string specified by *char*.
XMAX, YMAX, ZMAX=*n*	Specifies maximum scale value.

	MIN, XMIN, YMIN, ZMIN=*n*	Specifies minimum scale value.
	PIP, XPIP, YPIP, ZPIP=*n*	Specifies *n* pip marks between tick marks. The default value is 0.
	REV, XREV, YREV, ZREV	Reverses the scale.
Error	ERROR=[*var*]	Plots symmetric error bars with size specified by the values of *var*. If you do not specify a *var*, SYSTAT uses the standard deviation of the dependent variable.
	ERROR1=[*var*]	Plots one-sided error bars with size specified by the values of *var*. If you do not specify a *var*, SYSTAT uses the standard deviation of the dependent variable.
	SERROR	Plots symmetric error bars with length computed from the standard error of the mean of the dependent variable.
	SERROR1	Plots one-sided error bars with length computed from the standard error of the mean of the dependent variable.
Fill	FILL=*n1, n2, ...* I *varlist*	Specifies a fill pattern for symbols, bars, etc. Specify a fill pattern for each variable or group. Specifying a number between 0 and 1 produces an even gradation of shading between hollow and filled. Specifying an integer between 1 and 7, inclusive, produces one of SYSTAT's pre-set patterns. Specifying a variable name tells SYSTAT to use the values of that variable to determine shading.

Legend	LEGEND= *x unit, y unit*	Determines the location of the lower left corner of the legend. The *x* and *y* values refer to the distance from the origin. The default *unit* is % (percent). Other units available are IN (for inches) and CM (for centimeters). The default placement is at the lower right corner of the graph. To delete the legend all together, move it off the page (e.g. LEGEND=200,200)
	LLABEL='*label1*', '*label2*',... '*labeln*'	Allows labels up to 80 characters long for each value in the legend of a multivalued graph.
Line	LINE=*n1, n2, ...*	Connects plotting symbols with a line. The type of line is specified by *n*. Enter a number for each *y* variable plotted.
Log	LOG, XLOG, YOG, ZLOG=*n*	Logs the scale to the base *n* before plotting. The default is logging to the base *e*.
Power	POW, XPOW, YPOW, ZPOW=*n*	Specifies a scale to the power of *n*. The default value of *n* is .5.
Symbol	SYMBOL=*n1, n2, ...* | "*char1* " "*char2* " ... | *varlist*	Labels data points. Specify one number, character string, or variable for each *y* variable you plot. If you specify character variables, the first character is used as the plotting symbol for each case. If you specify numeric variables, their values are used the same way as numbers you specify.

		Numbers specify preset symbols ($1 \leq n \leq 21$). If you specify a character variable, SYSTAT uses the first letter of each value as the plotting symbol. Numeric variables should contain values between 1 and 128. Values between 1 and 21 are plotted with the corresponding SYGRAPH plotting symbols; values from 32 to 128 are plotted with the corresponding ASCII characters. Values that do not correspond to symbols are deleted.
	SIZE=n | *var*	Specifies a symbol size multiplier. If you specify a variable *var*, symbols are multiplied by the value of *var* for each case. If you specify SIZE=0, no points are printed.
Title	TITLE="*char*"	Prints *char* above the graph.
T'pose	TRANS	Transposes the plot.
Ruler	HEIGHT=n | n IN | n CM | n PT	Specifies physical height of plot. If you do not specify a metric (inches or centimeters), the plot will be n percent of the default height. For WRITE, you may give measurements in points (PT).
	WIDTH=n | n IN | n CM | n PT	Specifies physical width of plot. If you do not specify a metric (inches or centimeters), the plot will be n percent of the default width. For WRITE, you may give measurements in points (PT).
	ORIGIN *x unit, y unit*	This is actually a command. Specifies the origin for following plots. *X* and *y* refer to coordinates in the View window (or plotting page). The default *unit* is percentage of the total screen; you can also use IN or CM.

Bar	**BAR** *varlist* [* *gvar*]	Produces a bar chart of each numeric variable in *varlist*. If you omit *varlist*, all numeric variables are used. If you include a grouping variable, *gvar*, bar charts of *varlist* for each group of *gvar* are plotted.
	/BASE=*n*	Anchors bars at a selected level *n*.
	BWIDTH=*n*	Specifies bars of width *n*. All values falling within a bar's interval are added to that bar's total count. BWIDTH is useful for producing bar charts of continuous variables.
	FAT	Removes space from between bars.
	PERCENT	Produces a divided bar chart where each segment of the chart represents the percentage of that group's contribution to the total. You may want to use STACK in conjunction with this option.
	RANGE	Plots the range of two variables against a categorical variable.
	STACK	When you specify multiple variables in *varlist* against a grouping variable, the bars are stacked instead of displayed next to each other.

Common options			
	AXES	PIP	XLABEL
	COLOR	POW	XMAX
	ERROR	SCALE	XMIN
	ERROR1	SORT	XREV
	FILL	STICK	YLABEL
	GRID	TICK	YMAX
	HEIGHT	TITLE	YMIN
	LIMIT	TRANS	YREV
	LOG	WIDTH	

Category   **CPLOT** *varlist* [* *gvar*]   Plots categorical plots of all variables in *varlist*. If *varlist* is omitted, all numeric variables are used. If a grouping variable *gvar* is included, SYGRAPH plots the mean of each variable in *varlist* within each group of *gvar*.

/BWIDTH=*n*   Specifies categories of width *n*. All values falling within a category's interval are added to that category's total count. BWIDTH is useful for producing category plots of continuous variables.

HILO   Plots a high-low-close plot. You must specify three numeric variables and one grouping variable. The first variable represents the high value, the second represents the low value, and the third represents the close value.

PERCENT   Produces a multi-variable percentage or divided line graph. You may want to use STACK in conjunction with this option.

POLAR   Produces a polar coordinate category plot.

STACK   Produces stacked or cumulative line graphs.

Common options

AXES	PIP	TITLE
COLOR	POW	TRANS
ERROR	REV	WIDTH
ERROR1	SCALE	XLABEL
FILL	SIZE	XMAX
GRID	SORT	XMIN
HEIGHT	STICK	YLABEL
LIMIT	SYMBOL	YMAX
LINE	TICK	YMIN
LOG		

Pie	**PIE** *gvarlist	varlist * gvar*	Produces a pie chart of counts within grouping variables or continuous variables against a categorical variable. If you specify PIE with no argument, pie charts of all numeric variables are produced.
	/RING	Draws ring (attention) plots.
	SCALE=0	Prints no labels around the pie.

Common options

COLOR	LOG	TITLE
FILL	POW	WIDTH
HEIGHT	SORT	

Box   **BOX** *varlist* [* *gvar*]   Plots box-and-whiskers plots of all variables in *varlist*. If *varlist* is omitted, all numeric variables are used. If a grouping variable *gvar* is included, a separate box for each group of *gvar* is displayed.

/NOTCH   Produces notched box plots.

Common options

AXES	MIN	TICK
COLOR	PIP	TITLE
HEIGHT	POW	TRANS
LIMIT	REV	WIDTH
LOG	SCALE	XLABEL
MAX	SORT	YLABEL

Density	**DENSITY** *varlist*	Plots the density of all variables in *varlist*. If you omit *varlist*, all numeric variables are plotted.
	/FUZZY I <u>HIST</u> I JITTER I POLY I STRIPE	FUZZY produces a fuzzygram, HIST, the default, produces histograms, JITTER produces jittered density graphs, POLY produces frequency polygons, and STRIPE produces density stripes.
		The following options are available only for histograms.
	BARS=*n*	Specifies the number of bars to use in a histogram.
	BWIDTH=*n*	Specifies the width of bars in a histogram.
	NORMAL	Plots normal smooth *without* histogram.
	CUM	Produces cumulative histograms.
	SMOOTH= <u>NORMAL</u> I KERNEL	Smooths the histogram with a normal curve using the sample mean and standard deviation.

Common options	AXES	MAX	TITLE
	COLOR	MIN	TRANS
	FILL	POW	WIDTH
	HEIGHT	REV	XLABEL
	LOG	SCALE	YLABEL

Stem	**STEM** *varlist*	Plots a stem-and-leaf diagram of all variables in *varlist*. If you omit *varlist*, all numeric variables are used.
	/LINES=*n*	Specifies the number of lines *n* used to draw the plot.

Common options	HEIGHT	POW	WIDTH
	LOG	TITLE	

Plot, 3-D Plot, and Function	**SPIN** *zvar * yvar * xvar*	Plots a 3-D scatterplot in the Spin window where the point cloud can be rotated around the X, Y, or Z axis. Only the COLOR and SIZE options may be used with this command.
	PLOT *yvarlist * xvar | zvarlist * yvar * xvar | function*	Graphs a single 2-D scatterplot with *yvarlist* as dependent variable(s) and *xvar* as the independent variable, or graphs a 3-D scatterplot with *zvarlist* plotted on the vertical *z* axis against *xvar* and *yvar* on the horizontal plane. To plot mathematical functions, specify the equation .
	/ | !	*For function plots, use an exclamation point (!) before the option list rather than the usual slash (/).* For all data plots, use the slash.
	COLOR	Produces color-shaded 3-D surfaces. Low values of the Z variable are colored blue and high values are red. The number of colors available and the number of cuts determine the smoothness of the shading. The range of shading is controlled by ZMAX and ZMIN.
	CONTOUR	Draws a contour plot.
	SMOOTH= LINEAR | DWLS | INVERSE | KERNEL | NEXPO | QUAD	Specifies smoothing for the plot. See below for descriptions of these smoothing methods. NEXPO is the default.
	COLOR	Produces color contour plots with colors ranging from blue (low) to red (high).
	FILL	Produces shaded contour plot.
	TRI	Contours in triangular coordinates.
	CUT=*n*	Specifies number of lines used in contours and surface smooths (for surface smoothing, produces an $n \times n$ grid). The default value of *n* is 30 ($2 \le n \le 100$).

511

ELL=*n*	Draws a Gaussian bivariate ellipsoid over the scatterplot using the *p* value specified by *n* (0 ≤ *n* ≤ 1). The default value of *n* is .5.
ELM=*n*	Draws a Gaussian confidence interval of the bivariate centroid using the *p* value specified by *n* (0 ≤ *n* ≤ 1). The default value of *n* is .95.
FLOWER	Produces a sunflower plot where the density of symbols is determined by the number of observations falling on each point.
FOURIER	Plots Andrews' Fourier components (one waveform for each case).
HIDE	Hides overlapped portions of 3-D plots.
HILO	Produces a high-low-close plot. Specify three continuous variables against a categorical variable. The first variable gives the high value, the second specifies the low value, and the third specifies the close value.
INFLUENCE	Produces a plot where the size of each point represents the influence of that point on the correlation between the two variables. Hollow symbols represent positive influence and filled symbols represent negative influence.
JITTER	Moves data points by small uniform random amounts to show points that overlap.
LABEL=*var$*	Labels points with the values of *var$*.
PARALLEL	Produces parallel coordinate plots.

POLAR	Plots data in polar coordinates. The *y* scale is the distance of a point from the origin and the *x* scale is the angle between the horizontal axis and a line from the origin to the point.
PROJECT=GNOMON | STEREO | MERCATOR | ORTHO	Specifies a mapping projection for the plot. GNOMON specifies gnomonic projection, STEREO specifies stereographic projection, MERCATOR, the default, specifies mercator conformal projection, and ORTHO specifies orthographic projection.
SLOPE	Adjusts the size of the graph so that the median absolute physical slope of the line segments is one. Recommended for time series plots.
SMOOTH=DWLS | INVERSE | KERNEL | LINEAR | LOG | LOWESS | NEXPO | POWER | QUAD | SPLINE | STEP	Plots a smoothed function through the data. DWLS specifies distance weighted least squares smoothing. LINEAR, the default, specifies linear regression smoothing. LOWESS, available only for 2-D plots, specifies locally weighted scatterplot smoothing. NEXPO specifies negative exponentially weighted smoothing. QUAD specifies quadratic smoothing. SPLINE, available only for 2-D plots, specifies spline smoothing. STEP, available only for 2-D plots, specifies step smoothing.
CONFI=*n*	Draws confidence intervals at level *n*. Available only with 2-D linear smooth.
SHORT	Limits the domain of a smooth to the extreme data values on the horizontal axis. Available only with 2-D plots.

TENSION=*n*	Controls a stiffness parameter for DWLS, KERNEL, LOWESS, or SPLINE smoothing. A higher value of *n* uses more data points to smooth each value on the curve, and makes the smooth stiffer. A lower *n* makes the smooth looser and more susceptible to the influence of individual data points.
	For DWLS smoothing, $0 \le n \le 10$, and the default value is the inverse of the number of cases.
	For KERNEL, the default is $N^{(-1/5)}$ for univariate smoothing and $2N^{(-1/6)}$, where N is the number of cases.
	For LOWESS smoothing, $0 \le n \le 1$, and the default value is .5.
	For SPLINE smoothing, $0 \le n \le 10$, and the default value is 2.
SPAN	Plots a minimum spanning tree.
SPIKE=*n*	Draws a vertical line from each point to the level on the vertical axis corresponding to *n*. The default value of *n* is 0.
SURFACE=XCUT | YCUT | ZCUT	XCUT produces lines parallel to the X axis, YCUT produces lines parallel to the Y axis, and ZCUT produces contours along the Z axis. HIDE is not available with SURFACE=ZCUT.
TRI	Plots the data in triangular coordinates.
VECTOR=*x, y,* [*z*]	Draws a vector plot. Lines are drawn from the point *x,y* (and *z* for 3-D plots) to each data point. If you do not specify *x, y,* or *z,* lines are drawn from the origin of the graph.
VORONOI	Plots a Voronoi tesselation.

| | ZHEIGHT=*n* \| *n* IN \| *n* CM | Specifies the physical height of the *z* (vertical) axis in a 3-D plot. |

Common options			
	AXES	WIDTH	YMIN
	COLOR	XLABEL	YPIP
	ERROR	XLIMIT	YPOW
	ERROR1	XLOG	YREV
	FILL	XMAX	YTICK
	GRID	XMIN	ZLABEL
	HEIGHT	XPIP	ZLOG
	LINE	XPOW	ZMAX
	SCALE	XREV	ZPMIN
	SIZE	XTICK	ZPIP
	STICK	YLABEL	ZPOW
	SYMBOL	YLIMIT	ZREV
	TITLE	YLOG	ZTICK
	TRANSPOSE	YMAX	

SPLOM	**SPLOM** *varlist1* [* *varlist2*	Plots a full symmetric scatterplot matrix of all variables in *varlist1*. If you include *varlist2*, plots all variables in *varlist1* (vertical axis) against all variables in *varlist2* (horizontal axis). If you specify SPLOM with no argument, plots a symmetric matrix of all numeric variables.
	/AXES=0	Prints no axes. The default value is 4. The other values (1, 2, and 3) are not available.
	DENSITY=<u>HIST</u> | JITTER | STRIPE	Plots density graphs of the variables in the diagonal cells of the matrix. HIST, the default, specifies histograms. JITTER specifies jittered density graphs. STRIPE specifies density stripes.
	ELL=*n*	Draws a Gaussian bivariate ellipsoid in each scatterplot using the *p* value specified by *n* ($0 \le n \le 1$). The default value of *n* is .5.
	ELM=*n*	Draws a Gaussian confidence interval of the bivariate centroid in each scatterplot using the *p* value specified by *n* ($0 \le n \le 1$). The default value of *n* is .95.

FLOWER	Produces sunflower plots where the density of symbols is determined by the number of observations falling on each point.
HALF	Plots only the lower half of the matrix in a fully symmetric matrix.
INFLUENCE	Produces plots where the size of each point represents the influence of that point on the correlation between the two variables. Hollow symbols represent positive influence and filled symbols represent negative influence.
JITTER	Moves data points by small uniform random amounts to show points that overlap.
SMOOTH=DWLS | LINEAR | LOWESS | NEXPO | QUAD | SPLINE | STEP	Plots a smoothed function through data. DWLS specifies distance weighted least squares smoothing. LINEAR, the default, specifies linear regression smoothing. LOWESS specifies locally weighted scatterplot smoothing. NEXPO specifies negative exponentially weighted smoothing. QUAD specifies quadratic smoothing. SPLINE specifies spline smoothing. STEP specifies step smoothing.
CONFI=n	Draws confidence intervals at level n. Available only with linear smooth.
SHORT	Limits domain of a smooth to the extreme data values on the horizontal axis.

TENSION=*n*		Controls a stiffness parameter for LOWESS, spline, or DWLS smoothing. A higher value of *n* uses more data points to smooth each value on the curve, and makes the smooth stiffer. A lower *n* makes the smooth looser and more susceptible to the influence of individual data points.

For LOWESS smoothing, $0 \leq n \leq 1$, and the default value is .5.

For spline smoothing, $0 \leq n \leq 10$, and the default value is 2.

For DWLS smoothing, $0 \leq n \leq 10$, and the default value is the inverse of the number of cases.

SPAN	Plots minimum spanning trees.
SPIKE=*n*	Draws a vertical line from each point to the level on the vertical axis corresponding to *n*. The default value of *n* is 0.
VECTOR=*m, n*	Draws a vector plot. Lines are drawn from the point *m, n* to each data point. If you do not specify *m* or *n* lines are drawn from the origin of the graph.

Common options

COLOR	TITLE	XPOW
FILL	WIDTH	YLOG
HEIGHT	XLOG	YMAX
LINE	XMAX	YMIN
SIZE	XMIN	YPOW
SYMBOL		

Quantile

QPLOT *varlist* [* *var*]

Plots quantile plots of all variables in *varlist*. If you include *var*, plots two-sample quantile plots. If you specify PPLOT with no argument, all numeric variables are plotted.

/SMOOTH=<u>LINEAR</u> | QUAD

Smooths the quantile plot. LINEAR, the default, specifies a linear smooth. QUAD specifies a quadratic smooth.

SHORT

Limits the domain of a smooth to the extreme data values on the horizontal axis.

Common options

AXES	SYMBOL	XPOW
COLOR	TITLE	YTICK
FILL	TRANS	YLABEL
GRID	WIDTH	YLIMIT
HEIGHT	XLABEL	YLOG
LINE	XLIMIT	YPIP
SCALE	XLOG	YPOW
SIZE	XPIP	YTICK
STICK		

Icon	**ICON** *varlist*	Produces icon plots with the specified variables.
	/ ARROW	BLOB	FACE	HIST	PROFILE	RECT	STAR	VANE	ARROW produces arrow icons, BLOB produces Fourier blob icons, FACE produces Chernoff's faces, HIST produces histogram icons, PROFILE produces profile icons, RECT produces framed rectangle icons, STAR, the default, produces star icons, and VANE produces weather vane icons.
	COLS=*n*	Specifies the number of columns in which to print output.
	LABEL=*var$*	Labels each case with the value of *var$*.
	ROWS=*n*	Specifies the number of rows in which to print output.
	STAND	Standardizes data before plotting.
	X=*var1*, Y=*var2*	Centers icons on the X and Y coordinates specified by *var1* and *var2*.

Common options			
	COLOR	SIZE	XMIN
	FILL	TITLE	YMAX
	HEIGHT	XMAX	YMIN

Map	**MAP**	Produces a map of previously specified items.
	/LABEL=*var$*	Labels each state or polygon with the value contained in *var$*.
	LINE=*n*	Specifies the type of line to separate states or polygons ($1 \leq n \leq 11$). The default is *n*=1, a solid line.
	PROJECT=GNOMON | STEREO | MERCATOR | ORTHO	Specifies the type of mapping projection to use. GNOMON specifies gnomonic projection, STEREO specifies stereographic projection, MERCATOR, the default, specifies mercator conformal projection, and ORTHO specifies orthographic projection.

Common options	COLOR	TRANS	XMIN
	FILL	WIDTH	YMAX
	HEIGHT	XMAX	YMIN
	TITLE		

Prob'y	**PPLOT** *varlist*	Plots a normal probability plot of each variable in *varlist*. If you omit *varlist*, all numeric variables are used.
	/CHISQ=*n* I EXPO I GAMMA=*n* I HALF I <u>NORM</u> I UNIFORM I WEIBULL	Specifies the distribution against which data is plotted. CHISQ specifies a chi-square distribution with *n* degrees of freedom. EXPO specifies an exponential distribution. GAMMA plots data against the quantiles of a gamma distribution with shape parameter *n*. HALF specifies a half-normal distribution. NORM, the default, specifies a normal distribution. UNIFORM specifies a uniform distribution. WEIBULL specifies the Weibull distribution.
	SMOOTH=<u>LINEAR</u> I QUAD	Smooths the probability plot. LINEAR, the default, specifies a linear smooth. QUAD specifies a quadratic smooth.
	SHORT	Limits the domain of a smooth to the extreme data values on the horizontal axis.

Common options	AXES	POW	XLABEL
	COLOR	SCALE	XLIMIT
	FILL	SIZE	XPIP
	GRID	STICK	XTICK
	HEIGHT	SYMBOL	YLABEL
	LINE	TITLE	YLIMIT
	LOG	TRANS	YPIP
	PIP	WIDTH	YTICK

Appendix II: Command equivalents for examples

Mouse instructions are given for all examples in the manual. Here we provide the equivalent keyboard commands for those examples. Examples are numbered within each chapter; "5.3" means the third example of Chapter 5.

1 Tutorial

1.1

Open a data file

```
EDIT US
```

1.2

Draw a bar graph

```
BAR INCOME*REGION$
```

1.3

Printing your graph

```
OUTPUT=PRINTER
BAR INCOME*REGION$
```

1.4

Changing the axes

```
BAR INCOME*REGION$/AXES=1
```

1.5

Changing scales

```
BAR INCOME*REGION$,
 /AXES=0,SCALE=2,
```

1.6

Labeling axes

```
BAR INCOME*REGION$,
 /AXES=0,SCALE=2,
  XLABEL='Census Region',
  YLABEL='Per Capita Income'
```

1.7

Scale limits

```
BAR INCOME*REGION$/YMIN=0
```

Appendix II: Command equivalents for examples

1.8   Tick marks

      `BAR INCOME*REGION$/YMIN=0,TICK=8`

1.9   Pip marks

      `BAR INCOME*REGION$/YMIN=0,PIP=4`

1.10   Ticks inside or outside

      `BAR INCOME*REGION$/YMIN=0,PIP=4,STICK`

1.11   Reversing a scale

      `BAR INCOME*REGION$/YMIN=0,YREV`

1.12   Transposing a graph

      `BAR INCOME*REGION$/TRANS,AXES=1,YMIN=0`

1.13   Filling a graph

      `BAR INCOME*REGION$/FILL=7`

1.14   Coloring a graph

      `BAR INCOME*REGION$/COLOR=GREEN,FILL=1`

1.15   Making a pie chart

      `PIE INCOME*REGION$`

1.16   Making a scatterplot

      `PLOT INCOME*POPDEN`

1.17   Smoothing a scatterplot

      `PLOT INCOME*POPDEN/SMOOTH=LOWESS`

1.18   Transforming a plot scale

```
PLOT INCOME*POPDEN/SMOOTH=LINEAR,CONFI=.95,XLOG=10
```

1.19   Labeling points

```
PLOT INCOME*POPDEN,
 /SMOOTH=LINEAR,XLOG=10,LABEL=STATE$
```

1.20   Influence plots

```
PLOT INCOME*POPDEN/XLOG=10,INFLUENCE
```

1.21   Plotting symbols

```
PLOT INCOME*POPDEN/XLOG=10,SYMBOL=2,FILL=1
```

1.22   Symbols from data values

```
PLOT LABLAT*LABLON,
 /SYMBOL=STATE$,HEIGHT=3IN,WIDTH=4IN
```

1.23   Varying symbol sizes

```
PLOT PERSON*PROPERTY,
 /SYMBOL=10,SIZE=1.5
```

1.24   Varying symbol sizes with a variable

```
PLOT LABLAT*LABLON,
 /SYMBOL=2,SIZE=RAI,HEIGHT=3IN,WIDTH=4IN
```

1.25   Grid marks

```
PLOT INCOME*POPDEN,
 /XLOG=10,SYMBOL=2,GRID=3,XPIP=9,YPIP=10,
  XLABEL='Log of Population Per Square Mile',
  YLABEL='Per Capita Income'
```

1.26   Plotting a curve

```
PLOT Y=X^3
```

Appendix II: Command equivalents for examples

1.27   3-D function plot

      ```
PLOT Z=X^2-Y^2!HIDE
```

1.28   3-D spike plot

      ```
PLOT INCOME*LABLAT*LABLON/SYMBOL=2,SPIKE
```

4 Common options

4.1   Basic bar chart
    ```
BAR INCOME*REGION$
```

4.2   Data limits

    ```
BAR INCOME*REGION$/YMIN=0
```

4.3   Pips

    ```
BAR INCOME*REGION$/YMIN=0 TICK=4 PIP=4
```

4.4   Labeling axes

    ```
BAR INCOME*REGION$/XLABEL='Census Region',
YLABEL='Income'
```

4.5   Control limits

    ```
BAR INCOME*REGION$/YLIMIT=-1,3464.5
```

4.6   Axes

    ```
BAR INCOME*REGION$/AXES=1
```

4.7   Scales

    ```
BAR INCOME*REGION$/AXES=0 SCALE=2
```


4.8   Grids

```
BAR INCOME*REGION$/GRID=3
```

4.9   Reversing scales

```
BAR INCOME*REGION$/YREV
```

4.10   Colored bars

```
BAR INCOME*REGION$/COLOR=GREEN
```

4.11   Solid colored bars

```
BAR INCOME*REGION$/FILL=1 COLOR=GREEN
```

4.12   Filled bars

```
BAR INCOME*REGION$/FILL=.5
```

4.13   Two-variable bar chart

```
BAR SUMMER,WINTER*REGION$/FILL=1,7
```

4.14   Category plot with line

```
CPLOT INCOME*REGION$/LINE=11
```

4.15   Logged bar chart

```
BAR SUMMER WINTER*REGION$/LOG=10,FILL 1,7
```

4.16   Unsorted bars

```
BAR SUMMER WINTER*REGION$/SNORT,FILL 1,7
```

4.17   Filled symbols

```
CPLOT INCOME*REGION$/SYMBOL=21 FILL=6
```

4.18   Titled bar chart

```
BAR INCOME*REGION$/TITLE='Income within Region'
```

4.19   Transposed bar chart

```
BAR INCOME*REGION$/TRANSPOSE
```

4.20   Looking up at a surface

```
EYE -5,-2,-1
TYPE=STROKE
PLOT Z=X^2-Y^2 ! HIDE
```

4.21   Thickness

```
THICK=5
BAR SUMMER WINTER*REGION$
```

5 Bar

5.1   Bar chart of counts

```
BAR REGION$/SNORT
```

5.2   Using a count variable

```
WEIGHT=COUNT
BAR REGION$/SNORT
```

5.3   Bar chart of means

```
BAR SUMMER*REGION$/YMIN=0,SNORT
```

5.4   Multi-variable bar chart

```
BAR SUMMER,WINTER*REGION$/FILL=7,4,YMIN=0,SNORT
```

5.5   Creating categories from a continuous variable

```
BAR SUMMER/XMIN=0,BWIDTH=10
```

5.6   Divided bar graph

```
BAR INCOME*REGION$/PERCENT,SNORT
```

5.7   Multi-variable divided bar graph

```
BAR DEFENSE,INTEREST,OTHER*YEAR$,
/STACK,FILL=1,2,7,PERCENT
```

5.8   Range chart

```
BAR LOW,HIGH*CITY$/RANGE
```

5.9   Anchored bar chart

```
BAR SUMMER*REGION$/BASE=75.6, SNORT
```

5.10   Symmetric error bars

```
TYPE=HERSHEY
BAR DENSITY*ENERGY$/ERROR=SE
```

5.11   Fat bars

```
BAR SUMMER*REGION$/FAT,SNORT
```

5.12   Stacked percentage chart

```
BAR DEFENSE,INTEREST,OTHER*YEAR$
/STACK,FILL=1,2,7
```

6 Category

6.1   Category plot of counts

```
CPLOT REGION$/SNORT
```

Appendix II: Command equivalents for examples

6.2   Using a count variable

```
WEIGHT=COUNT
CPLOT REGION$/SNORT
```

6.3   Category plot of means

```
CPLOT SUMMER*REGION$/SYMBOL=2,SNORT
```

6.4   Multi-variable category plot

```
CPLOT SUMMER,WINTER*REGION$/SYMBOL=2,3,SNORT
```

6.5   Creating categories from a continuous variable

```
CPLOT SUMMER/XMIN=0,BWIDTH=10,SYMBOL=2,FILL=1
```

6.6   High-low-close plot

```
CPLOT HIGH,LOW,CLOSE*MONTH$,
  /HILO,YLABEL='PRICE',SYMBOL=12
```

6.7   Profile plot

```
THICK=7
CPLOT INCOME*REGION$/LINE,SNORT
```

6.8   Multi-variable profile plot

```
CPLOT SUMMER,WINTER*REGION$,
  /LINE=1,10,SIZE=0,SNORT
```

6.9   Multi-variable divided line plot

```
CPLOT DEFENSE,INTEREST,OTHER*YEAR$,
  /STACK,FILL=1,2,7,LINE,PERCENT,STICK,SIZE=0
```

6.10   Star plot

```
CPLOT INCOME*REGION$/SIZE=0,POLAR,LINE,SNORT
```

6.11   Symmetric error bars

```
TYPE=HERSHEY
CPLOT DENSITY*ENERGY$,
  /ERROR=SE,SYMBOL=3,FILL=1
```

6.12   Stacked line plot

```
CPLOT DEFENSE,INTEREST,OTHER*YEAR$,
  /STACK,FILL=1,2,7,LINE,YMIN=0,YMAX=600000,SIZE=0
```

7 Pie
_____

7.1   Pie chart of counts

```
PIE REGION$/SNORT
```

7.2   Using a count variable

```
WEIGHT=COUNT
PIE REGION$/SHORT,SNORT
```

7.3   Pie chart of means

```
TYPE=BRITISH
PIE SALES*REGION$/SNORT
```

7.4   Attention map

```
TYPE=BRITISH/ITALIC
PIE PERCENT*LOCUS$/RING,SNORT
```

7.5   Logged data pie chart

```
TYPE=STROKE/ITALIC
PIE SALES*REGION$/LOG=10,SNORT
```

7.6   Powered data pie chart

```
TYPE=HERSHEY
PIE SALES*REGION$/POW=2,SNORT
```

8 Box

8.1   Box plot

```
BOX POPDEN
```

8.2   Grouped box plot

```
BOX INCOME*REGION$/SNORT
```

8.3   Notched box plot

```
BOX INCOME*REGION$/NOTCH,SNORT
```

9 Density

9.1   Histogram

```
DENSITY INCOME
```

9.2   Cumulative histogram

```
DENSITY INCOME/CUM
```

9.3   Fuzzygram

```
DENSITY WINTER/FUZZY
```

9.4   Jittered density

```
DENSITY POPDEN/JITTER
```

9.5   Frequency polygon

```
DENSITY INCOME/POLY,FILL=7
```

9.6   Stripe plot

```
DENSITY POPDEN/STRIPE
```

9.7   Dit plot

```
DENSITY SUMMER/DIT
```
9.8   Grouped dot plot

```
DENSITY INCOME*REGION$/DOT
```

9.9   More bars

```
TYPE=HERSHEY
DENSITY INCOME/BARS=15
```

9.10   Choosing bar widths

```
DENSITY INCOME/MIN=2000,BWIDTH=150
```

9.11   Histogram smoothed with normal density

```
TYPE=BRITISH
DENSITY WINTER/SMOOTH=NORMAL
```

10 Stem

10.1   Stem-and-leaf display

```
STEM INCOME
```

10.2   More lines

```
STEM INCOME/LINES=30,HEIGHT=3.5IN,WIDTH=2IN
```

11 Plots

11.1   Scatterplot

```
TYPE=BRITISH
PLOT SUMMER*LABLAT
```


Appendix II: Command equivalents for examples

11.2   Multiple Y variable scatterplot

```
PLOT SUMMER,WINTER*LABLAT/SYMBOL=2,3
```

11.3   Scatterplot with box plot

```
TYPE=HERSHEY
BEGIN
PLOT RAIN*SUMMER,
 /HEIGHT=3IN,WIDTH=1.5IN,SYMBOL=2
ORIGIN=2.5IN,0
PLOT RAIN*WINTER,
 /AXES=4,HEIGHT=3IN,WIDTH=1.5IN,SYMBOL=2
ORIGIN=4IN,0
BOX RAIN,
 /TRANS,AXES=0,SCALE=0,HEIGHT=3IN,WIDTH=1.5IN,
  XLABEL=' '
ORIGIN=2.5IN,3IN
BOX WINTER,
 /AXES=0,SCALE=0,HEIGHT=1.5IN,WIDTH=1.5IN,
  XLABEL=' '
ORIGIN=0,3IN
BOX SUMMER,
 /AXES=0,SCALE=0,HEIGHT=1.5IN,WIDTH=1.5IN,
  XLABEL=' '
END
```

11.4   Contour plot with lines

```
PLOT RAIN*LABLAT*LABLON,
 /ZTICK=10,SMOOTH=DWLS,CONTOUR
```

11.5   Contour plot with shading

```
PLOT Z=X^2-Y^2,
 !CONTOUR,FILL,ZTICK=10,ZMIN=-2,ZMAX=2,CUT=60
```

11.6   Contour plot with color

```
PLOT Z=X^2-Y^2,
 !CONTOUR,COLOR,ZTICK=10,ZMIN=-2,ZMAX=2,CUT=60
```

11.7   Fourier plot

```
TYPE=HERSHEY
PLOT/FOURIER,LABEL=FOOD$
```

11.8   High-low-close plot

```
PLOT HIGH,LOW,CLOSE*MONTH/HILO,SYMBOL=12
```

11.9   Influence plot

```
TYPE=HERSHEY
PLOT RAIN*SUMMER/INFLUENCE
```

11.10   Profile plot

```
PLOT/PARALLEL
```

11.11   Voronoi plot

```
PLOT Y*X,
 /SYMBOL='M',AXES=0,SCALE=0,
  XLABEL=' ',YLABEL=' ',VORONOI
```

11.12   Bubble plot

```
DATA
USE US
SAVE US2
LET DEN=4*SQR(POPDEN/1000)
RUN
QUIT

GRAPH
USE US
PLOT PERSON*PROPERTY/SYMBOL=2,SIZE=DEN
```

11.13   Scatterplot with bivariate confidence interval

```
TYPE=HERSHEY
PLOT PERSON*PROPERTY/SYMBOL=2,ELM=.95
```

Appendix II: Command equivalents for examples

11.14   Scatterplot with ellipse

```
TYPE=HERSHEY
PLOT PERSON*PROPERTY/SYMBOL=2,ELL=.5
```

11.15   Polar scatterplot

```
PLOT FREQ*ANGLE,
 /POLAR,SMOOTH=SPLINE,SYMBOL=2,XMIN=0,XMAX=360
```

11.16   Triangular scatterplot

```
TYPE=SWISS
PLOT RED*GREEN*BLUE/TRI,SYMBOL=COLOR$
```

11.17   Scatterplot with error bars

```
PLOT GROWTH*DOSE/SYMBOL=2,FILL=1,ERROR=SE
```

11.18   Time series plot

```
PLOT GNP*YEAR/LINE,SLOPE,SIZE=0
```

11.19   Multi-variable line graph

```
TYPE=HERSHEY
PLOT RECEIPT,EXPENSE*YEAR/LINE=1,3
```

11.20   Filled line plot

```
PLOT GROWTH*DOSE/FILL=5,SIZE=0,LINE,YMIN=0
```

11.21   Map with plot overlaid

```
PLOT LABLAT*LABLON,
 /XMIN=-125,XMAX=-65,YMIN=25,YMAX=50,
  PROJECT=GNOMON,SYMBOL=2,SIZE=.5,
  HEIGHT=3IN,WIDTH=5IN,AXES=0,SCALE=0,
  XLABEL=' ',YLABEL=' '
MAP,
 /XMIN=-125,XMAX=-65,YMIN=25,YMAX=50,
  PROJECT=GNOMON,HEIGHT=3IN,WIDTH=5IN
```

11.22   Linear regression

```
PLOT RAIN*LABLAT*LABLON/SMOOTH=LINEAR,SIZE=0
```

11.23   Regression with confidence intervals

```
TYPE=HERSHEY
PLOT WINTER*LABLAT/SMOOTH=LINEAR,CONFI=.95
```

11.24   LOWESS scatterplot smoothing

```
PLOT PROPERTY*LABLON/SMOOTH=LOWESS,SYMBOL=2
```

11.25   Negative exponentially weighted smoothing

```
PLOT ENGLAND*YEAR/SMOOTH=NEXPO,SYMBOL=2,FILL
```

11.26   Inverse squared distance smoothing

```
PLOT ENGLAND*YEAR/SMOOTH=INVERSE,SYMBOL=2,FILL
```

11.27   Quadratic smoothing

```
PLOT INCOME*POPDEN/SMOOTH=QUAD,SYMBOL=2,SIZE=.5
```

11.28   Distance weighted least squares smoothing

```
PLOT INCOME*POPDEN/SMOOTH=DWLS,SYMBOL=2,SIZE=.5
```

11.29   Spline smoothing

```
PLOT Y*X/SMOOTH=SPLINE,SYMBOL=2,FILL=1
```

11.30   Step smoothing

```
PLOT Y*X/SMOOTH=STEP SYMBOL=2 FILL=1
```

11.31   Log smoothing

```
PLOT INCOME*POPDEN/SMOOTH=LOG SYMBOL=2 SIZE=.5
```

Appendix II: Command equivalents for examples

11.32   Power smoothing

               `PLOT INCOME*POPDEN/SMOOTH=POWER SYMBOL=2 SIZE=.5`

11.33   Kernel density estimators

               `PLOT SUMMER*WINTER/SMOOTH=KERNEL, CONTOUR`

11.34   Shortening the domain of smoothing

               `PLOT WINTER*LABLAT/SMOOTH=LINEAR,CONFI=.95,SHORT`

11.35   Tension parameter

               `PLOT PROPERTY*LABLON/SMOOTH=LOWESS,TENSION=.9`

11.36   Spanning tree

               `PLOT LABLAT*LABLON/SPAN,HEIGHT=2IN,WIDTH=4IN`

11.37   Spike plot

               `PLOT RESIDUAL*ESTIMATE/SPIKE=0,YMIN=-20,YMAX=20`

11.38   Sunflower plot

               `WEIGHT=COUNT`
               `PLOT PERSON*PROPERTY/FLOWER,SIZE=2`

11.39   Vector plot of factor loadings

```
FACTOR
USE US
NUMBER=3
ROTATE=VARIMAX
SAVE TEMP/LOADINGS
FACTOR
QUIT

DATA
USE TEMP
SAVE LOAD
TRANS
RUN
QUIT

GRAPH
USE LOAD
PLOT COL(2)*COL(1)/VECTOR=0,LABEL=LABEL$
```

11.40   Jittered scatterplot

```
WEIGHT=COUNT
PLOT PERSON*PROPERTY/SYMBOL=2,JITTER
```

12 3-D Plot

12.1   3-D scatterplot

```
PLOT INCOME*LABLAT*LABLON/SYMBOL=2,FILL=1
```

12.2   3-D bubble plot

```
PLOT RAIN*LABLAT*LABLON/SIZE=DEN,SYMBOL=2,AXES=5
```

12.3   3-D line graph

```
PLOT Z*Y*X/LINE
```

Appendix II: Command equivalents for examples

12.4   3-D polar plot

```
PLOT RAIN*LABLAT*LABLON/SPIKE, LABEL=STATE$,
   XMIN=-180 XMAX=180 YMIN=0 YMAX=90 XREV YREV,
   GRID=3 POLAR
```

12.5   3-D minimal spanning tree

```
PLOT RAIN*LABLAT*LABLON/SPAN
```

12.6   3-D spike plot

```
PLOT RAIN*LABLAT*LABLON/SYMBOL=18,SPIKE
```

12.7   Linear smoothing

```
PLOT PROPERTY*LABLAT*LABLON/SMOOTH=LINEAR,SIZE=0
```

12.8   Negative exponentially weighted smoothing

```
PLOT Z*Y*X,
   /SMOOTH=NEXPO,XREV,YREV,SIZE=0,
   XMIN=0,XMAX=25,YMIN=0,YMAX=20
```

12.9   Inverse squared distance smoothing

```
PLOT RAIN*LABLAT*LABLON /SMOOTH=INVERSE SIZE=0
```

12.10   Quadratic smoothing

```
PLOT RAIN*LABLAT*LABLON/SMOOTH=QUAD,SIZE=0
```

12.11   Distance weighted least squares smoothing

```
PLOT RAIN*LABLAT*LABLON/SMOOTH=DWLS,SIZE=0,HIDE
```

12.12   Step smoothing

```
PLOT RAIN*LABLAT*LABLON/SMOOTH=STEP,SIZE=0
```

12.13   Kernel density estimators

    ```
    PLOT SUMMER*WINTER /SMOOTH=KERNEL
    ```

12.14   Tension parameter

    ```
    PLOT RAIN*LABLAT*LABLON/SMOOTH=DWLS SIZE=0 TENSION=1
    ```

12.15   3-D vector plots

    ```
    PLOT COL(3)*COL(2)*COL(1)/LABEL=LABEL$,VECTOR=0
    ```

13 Splom

13.1   Full symmetric SPLOM

    ```
    SPLOM
    ```

13.2   Asymmetric SPLOM

    ```
    SPLOM SUMMER,WINTER,RAIN*PERSON,PROPERTY
    ```

13.3   Half symmetric SPLOM

    ```
    TYPE=SWISS
    SPLOM/HALF
    ```

13.4   Splom with histograms

    ```
    SPLOM SUMMER,WINTER,RAIN/DENSITY=HISTOGRAM
    ```

13.5   Splom with density stripes

    ```
    SPLOM SUMMER,WINTER,RAIN/DENSITY=STRIPE
    ```

13.6   Splom with jitter plots

    ```
    WEIGHT=COUNT
    SPLOM SUMMER,WINTER,RAIN/SYMBOL=2,JITTER
    ```

13.7   Splom with bubbles

```
DATA
USE US
SAVE US2
LET DEN=POPDEN/300
RUN

GRAPH
USE US2
SPLOM SUMMER,WINTER,RAIN/SIZE=DEN,SYMBOL=2
```

13.8   Splom with centroids

```
TYPE=SWISS
SPLOM SUMMER,WINTER,RAIN/ELM=.99,DENSITY=HIST
```

13.9   Splom with ellipses

```
SPLOM SUMMER,WINTER,RAIN/ELL
```

13.10   Influence SPLOM

```
SPLOM SUMMER,WINTER,RAIN/INFLUENCE
```

13.11   Splom with lines

```
SPLOM
US,CANADA,JAPAN,GERMANY,ENGLAND*YEAR/LINE,SIZE=0,
YMIN=0,YMAX=200
```

13.12   Linear regression

```
SPLOM SUMMER,WINTER,RAIN/SMOOTH=LINEAR
```

13.13   Regression with confidence bands

```
SPLOM SUMMER,WINTER,RAIN,
 /SMOOTH=LINEAR,CONFI=.95,DENSITY=JITTER
```

13.14   LOWESS smoothing

```
SPLOM SUMMER,WINTER,RAIN/SMOOTH=LOWESS
```

13.15   Negative exponentially weighted smoothing

```
SPLOM US,CANADA,JAPAN,GERMANY,ENGLAND*YEAR,
/SMOOTH=NEXPO,SIZE=0,HEIGHT=3IN,WIDTH=4IN,
YMIN=0,YMAX=200
```

13.16   Inverse squared distance smoothing

```
SPLOM US,CANADA,JAPAN,GERMANY,ENGLAND*YEAR,
/HEIGHT=3IN WIDTH=4IN SMOOTH=INVERSE YMIN=0,
YMAX=200
```

13.17   Quadratic smoothing

```
SPLOM SUMMER,WINTER,RAIN/SMOOTH=QUAD
```

13.18   Distance weighted least squares smoothing

```
SPLOM SUMMER,WINTER,RAIN/SMOOTH=DWLS,SHORT
```

13.19   Spline smoothing

```
SPLOM US,CANADA,JAPAN,GERMANY,ENGLAND*YEAR,
/SMOOTH=SPLINE,SIZE=0,HEIGHT=3IN,WIDTH=4IN,
YMIN=0,YMAX=200
```

13.20   Step smoothing

```
SPLOM US,CANADA,JAPAN,GERMANY,ENGLAND*YEAR,
/SMOOTH=STEP,SIZE=0,HEIGHT=3IN,WIDTH=4IN,
YMIN=0,YMAX=200
```

13.21   Log smoothing

```
SPLOM SUMMER WINTER RAIN/SMOOTH=LOG
```

Appendix II: Command equivalents for examples

13.22   Power smoothing

```
SPLOM SUMMER WINTER RAIN/SMOOTH=POWER
```

13.23   Shortening the domain of smoothing

```
SPLOM SUMMER,WINTER,RAIN,
 /SMOOTH=LINEAR,CONFI,SHORT
```

13.24   Tension parameter for LOWESS, spline, or DWLS smoothing

```
SPLOM SUMMER,WINTER,RAIN/SMOOTH=LOWESS,TENSION=.9
```

13.25   Super-duper span SPLOM

```
CORR
USE US
SAVE UCOR
PEARSON
QUIT

MDS
USE UCOR
SAVE UCON/CONFIG
DIMENSION=3
SCALE

GRAPH
USE UCON
SPLOM DIM(1-3),
 /SPAN,SYMBOL=NUM$,SIZE=3,
   XMIN=-1.5,XMAX=1.5,YMIN=-1.5,YMAX=1.5
```

13.27   Splom with spikes

```
MGLH
USE US
MODEL SUMMER,WINTER,RAIN=CONSTANT+LABLAT+LABLON
SAVE RESID
ESTIMATE

GRAPH
USE RESID
SPLOM RESIDUAL(1-3)*ESTIMATE(1-3)/SPIKE=0
```

13.27   Sunflower SPLOM

```
WEIGHT=COUNT
SPLOM SUMMER,WINTER,RAIN/FLOWER,SIZE=2
```

13.28   Splom with vectors

```
SPLOM COL(1-3),
 /XMIN=-1,XMAX=1,YMIN=-1,YMAX=1,
  SYMBOL=NUM$,SIZE=2,VECTOR=0,0
```

13.29   Jittered SPLOM

```
WEIGHT=COUNT
SPLOM SUMMER,WINTER,RAIN/JITTER,SYMBOL=0
```

14 Function

14.1   2-D function plot

```
TYPE=HERSHEY
PLOT P=SQR(R)*EXP(-R)!XMIN=0,XMAX=10,YMIN=0,YMAX=.5
```

14.2   Three-Dimensional Function Plots

```
PLOT Z=2*SIN(2*SQR(X^2+Y^2))/SQR(X^2+Y^2),
 !XMIN=-5,XMAX=5,
  YMIN=-5,YMAX=5,
  ZMIN=-5,ZMAX=5,HIDE
```

14.3	Smooth, hidden surface

```
TYPE=HERSHEY
PLOT Z=EXP(-X^2-Y^2)!ZMIN=0,ZMAX=1,HIDE,CUT=60
```

14.4	Contour plotting with lines

```
PLOT Z=SIN(X)*COS(Y) ! CONTOUR, HIDE
```

14.5	Contour plotting with shading

```
PLOT Z=SIN(X)*COS(Y) ! CONTOUR, FILL, HIDE, CUT=60
```

14.6	Contour plotting with color

```
PLOT Z=SIN(X)*COS(Y) ! CONTOUR, HIDE, COLOR, CUT=60
```

14.7	Contouring with triangular coordinates

```
PLOT U=V+W^2+X^3-2.5*V*W*X ! CONTOUR, TRI, ZTICK=10,
    ZMIN=0 ZMAX=1
```

14.8	Filled function plot

```
PLOT Y=SIN(X) ! XMIN=0 XMAX=6.28, YMIN=-1, YMAX=1
```

14.9	Polar function plot

```
PLOT Y=SIN(8*X),
  !POLAR,YMAX=1,XMIN=0,XMAX=6.28,AXES=0,SCALE=0,
  XLABEL=' ',YLABEL=' '
```

14.10	Spherical function plot

```
PLOT Z=SIN(X) + COS(Y) ! SPHERE, FILL
```

15 Prob'y

15.1	Normal probability plot

```
PPLOT PERSON
```

15.2   Normal random data

```
DATA
SAVE RAND
RSEED=1339
LET Z=SRN
REPEAT 500
RUN

GRAPN
USE RAND
PPLOT Z/NORM
```

15.3   Chi-square probability plot

```
MGLH
USE US
MODEL PERSON,PROPERTY=CONSTANT
ESTIMATE
HYPOTHESIS
SAVE CANON
TEST

GRAPH
PPLOT DISTANCE/POW=2,SMOOTH=LINE,CHISQ=2
```

15.4   Exponential probability plot

```
WEIGHT=COUNT
PPLOT MONTH/TRANS,SMOOTH=LINEAR,EXPO
```

15.5   Gamma probability plot

```
WEIGHT=COUNT
PPLOT MONTH/TRANS,SMOOTH=LINEAR,GAMMA=.5
```

15.6   Half-normal probability plot

```
PPLOT POPDEN/HALF
```

Appendix II: Command equivalents for examples

15.7   Uniform probability plot

```
DATA
SAVE URAND
RSEED=1339
LET X=URN
REPEAT 500
RUN

GRAPH
PPLOT X/UNIFORM
```

15.8   Weibull probability plot

```
WEIGHT=COUNT
PPLOT MONTH,
 /TRANS,SMOOTH=LINEAR,WEIBULL,
  XLABEL='Log of Recidivism Month',
  YLABEL='Log Weibull Quantiles'
```

15.9   Probability plot with bubbles

```
DATA
USE US
SAVE US2
LET WIN=WINTER/25
RUN

GRAPH
PPLOT SUMMER/NORMAL,SYMBOL=2,SIZE=WIN
```

15.10   Linear regression

```
PPLOT WINTER/TRANS,SMOOTH=LINEAR
```

15.11   Quadratic smoothing

```
PPLOT WINTER/TRANS,SMOOTH=QUAD
```

15.12   Shortening the domain of smoothing

```
PPLOT WINTER/TRANS,SMOOTH=QUAD,SHORT
```

16 Quantile

16.1   Quantile plot

```
QPLOT INCOME
```

16.2   Q-Q plot

```
QPLOT PERSON*PROPERTY
```

16.3   Bubble quantile plot

```
DATA
USE US
SAVE US2
LET DEN=4*SQR(POPDEN/1000)
RUN

GRAPH
USE US2
QPLOT SUMMER/SYMBOL=2,SIZE=DEN
```

16.4   Linear regression

```
QPLOT PERSON/SMOOTH=LINEAR
```

16.5   Quadratic smoothing

```
QPLOT PERSON/SMOOTH=QUAD
```

17 Icon

171   Blob plot

```
SELECT REGION$='New England'
ICON INCOME,POPDEN,PROPERTY,PERSON,RAIN,WINTER,
   SUMMER/LABEL=STATE$,STAND,BLOB
```

17.2   Chernoff plot

```
SELECT REGION$='New England'
ICON INCOME,POPDEN,PROPERTY,PERSON,RAIN,WINTER,
  SUMMER/LABEL=STATE$,STAND,FACE
```

17.3   Histogram icon plot

```
SELECT REGION$='New England'
ICON INCOME,POPDEN,PROPERTY,PERSON,RAIN,WINTER,
  SUMMER/LABEL=STATE$,STAND,HIST
```

17.4   Profile icon plot

```
SELECT REGION$='New England'
ICON INCOME,POPDEN,PROPERTY,PERSON,RAIN,WINTER,
  SUMMER/LABEL=STATE$,STAND,PROF
```

17.5   Star icon plot

```
SELECT REGION$='New England'
ICON INCOME,POPDEN,PROPERTY,PERSON,RAIN,WINTER,
  SUMMER/LABEL=STATE$,STAR,STAND
```

17.6   Rectangule icon plot

```
ICON INCOME,WIDTH/LABEL=REGION$,RECT
```

17.7   Arrow plot

```
USE ROTATE
ICON RT,ANGLE/ARROW STAND
```

17.8   Weathervane plot

```
ICON RAIN SUMMER WINTER/VANE
```

17.9   Unstandardized icons

```
SELECT REGION$='New England'
ICON INCOME,POPDEN,PROPERTY,PERSON,RAIN,WINTER,
  SUMMER/LABEL=STATE$,HIST
```

17.10   Four column star plot

```
ICON INCOME,POPDEN,PROPERTY,PERSON,RAIN,WINTER,
    SUMMER/LABEL=STATE$,STAND,COLS=4
```

17.11   Icons overlayed on a mop

```
BEGIN
SELECT REGION$='Mountain'
ICON INCOME,POPDEN,PROPERTY,PERSON,RAIN,WINTER,
    SUMMER/FACE,STAND,SIZE=2,X=LABLON,Y=LABLAT
    XMIN=-120,XMAX=-105,YMIN=30,YMAX=50
MAP/XMIN=-120,XMAX=-105,YMIN=30,YMAX=50
END
```

18 Maps

181   Map of the United States

```
MAP
```

18.2   Map with stereographic projection and grid lines

```
MAP / GRID=7,XMIN=-130,XMAX=-60,YMIN=20,YMAX=55,
    HEIGHT=3IN,WIDTH=4IN,PROJECT=STEREO
```

18.3   Squished map

```
MAP/XMIN=-140,XMAX=-60,YMIN=20,YMAX=50
```

18.4   The world

```
MAP/SPHERE, GRID, HIDE
```

Appendix II: Command equivalents for examples

Appendix III: Data files

All the datasets used in the examples for this manual are listed below. In the right margin are the filename and reference for each dataset. The text gives background information and details about variables.

AGESEX
1980 U.S. Census

These data show the distribution of males and females within age groups. Each age group is labeled by the upper age limit of its members.

AKIMA
Akima (1978), SAS (1986)

These data are topological measurements of a three-dimensional surface.

ANOVA
Winer (1971)

These artificial data are the cell means from a repeated measures example in Winer, p. 525.

CIGARETTE
Harris (1987)

These data record the PRICE in U.S. dollars for a package of cigarettes in 1986 U.S. dollars (PRICE) and consumption in packs per person per day (CONSUMP) in 1986.

COLOR

These data provide the proportions of RED, GREEN, and BLUE that will produce the color specified in COLOR$.

EXPEND
The World Almanac, 1971

These data are the U.S. expenditures in millions of dollars for defense (DEFENSE), interest on public debt (INTEREST), and all other (OTHER).

FADE
Giloh and Sedat (1982)

Giloh and Sedat used these data to show that the chemical *n*-propyl gallate reduces the rate of fading of fluorescence of cell structures labeled with tetramethylrhodamine for microscopy. T_HALF represents the fluorescence halftime in minutes: the time elapsed before 50 percent loss of initial fluorescence; and CONCENT represents concentration of propyl gallate (percentage, weight to volume).

FOSSILS
Warner, Mathewes, Claque (1982)

These data give the incidence in macrofossils per 100cc of fossil specimens of various flora found at various elevations of a site in British Columbia.

HILO
SYSTAT

These are some hypothetical price data for a stock. HIGH is the highest price for that month, LOW is the low price, and CLOSE is the closing price at the end of the month.

LABOR
U.S. Bureau of
Labor Statistics

These data show output productivity per labor hour in 1977 U.S. dollars for a 25 year period.

LOAD

These data result from running the specified principal components analysis on the US dataset.

LOTUS
Nelson (1987)

These data are the results of a Lotus 1-2-3 analysis using the @IRR (internal rate of return) and @NPV (net present value) Lotus functions on figures from an undeveloped land holding. Nelson standardized both measures to allow a common vertical scale on his graph.

NUTRIENTS
USDA

These data are the percentages of selected nutrients in a typical computer programmer's diet, estimated from figures supplied by the U.S. Department of Agriculture.

PAROLE
Maltz (1984)

These data record the number of Illinois parolees who failed conditions of their parole after a certain number of months. An additional 149 parolees failed after 22 months, but we do not use these.

POLYNOMIAL

X and Y were created in SYSTAT using the equations:

$$x = u + i - 10$$
$$y = 2 + 3x + 4x^2 + 5x^3 + 500z$$

where u is a uniform random variable, i is an index running from 1 to 20, and z is a standard normal random variable. ESTIMATE was estimated from a cubic regression model computed with the **MGLH** regression program in SYSTAT. Finally, the variables UPPER and LOWER were computed in DATA from the variable SEPRED (standard error of the predicted values) created by **MGLH**. UPPER is two standard errors above ESTIMATE and LOWER is two standard errors below.

ROTATE
Metzler and
Shepard (1974)

These data measure reaction time in seconds (RT) versus angle of rotation in degrees (ANGLE) in a perception study. The experiment measured the time it took subjects to make "same" judgements when comparing a picture of a three-dimensional object to a picture of possible rotations of the object.

SPECTRAL
Michalske,
Bunker (1987)

These data are the Fourier transformed infrared spectroscopy data for a chemical reaction involving methanol. They were estimated by interpolating a graph at several points. The vertical scale was not given in the article, so it has been standardized it to 1.0 maximum.

SPLINE
Brodlie (1980)

These data are X and Y coordinates taken from a figure in Brodlie's discussion of cubic spline interpolation.

TEMP

These data are the high (HIGH) and low (LOW) temperatures for eight U.S. cities in July, 1983.

TREASURY
U.S. Treasury
Annual Reports

These data are U.S. receipts (RECEIPT) and expenditures (EXPENSE) in dollars from 1960 to 1970.

US
US.MAP
State and Metro-
politan Area Data
Book, 1986;
Bureau of the
Census; The
World Almanac,
1971.

POPDEN is people per square mile; PERSON is F.B.I. reported incidences, per 100,000 people, of personal crimes (murder, rape, robbery, assault); PROPERTY is incidences, per 100,000 people, of property crimes (burglary, larceny, auto theft); INCOME is per-capita income. SUMMER is average summer temperature; WINTER is average winter temperature; RAIN is average inches of rainfall per year; LABLAT is latitude in degrees of the center of each state; LABLON is the longitude of the center of each state.

Appendix III: Data files

Appendix IV: Typefaces

SYGRAPH contains five typefaces: Stroke, Swiss, British, Hershey, and Greek. Allen V. Hershey (Hershey, 1972) digitized the Hershey font and SYSTAT, Inc. digitized the others. Their sizes are infinitely variable with the sizing options in **Draw, Write,** and other procedures. The figures in this appendix show each typeface with equal height and width.

Control

You can produce superscripts, subscripts, and other special features by embedding control characters in a string. All control characters begin with a back slash (\). The next character following the back slash controls how subsequent characters in the string are printed. Here are the options:

```
\1                  Stroke font
\2                   Swiss font
\3                 British font
\4                 Hershey font
\5                   Greek font

\H               Double height
\h                 Half height
\W                Double width
\w                 Half width

\*                   Overstrike

\>                 Superscript
\<                   Subscript
\+               Up one level
\-             Down one level
\=   Normal level and size

\/                      Italic
\|                       Roman

\\                   Backslash
```

Superscripts and subscripts are automatically half size. Up one level and Down one level raise or lower characters one full character height without changing their size. The equal sign returns size and level settings to normal.

Height, width, superscripts, and subscripts are multiplicative. For example, superscripts of superscripts will be half-half (quarter) sized. Up and down levels are additive. To go up two levels, for example, type \+\+.

Here are some examples and their output. Notice how the operators can be combined to move in fractional increments. In the summation example, the "x" is moved up in fractional increments by first halving its height. Then its height is doubled (to return to normal) for printing.

```
'\4Hello\2\/World'
```

Hello **WORLD**

```
'\5\H\HS\*\3\=\+\+\+\+\h\w\+n\=\-\h\w\*i=1\=\h\+\+\+\H\x\<i'
```

```
'Equation is
\3y\/\<i\=\|=\/\5b\<0\|\=+\/b\<1\=\3\|x\/\<i\=\*\>2=\|+\/\5e\3\<i'
```

Equation is $\mathbf{y}_i = \beta_0 + \beta_1 \mathbf{x}_i^2 + \varepsilon_i$

Stroke

!"#$%&(
)*+,-./0
12345678
9:;<=>?@
ABCDEFGH
IJKLMNOP
QRSTUVWX
YZ[\]^_`
abcdefgh
ijklmnop
qrstuvwx
yz{|}~

Stroke italic

!"#$%&(
)*+,-./0
12345678
9;:<=>?@
ABCDEFGH
IJKLMNOP
QRSTUVWX
YZ[\]^_`
abcdefgh
ijklmnop
qrstuvwx
yz{|}~

Swiss

!"#$%&(
)*+,-./0
12345678
9:;<=>?@
ABCDEFGH
IJKLMNOP
QRSTUVWX
YZ[\]^_'
abcdefgh
ijklmnop
qrstuvwx
yz{|}~

Swiss italic

!"#$%&(
)*+,-./0
12345678
9:;<=>?@
ABCDEFGH
IJKLMNOP
QRSTUVWX
YZ[\]^_'
abcdefgh
ijklmnop
qrstuvwx
yz{|}~

British

!"#$%&(
)*+,−./0
12345678
9:;<=>?@
ABCDEFGH
IJKLMNOP
QRSTUVWX
YZ[\]^_
abcdefgh
ijklmnop
qrstuvwx
yz{|}~

British italic

!"#$%&(
)*+,-./0
12345678
9:;<=>?@
ABCDEFGH
IJKLMNOP
QRSTUVWX
YZ[\]^_
abcdefgh
ijklmnop
qrstuvwx
yz{|}~

Hershey

!"#$%&(
)*+,−./0
1234567 8
9:;<=>?@
ABCDEFGH
IJKLMNOP
QRSTUVWX
YZ[\]^_'
abcdefgh
ijklmnop
qrstuvwx
yz{|}~

Hershey italic

!"#$%&(
)*+,−./0
12345678
9:;<=>?@
ABCDEFGH
IJKLMNOP
QRSTUVWX
YZ[\]^_'
abcdefgh
ijklmnop
qrstuvwx
yz{|}~

Greek

!∀#∃%&(
)*+,−./0
12345678
9:;<=>?≅
ΑΒΧΔΕΦΓΗ
ΙJΚΛΜΝΟΠ
ΘΡΣΤΥςΩΞ
ΨΖ[∴]⊥__ ̄
αβχδεφγη
ιφκλμνοπ
θρστυϖωξ
ψζ{|}~

Greek italic

!∀#∃%&(
)*+,−./0
12345678
9.;<=>?≅
ΑΒΧΔΕΦΓΗ
ΙJΚΛΜΝΟΠ
ΘΡΣΤΥςΩΞ
ΨΖ[∴]⊥‾
αβχδεφγη
ιφκλμνοπ
θρστυϖωξ
ψζ{|}~

Appendix V: Map boundary files

SYGRAPH plots maps using two files at the same time. One has a .MAP extension and contains the coordinates of the boundaries of each polygon (state, precinct, etc.) in the file. The other is a regular SYSTAT data file that contains data about each polygon. Both files are binary. The MAP file has a special format that cannot be read by DATA. The other file can be edited or created with the Data Editor or DATA.

The data file can have any name (subject to the usual Macintosh restrictions for filenames). The MAP file must have that same name *exactly*, plus the four characters .MAP (period and extension) appended immediately after the last character of the data file's name.

The following are valid filename pairs:

```
MYDATA             MYDATA.MAP
Map stuff          Map stuff.MAP
Sara's_data_12     Sara's_data_12.MAP
```

The MAP file

File/Import... will convert an ASCII (character) file containing latitude and longitude coordinates to a MAP file. This file must have a structure like the following:

```
ID  NP    X      Y      X     Y     X    Y
ID  NP    X      Y      X     Y     ID   NP    X     Y
X   Y     ID     NP     X     Y     X    Y     X     Y ...
```

and so on. *ID* is an ID number for each polygon. *NP* is the number of points in the polygon (X,Y pairs). *X* and *Y* are the longitude and latitude, respectively, of each point on the boundary of the polygon. SYGRAPH plots a "map" for any arbitrary polygon with X,Y coordinates in any units, but most geographical data files use longitude and latitude in decimal degrees.

569

The records in this file can be unequal lengths (up to 999 characters) and the data may be integer or real or exponential. If you are uncertain about a format, the simplest is one with two numbers per record, separated by a blank or comma:

```
ID  NP
X   Y
X   Y
X   Y
ID  NP
X   Y
      etc.
```

The ID variable

The ID variable should be sorted in ascending order of absolute values in the file (early ID values smaller than later values). Several polygons may have the same ID. The Massachusetts map in the US.MAP file, for example, has three polygons for the mainland, Nantucket, and Martha's Vineyard, respectively. ID's need not be sequential numbers (i.e. you can skip a number), but they must be integers or they will be truncated to integers (decimals discarded).

If an ID is negative, then its associated polygon will not be filled with color or fill pattern. This is a useful device for representing rivers or roads within a state or polygon. A Massachusetts map, for example could have the following ID's: 4 (mainland), 4 (Martha's Vineyard), 4 (Nantucket), 4 (Cape Cod), –4 (Mass Turnpike), –4 (Concord River), –4 (Route 128). All of the points following these ID's would be plotted as Massachusetts.

Islands

Islands are represented as part of their surrounding polygon. The following figure shows an example of an island surrounded by an irregular polygon. If you trace the numbers, you can see that the filled area will exclude the triangular island in the center. The path from 6 to 7 and 10 to 11 is called a "zero width corridor." To represent this polygon and its island, you should enter 11 X,Y coordinates into the map file. The corridor will show on maps drawn with SYGRAPH unless you use "Fill" to conceal it. Otherwise, you should represent the island and the outer polygon as two separate polygons.

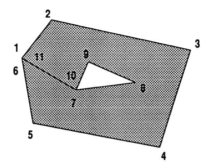

The data file

You can use the Data Editor or DATA to create the data file. The data file contains the following variables:

MAPNUM	ID number of each polygon
MINLAT	Minimum latitude of polygon
MAXLAT	Maximum latitude of polygon
MINLON	Minimum longitude of polygon
MAXLON	Maximum longitude of polygon
LABLAT	Latitude of label for polygon
LABLON	Longitude of label for polygon

These variables may be in any order in the file, but if they are missing, **Map** will not work. The data file may contain additional variables on each record. The variable names must be spelled exactly as they appear above.

How SYGRAPH plots a map

To plot a map, an ID for a polygon is selected by reading the MAPNUM variable in the first record of the data file (or the first appropriate record selected with **By groups...** or **Select...**). Next, the MAP file is read until a matching ID variable absolute value is found. The subsequent NP points of the polygon corresponding to that ID are plotted and, possibly, filled with color and fill pattern and labeled. Next, the MAP file is read further to check for remaining ID's which match the current MAPNUM. Any polygons with ID's corresponding in absolute value to the current value of MAPNUM are similarly plotted. If an ID is negative and its absolute value corresponds to the current value of MAPNUM, its associated polygon is plotted but not filled. When no further ID's corresponding to MAPNUM's value are found, the next appropriate record in the data file is selected. Polygon(s) for this ID are plotted and the process continues until no further appropriate records are available in the data file. The MINLAT, MAXLAT, MINLON, and MAXLON variables are used for scaling maps in the viewing window and the LABLAT and LABLON variables are used for labeling polygons. Up to 200 polygons can be labeled in a single MAP command.

Drawing other stuff

You may have figured out that the MAP file is a way to plot any filled or empty shape in SYGRAPH. You can take a digitizer tablet, for example, and trace letters, figures, and symbols from published material or laboratory data. Most CAD programs convert these digitized tracings into X,Y coordinate ASCII files. If you import these files into a MAP file, you can plot irregular shapes with SYGRAPH.

Sources of map files

Contact SYSTAT, Inc. for information on map files. The following companies distribute ASCII map files and associated information which can be plotted in SYGRAPH.

Geographic Data Technology, Inc.
13 Dartmouth College Highway
Lyme, NH 03768
603.**795.2183**

National Planning Data Corporation
P.O. Box 610
Ithaca, New York 14851
607.**273.8208**

Appendix VI: References

Akima, H. (1978). A method of bivariate interpolation and smooth surface fitting for irregularly distributed data points. *ACM Transactions on Mathematical Software, 4,* 148-159.

Andrews, D.F. (1972). Plots of high-dimensional data. *Biometrics, 28,* 125-136.

Baird, J.C. (1970). *Psychophysical Analysis of Visual Space.* New York: Pergamon Press.

Bertin, J. (1983). *Semiology of Graphics.* Madison, Wisconsin: University of Wisconsin Press. (English translation of *Semiologie Graphique,* Paris: Gauthier-Villars, 1967).

Bickel, P.J., Hammel, E.A., O'Connell, J.W. (1975). Sex bias in graduate admissions: Data from Berkeley. *Science, 187,* 398-404.

Bornstein, M.H., Kessen, W., and Weiskopf, S. (1976). Color vision and hue categorization in young human infants. *Journal of Experimental Psychology: Human Perception and Performance, 2,* 115-129.

Brodlie, K.W. (1980). A review of methods for curve and function drawing. In K.W. Brodlie (Ed.), *Mathematical Methods in Computer Graphics and Design.* London: Academic Press, Inc.

Bruntz, S.M., Cleveland, W.S., Kleiner, B., and Warner, J.L. (1974). The dependence of ambient ozone on solar radiation, wind, temperature, and mixing height. *Proc. Symp. Atmos. Diffus. Air Pollution, American Meteorological Society.* 125–8.

Chambers, J.M., Cleveland, W.S., Kleiner, B., and Tukey, P.A. (1983). *Graphical Methods for Data Analysis.* Boston: Duxbury Press.

Chernoff, H. (1973). Using faces to represent points in k-dimensional space graphically. *Journal of the American Statistical Association, 68,* 361-368.

Chernoff, H., and Rizvi, M.H. (1975). Effect on classification error of random permutations of features in representing multivariate data by faces. *Journal of the American Statistical Association, 70,* 548-554.

Cleveland, W.S. (1979). Robust locally weight regression and smoothing scatterplots. *Journal of the American Statistical Association, 74,* 829-836.

Cleveland, W.S. (1981). LOWESS: A program for smoothing scatterplots by robust locally weighted regression. *The American Statistician, 35,* 54.

Cleveland, W.S. (1984). Graphs in scientific publications. *The American Statistician, 38,* 261-269.

Cleveland, W.S. (1984). Graphical methods for data presentation: Full scale breaks, dot charts, and multi-based logging. *The American Statistician, 38* 270-280.

Cleveland, W.S. (1985). *The Elements of Graphing Data.* Monterey, CA: Wadsworth Advanced Books.

Cleveland, W.S., Kleiner, B., McRae, and Warner (1976). Photochemical Air Pollution: Transport from the New York City Area into Conn. and Mass. *Science, 191,* 179-181.

Cleveland, W.S., Diaconis, P., and McGill, R. (1982). Variables on scatterplots look more highly correlated when the scales are increased. *Science, 216,* 1138-1141.

Cleveland, W.S., Harris, C.S., and McGill, R. (1982). Judgments of circle sizes on statistical maps. *Journal of the American Statistical Association, 77,* 541-547.

Cleveland, W.S. and McGill, R. (1983). A color caused optical illusion on a statistical graph. *American Statistician , 37,* 101-105.

Cleveland, W.S. and McGill, R. (1984). Graphical perception: theory, experimentation, and application to the development of graphical methods. *Journal of the American Statistical Association, 79,* 531-554.

Cleveland, W.S. and McGill, R. (1985). The many faces of a scatterplot. *Journal of the American Statistical Association, 79,* 807-822.

Cleveland, W.S. and McGill, R. (1987). Graphical perception: The visual decoding of quantitative information on graphical displays of data. Unpublished paper. AT&T Bell Laboratories.

Cleveland, W.S., McGill, R., and McGill, M.E. (1988). The shape parameter of a two-variable graph. *Journal of the American Statistical Association*, in press.

Coombs, C.H. (1964). *A Theory of Data*. New York: John Wiley and Sons.

Coren, S. and Girgus, J.S. (1978). *Seeing is Deceiving: The Psychology of Visual Illusions*. Hillsdale, NJ: Lawrence Erlbaum Associates.

Croley, T.E. and Hartmann, H.C. (1985). Resolving Thiessen polygons. *Journal of Hydrology, 76*, 363-379.

Croxton, F.E. and Struker, R.E. (1927). Bar charts versus circle diagrams. *Journal of the American Statistical Association, 22*, 473-482.

Curtis, D.B., Burton, R.P. , and Campbell, D.M. (1987). An alternative to Cartesian graphics. *Computer Graphics World , 40*, 95-98.

Daniel, C., and Wood, F.S. (1971). *Fitting Equations to Data*. New York: John Wiley & Sons.

Diamond, W.J. (1981). *Practical Experiment Designs for Engineers and Scientists*. Belmont, CA: Wadsworth.

Doane, D.P. (1976). Aesthetic frequency classifications. *The American Statistician, 30*, 181-183.

Dunn, R. (1987). Variable-width framed rectangle charts for statistical mapping. *The American Statistician, 41*, 153-156.

Durrett, H.J. (Ed.) (1987). *Color and the Computer*. New York: Academic Press.

Eels, W.C. (1926). The relative merits of circles and bars for representing component parts. *Journal of the American Statistical Association, 21*, 119-132.

Everitt, B. (1978). *Graphical Techniques for Multivariate Data*. London: Heinemann Educational Books.

Fienberg, S.E. (1979). Graphical methods in statistics. *The American Statistician, 33*, 165-177.

Freedman, D., Pisani, and Purves (1980). *Statistics*. New York: W.W. Norton & Co.

Freni-Titulaer, L.W.J. and Louv, W.C. (1984). Comparisons of some graphical methods for exploratory multivariate data analysis. *The American Statistician, 38*, 184-188.

Frisby, J.P. (1980). *Seeing: Illusion, Brain and Mind*. Oxford: Oxford University Press.

Gale, N . and Halperin, W.C. (1982). A case for better graphics: the unclassified choropleth map. *The American Statistician, 36*, 330-336.

Garner, W.R. (1974). *The Processing of Information and Structure*. Hillsdale, N .J.: Lawrence Erlbaum.

Garner, W.R. and Felfoldy, G.L. (1970). Integrality of stimulus dimensions in various types of information processing. *Cognitive Psychology, 1*, 225-241.

Gilbert, E.N. (1962). Random subdivisions of space into crystals. *Annals of Mathematical Statistics, 33*, 958-972.

Giloh, H. and Sadat, J.W. (1982). Fluorescence microscopy: Reduced photobleaching of rhodamine and flourescein protein conjugates by n-propyl gallate. *Science, 217*, 1252-1255.

Gnanadesikan, R. (1977). *Methods for Statistical Data Analysis of Multivariate Observations*. New York: John Wiley & Sons.

Green, P.J. and Sibson, R. (1978). Computing Dirichlet tesselations in the plane. *Computer Journal, 21*, 168-173.

Gregory, R.L. (1969). *Eye and Brain*. New York: McGraw-Hill.

Haber, R.N . and Hershenson, M. (1980). *The Psychology of Visual Perception*. 2nd. Ed. New York: Holt, Rinehart and Winston.

Haber, R.N . and Wilkinson, L. (1982). Perceptual components of computer displays. *IEEE Computer Graphics and Applications, 2*, 23-36.

Harris, J.E. (1987). "Who should profit from cigarettes?" *The New York Times*. Sunday, March 15, Section C, 3.

Hartigan, J.H. (1975a). Printer graphics for clustering. *Journal of Statistical Computation and Simulation, 4*, 187-213.

Hartigan, J.H. (1975b). *Clustering Algorithms*. New York: John Wiley & Sons.

Hershey, A.V. (1972). A computer system for scientific typography. *Computer Graphics and Image Processing, 1*, 373-385.

Inselberg, A. (1985). The plane with parallel coordinates. *The Visual Computer, 1*, 69-91.

Jacob, R.J.K. (1983). Investigating the space of Chernoff faces. In M.H. Rizvi, J.S. Rustaqi, and D. Siegmund (Eds.), *Recent Advances in Statistics: A Festschrift in Honor of Herman Chernoff's Sixtieth Birthday*. New York: Academic Press.

Kosslyn, S.M. (1980). *Image and Mind*. Cambridge, MA: Harvard University Press.

Krumhansl, C.L., and Shepard, R.N. (1979). Quantification of the hierarchy of tonal functions within a diatonic context. *Journal of Experimental Psychology: Human Perception and Performance, 5*, 579-594.

Kruskal, W.H. (1982). Criteria for judging statistical graphics. *Utilitas Mathematica, 21B*, 283-310.

Levine, M.W. and Shefner, J.M. (1981). *Fundamentals of Sensation and Perception*. Reading, MA: Addison-Wesley.

Lodwick, G.D. and Whittle, J. (1970). A technique for automatic contouring field survey data. *Australian Computer Journal, 2*, 104-109.

Long, L.H. (Ed.) (1971). *The World Almanac and Book of Facts*. New York: Doubleday and Co., Inc.

Maltz, M.D. (1984). *Recidivism*. New York: Academic Press.

McGill, R., Tukey, J.W., and Larsen, W.A. (1978). Variations of box plots. *The American Statistician, 32*, 12-16.

McLain, D.H. (1974). Drawing contours from arbitrary data points. *The Computer Journal, 17*, 318-324.

Michalske, T.A., and Bunker, B.C. (1987). The fracturing of glass. *Scientific American, 257* (December), 122-129.

Miles, R.E. (1974). A synopsis of "Poisson flats in Euclidean spaces." In E.F. Harding and D.G. Kendall, Eds., *Stochastic Geometry*. New York: John Wiley & Sons, 202-227.

Miller, G.A. (1956). The magical number seven, plus or minus two. *Psychological Review, 63*, 81-97.

Nelson, S.L. (1987). Plotting investment profitability. *Lotus*, April, 1987, 61-68.

Preparata, F.P. and Shamos, M.I. (1985). *Computational Geometry: An Introduction*. New York: Springer Verlag.

Rhynsburger, D. (1973). Analytic delineation of Thiessen Polygons. *Geographical Analysis, 5*, 133-144.

Richardus, P. and Adler, R.K. (1972) *Map Projections for Geodesists, Cartographers, and Geographers*. New York: North-Holland/American Elsevier.

Ripley, B.D. (1981). *Spatial Statistics*. New York: John Wiley & Sons.

Rudnick, J. and Gaspari, G. (1987). The shapes of random walks. *Science, 237*, 384-389.

SAS Institute Inc. (1986) *SAS/GRAPH*. Cary, NC: SAS Institute Inc.

Scott, D.W. (1979). Optimal and data-based histograms. *Biometrika, a*, 605-610.

Shepard, R.N. (1978). The mental image. *American Psychologist, 33*, 125-137.

Silverman, B.W. (1986). *Density Estimation for Statistics and Data Analysis*. London: Chapman and Hall.

Simken, D. and Hastie, R. (1987). An information-processing analysis of graph perception. *Journal of the American Statistical Association, 82*, 454-465.

Spoehr, K.T. and Lehmkuhle, S.W. (1982). *Visual Information Processing.* San Francisco: W.H. Freeman.

Sturges, H.A. (1926). The choice of a class interval. *Journal of the American Statistical Association, 21,* 65.

Trumbo, B.E. (1981). A theory for coloring bivariate statistical maps. *The American Statistician, 35,* 220-226.

Tufte, E.R. (1983). *The Visual Display of Quantitative Information.* Cheshire, CT: Graphics Press.

Tukey, J.W. (1977). *Exploratory Data Analysis.* Reading, Mass: Addison-Wesley.

U.S. Bureau of the Census (1986). *State and Metropolitan Area Data Book.* U.S. Government Printing Office.

Velleman, P.F. and Hoaglin, D.C. (1981). *Applications, Basics, and Computing of Exploratory Data Analysis.* Boston: Duxbury Press.

Wainer, H. and Francolini, C.M. (1980). An empirical inquiry concerning human understanding of two-variable color maps. *The American Statistician, 34,* 81-93.

Wainer, H. and Thissen, D. (1981). Graphical data analysis. *Annual Review of Psychology, 32,* 191-241.

Wang, P.C.C. (Ed.) (1978). *Graphical Representation of Multivariate Data.* New York: Academic Press.

Warner, B.G., Mathewes, R.W., and Clague, J.J. (1982). Ice-free conditions on the Queen Charlotte Islands, British Columbia, at the height of late Wisconsin glaciation. *Science, 218,* 675-677.

Weber, R. (1982). *EDP auditing: Conceptual foundations and practices.* New York: McGraw-Hill.

Wegman, E.J. (1982). Density estimation. In S. Kotz and N .L. Johnson (Eds.), *Encyclopedia of Statistical Sciences. Vol. 2.* New York: John Wiley & Sons, 309-315.

Wegman, E.J. (1986). Hyperdimensional data analysis using parallel co-ordinates. *George Mason University Center for Computational Statistics and Probability Technical Report No. 1.*

Wilkinson, L. (1982). An experimental evaluation of multivariate graphical point representations. *Human Factors in Computer Systems: Proceedings*. Gaithersburg, Maryland, 202-209.

Wilkinson, L. (1983). *Fuzzygrams*. Cambridge, MA: Harvard Computer Graphics Week.

Winer, B.J. (1971). *Statistical principles in experimental design, 2nd. ed.* New York: McGraw-Hill.

Index

[X pow] (see [Power])
[X reverse] (see [Axes], Reversing scales)
[X tick] (see [Axes], Tick marks)
[X-Y] (see **Icons,** Locating)

[Y label] (see [Axes], Scale labels)
[Y limit] (see [Axes], Control limits)
[Y max] (see [Axes], Limits)
[Y min] (see [Axes], Limits)
[Y pip] (see [Axes], Pips)
[Y pow] (see [Power])
[Y reverse] (see [Axes], Reversing scales)
[Y tick] (see [Axes], Tick marks)

[Z label] (see [Axes], Scale labels)
[Z pip] (see [Axes], Pips)
[Z pow] (see [Power])
[Z reverse] (see [Axes], Reversing scales)
[Z tick] (see [Axes], Tick marks)

                                                        1989, SYSTAT, Inc.

Suggestions and problem report

_____
NAME

_____
ORGANIZATION

_____
CITY/STATE/ZIP/COUNTRY

_____
TELEPHONE #   FAX #

_____
MACHINE   RAM   VERSION OF SYSTEM/FINDER

_____
SYSTAT MENU ITEM OR COMMAND

_____
TYPE OF DATASET

Describe your problem or give details for your suggestion. If possible, enclose printouts of your commands and dataset, or provide explicit instructions for reproducing the problem.

Are there any new features you would like to see in future versions of SYSTAT for the Macintosh?

Send to SYSTAT, Inc., 1800 Sherman Avenue, Evanston, IL 60201-3793. Telephone 708.**864.5670**, FAX 708.492.3567.